A Publication Sponsored by
the Society for Industrial and Organizational Psychology, Inc.,
a division of the American Psychological Association

ᛒᛒᛒᛒᛒᛒᛒᛒᛒ

Career Development
in Organizations

ᛒᛒᛒᛒᛒᛒᛒᛒᛒᛒᛒᛒᛒᛒᛒᛒᛒᛒ

ℛℛℛℛℛℛℛℛℛ

Douglas T. Hall
and Associates

Foreword by Raymond A. Katzell

ℛℛℛℛℛℛℛℛℛℛℛℛℛℛℛℛℛℛℛ

Career Development in Organizations

Jossey-Bass Publishers

San Francisco • London • 1986

219159

650.14
H 175

CAREER DEVELOPMENT IN ORGANIZATIONS
by Douglas T. Hall and Associates

Library of Congress Cataloging-in-Publication Data

Hall, Douglas T. (date)
  Career development in organizations.

  (The Jossey-Bass management series) (The Jossey-Bass
social and behavioral science series)
  Includes bibliographies and indexes.
  1. Career development.   I. Title.   II. Series.
III. Series: Jossey-Bass social and behavioral science
series.
HF5549.5.C35H35   1986   650.1'4   86-2932
ISBN 0-87589-681-2 (alk. paper)

Manufactured in the United States of America

The paper in this book meets the guidelines for
permanence and durability of the Committee on
Production Guidelines for Book Longevity of the
Council on Library Resources.

JACKET DESIGN BY WILLI BAUM

FIRST EDITION

Code 8612

A joint publication in
The Jossey-Bass Management Series
and
The Jossey-Bass
Social and Behavioral Science Series

Frontiers of Industrial and Organizational Psychology

Series Editor

Raymond A. Katzell
New York University

Editorial Board

John P. Campbell
University of Minnesota

Richard J. Campbell
American Telephone and Telegraph Company

Edwin A. Fleishman
Advanced Research Resources Organization

Irwin L. Goldstein
University of Maryland

J. Richard Hackman
Yale University

Lyman W. Porter
University of California at Irvine

Victor H. Vroom
Yale University

ﾞﾞﾞﾞﾞﾞﾞﾞﾞﾞﾞﾞﾞﾞﾞﾞ

Foreword

One of the principal objectives of the Society for Industrial and Organizational Psychology is, according to its bylaws, to "advance the scientific status of the field." In 1982, Richard J. Campbell, then the president of the society, asked me to assume the chair of the Committee on Scientific Affairs, with the express charge of intensifying the society's pursuit of that objective. It was a charge that I, and the rest of the committee, embraced wholeheartedly.

Several new initiatives were undertaken during that year. The one that generated the greatest enthusiasm, not only in the committee but widely in the society, consisted of a plan to publish a series of volumes, each dealing with a single topic considered to be of major contemporary significance in industrial and organizational psychology. Each volume was to present cutting-edge theory, research, and practice in chapters contributed by about ten individuals doing pioneering work on the topic.

The proposal was unanimously adopted by the society's executive committee in 1983, and its implementation was entrusted to an editorial board, which I agreed to chair. It is further testimony to the vitality of the idea that every one of the distinguished and busy psychologists who was asked to join the board accepted the invitation.

Why has that plan been so favorably received? I think mainly because it is seen as filling a significant void in the media through which industrial and organizational psychologists advance their understanding of their field. Such volumes can be less kaleidoscopic than our journals and more focused than review chapters and yearbooks that scan developments in broad sectors of the field. By aiming to identify significant recent developments that may not yet have jelled into articulated patterns, these books can be more current than texts and professional works that seek to present integrated pictures of their subjects. It is that special and important niche among the publications in industrial and organizational psychology that this series is designed to occupy. The success of that endeavor should, it is hoped, facilitate progress in theory and research on the topics presented while also abetting the transition from science to practice.

The editorial board has further specified the plan in the following particulars:

- The subject matter of the volumes is to be aimed at the membership of the society, with the hope and expectation that scholars, professionals, and advanced students in cognate fields will also find it of value.
- Each volume is to be prepared under the editorship of a leading contributor to the topic it covers, who will also prepare integrating commentary, placing the chapters in a broader context.
- The choice of topics and editors will be made by the editorial board, which will also consult with the volume editors in planning each book. The chairman of the editorial board is to serve as series editor and coordinate the relationships and responsibilities of the volume editors, the editorial board, the series publisher, and the executive committee of the society.
- Volumes are to be issued when timely rather than on a fixed schedule, but at a projected rate of approximately one a year.
- The series is to be called *Frontiers of Industrial and Organizational Psychology*.

Among the first decisions that had to be made by the editorial board was the choice of a publisher. After careful consideration of several proposals, Jossey-Bass was chosen on the basis of criteria that included editorial support, production quality, marketing capability, and pricing.

Of the topics that were considered by the board for priority in publication, three struck us as especially relevant. The topic of careers in organizations was selected for the first volume not only because of its intrinsic merits and timeliness but also because we believed that it has received less attention in the field than is warranted by its theoretical and practical value. We were fortunate in securing the services of Douglas T. Hall, who is ideally qualified to be editor of a volume on this topic, and of the several prominent scholars and professionals who agreed to contribute chapters. The fruits of all those efforts are yours to savor in the rest of the book.

We look forward to the publication of two more volumes in the series: in 1987, a book on productivity, being edited by John P. Campbell, and another, on training and development, in 1988 under the editorship of Irwin L. Goldstein. Like the present volume, they will feature pioneer work in their respective areas. Topics for additional volumes are currently being explored.

This entire undertaking has required the cooperation and efforts of many able and dedicated people, most of whom must remain unnamed because of space limitations. I hope they know who they are and that they have our deep thanks. But I cannot refrain from acknowledging my colleagues on the editorial board, whose contributions have amply fulfilled our high expectations.

March 1986   Raymond A. Katzell
                                                                  New York University
                                                                  Series Editor

꘏꘏꘏꘏꘏꘏꘏꘏

Preface

This book examines the cutting edge of the rapidly changing field of organizational career development. Ten or fifteen years ago, it did not exist as a field. There were very few papers and symposia on career development at the annual meetings of the American Psychological Association and the Academy of Management, and there were few corporate human resource practitioners with the word "career" in their titles. Now there is a Careers Division of the Academy of Management, and such terms as *career specialist* and *manager of career development* are common in industry. The field has blossomed to the point that there is now a real need to take stock of where we are and to examine the source of the next developments.

Why does there need to be a book as a way of taking stock? First, to date, most of the literature in the field consists of articles scattered among the journals of a variety of disciplines: psychology, sociology, education, management, and others. Within each discipline, some publications focus on theory, some on research, and some on practice, hence even more diversity. This book provides the reader with a view that cuts across these different approaches to career work and consolidates key developments in areas that have been virtually isolated from each other.

Second, because the field of careers is at once theory-based and applied, our stocktaking needs to cover all of the three domains in which work takes place: theory, research, and innovative practice. Up to now, most publications on careers have dealt with only one or two of these areas. We have made the scope of this book broad enough to include all three domains.

Yet another impetus for this book has been that many of the important developments in the careers area have taken place in organizational activities that are not normally written up for publication. One of our objectives here was to seek out information on cutting-edge activities and present it to our readers, focusing on both individual career planning and organizational career management. Indeed, the basis of selecting chapter topics and authors was to sample from this span. Thus, taken altogether, the chapters of this book provide an overview of how organizations and individual employees are currently going about working on careers in organizational settings.

The primary audience for this book is people such as the members of the Society for Industrial and Organizational Psychology—people who are interested in research and creative practice in applied psychology. This group includes human resource management professionals and managers, industrial and counseling psychologists, students and academics in industrial and organizational psychology and organizational behavior programs in schools of business and education, organizational consultants, and line managers interested in new concepts in the management of people.

Overview of the Contents

Career Development in Organizations opens with an introduction that provides readers with an overview of the field at the present time. The rest of the chapters are grouped into four parts, each of which focuses on a different major arena: in Part One, the cultural and organizational contexts of careers; in Part Two, individual career development processes; in Part Three, career management programs in organizations; and in Part Four, the current and future outlook for work in the field of career development. However, the chapters of this book also work in another organizational structure that roughly separates into individual and organizational dimensions (which necessarily overlap). In the Introduction, I describe a spectrum of career development activities that ranges from individual career planning (micro) to organizational career management (macro). The chapters in Parts Two and Three reflect work spanning this spectrum from micro to macro career development.

On the individual side, Manuel London and Stephen Stumpf, in Chapter One, explore new employee attitudes toward careers and the ways these attitudes are shaping corporate career programs. Chapter Three by Donald Super (the "father" of career development, in my opinion) explores a new topic—leisure—as an end in itself and as a guide to identity exploration for career planning. (Incidentally, Super first wrote about this "new" topic in the 1940s!) In Chapter Four, Douglas Hall discusses how careers change in the middle and what forces trigger a shift from a previously rewarding career field into new areas. Frank Minor, in Chapter Six, explores computer-based career-planning systems, which help link micro and macro activities.

At the intersection of individual and organizational career activities, Kathy Kram (Chapter Five) explores mentoring and other helping relationships that promote career growth for the benefit of both the senior and junior parties. Moving more toward the macro or organizational side, Richard Campbell and Joseph Moses (Chapter Eight) describe the far-reaching career development programs that have been pioneered at American Telephone and Telegraph (particularly those regarding career progress of women). Chapter Two, by Thomas Gutteridge, describes the current state of the practice in organizational career development. This chapter shows how organizational career management practices can effectively be integrated with individual career-planning processes. Chapter Seven, by Robert Morrison and Roger Hock, reports on an integrative, multidisciplinary model that shows how a series of job assignments can be put together to gradually "grow" a desired profile of knowledge, skills, and abilities.

Edgar Schein, another pioneer in the field of careers, was asked to comment on the other chapters in this book and to state his own ideas on future needs for the field. In Chapter Nine, he provides a critical overview of the current status of work in careers, as well as a call for more descriptive research.

Acknowledgments

Many acknowledgments are in order for people who contributed to this book. The project has been completed in a fairly short time frame, thanks to the conscientious work of our chapter authors. Raymond Katzell, series editor, has been a critical partner in this project at all stages: in brainstorming the initial concept for the book, recruiting the authors, providing developmental feedback on drafts, acting as sounding board, consultant, and chief handholder for me in interacting with the publisher, and in general shepherding the book along to its final form. For me, getting to know Ray and having the opportunity to work with a person of his wisdom, integrity, and skill has been one of the most important rewards of this project.

Here at Boston University, I have been blessed with a supportive and efficient work environment. My thanks go to Henry Morgan, dean of the School of Management, and David Brown, chair of the Department of Organizational Behavior, for providing resources, time, and encouragement for scholarly pursuits. The department's secretaries, Sara Tarbox and Leslie Lomasson, have managed scheduling, communications with authors and the publisher, and countless other logistics with much more patience and grace than I deserve. A large thank you goes to the School of Management's word processors, Vince Mahler and Emily Phillips, for transforming reams of crossed-out, inserted, and ungrammatical hen scratching into attractive typed pages.

Much of my current work on the midcareer stages of career development was initiated during a visiting year at the Columbia University Center for Research in Career Development. The support of Mary Anne Devanna and Kirby Warren was especially important in getting this midcareer research underway. More recently, much of my learning has been stimulated by the Boston University Human Resources Policy Institute. My interactions with the thirty-five company human resources officers and with Fred Foulkes, the institute's director, have been a critical source of professional development for me.

Finally, I would like to thank the Society for Industrial and Organizational Psychology and its 1984-1985 president, Benjamin

Preface xvii

Schneider, for their work on this "Frontiers" series and for their confidence in and support for me as editor of Volume One. In particular, Ben has been a personal as well as professional friend for many years. It has been a long time since our priest study, and it was good to have the opportunity to work together again.

Boston, Massachusetts Douglas T. Hall
March 1986

Contents

ༀༀༀༀༀༀༀༀ

The Authors

Douglas T. "Tim" Hall is professor of organizational behavior in the School of Management at Boston University. He received his B.S. degree (1962) in industrial administration from the School of Engineering at Yale University and his M.S. (1964) and Ph.D. (1966) degrees in management from the Sloan School of Management at M.I.T. He has held faculty positions at Yale, York, Michigan State, and Northwestern Universities. At Northwestern he held the Earl Dean Howard Chair in Organizational Behavior and served a term as department chairman. He is the author of *Careers in Organizations* and co-author of *Organizational Climates and Careers, The Two-Career Couple, Experiences in Management and Organizational Behavior,* and *Human Resource Management: Strategy, Design, and Implementation.*

Hall is a recipient of the American Psychological Association's James McKeen Cattell Award for research design and is a fellow of the American Psychological Association and of the Academy of Management, where he served on the Board of Governors. He has served on the editorial boards of five scholarly journals. His research and consulting activities have dealt with career development, women's careers, career burnout, and two-career couples. He has served as a consultant to organizations such as Sears, American Telephone and Telegraph, American Hospital Supply, General Electric, Borg-Warner, Price Waterhouse, Ford Motor Company, Eli Lilly, and the World Bank.

Richard J. Campbell is director of management development, education, and work relationships at American Telephone
and Telegraph (AT&T). His main research interest is the
identification and development of managers. He is coauthor of the
book *Formative Years in Business* (1974) and has written articles on
assessment centers. In 1983 he was co-chair of the AT&T Policy
Advisory Committee responsible for the overall direction of the
assignment of people during the Bell System divestiture. Campbell
received his B.A. degree (1954) in psychology from Temple
University, his M.S. degree (1958) in psychology from Ohio State
University, and his Ph.D. degree (1960) in industrial psychology
(1960), also from Ohio State University.

Thomas G. Gutteridge is dean of the College of Business and
Administration and professor of administrative sciences at Southern
Illinois University at Carbondale. Prior to assuming these duties, he
was associate dean and associate professor of human resources and
industrial relations with the school of management at the State
University of New York at Buffalo. He received his degree in
industrial engineering from General Motors Institute, and his M.S.
and Ph.D. degrees from the Herman C. Krannert Graduate School
of Purdue University. Gutteridge is author, co-author, or
contributor to numerous publications, including *Career Planning
Practices* (with J. W. Walker), "A Guide for Career Development
Inquiry," and *Organizational Career Development: State of the
Practice.* Gutteridge is a consultant in career development and
human resource planning as well as a labor arbitrator for the
American Arbitration Association and the Federal Mediation and
Conciliation Services. He is a member of the American Society of
Personnel Administration, the American Society of Training and
Development, and the Industrial Relations Research Association.

Roger R. Hock is a doctoral candidate in experimental social
psychology at the University of California, San Diego. He also
teaches psychology at Palomar College in San Marcos, California.
He received his M.S. degree in industrial-organizational psychology
from San Diego State University in 1984 and was a student

contractor at the Navy Personnel Research and Development Center from 1984 to 1985.

Kathy E. Kram is an assistant professor in the department of organizational behavior at the Boston University School of Management, where she is also a research associate at the Center for Applied Social Science. She received her B.S. degree (1972) in behavioral science and management and her M.S. degree (1973) in behavioral science and management from the M.I.T. Sloan School of Management, and her Ph.D. degree (1980) in organizational behavior from Yale University. In addition to her ongoing teaching and research activities, she consults with private- and public-sector organizations on a variety of human resource management concerns.

Manuel London is a district manager in charge of personnel research for American Telephone and Telegraph (AT&T) Communications. He received his B.A. degree (1971) from Case Western Reserve University in philosophy and psychology and his M.A. (1972) and Ph.D. (1974) degrees from Ohio State University in industrial and organizational psychology. He is a consulting editor of the *Academy of Management Journal*. London's books include *Developing Managers* (1985) and *Managing Careers* (1982, with S. A. Stumpf).

Frank J. Minor is program manager of personnel research in the IBM Corporation Information Systems Group Headquarters, where he is responsible for personnel research and information systems development projects to support human resource development activities. He is also a faculty member of the Pace University Graduate School of Business Administration. Minor received his B.S. degree (1955) from Rutgers University in business administration, and his M.A. (1956) and Ph.D. (1958) degrees from Ohio State University in industrial psychology. He is a member of the American Psychological Association, Academy of Management, and International Association of Applied Psychology.

Robert F. Morrison is the head of the Career Development Systems Division at the Navy Personnel Research and Development Center and an adjunct professor of systems management at the University of Southern California. He received his B.S. (1952) and M.S. (1956) degrees from Iowa State University in general science and applied psychology respectively, and his Ph.D. degree (1961) from Purdue University in industrial psychology. In 1982, he received the James McKeen Cattell award for research design from the Society for Industrial and Organizational Psychology, a division of the American Psychological Association.

Joseph L. "Joel" Moses is division manager, Management Continuity Research and Programs, at American Telephone and Telegraph (AT&T) corporate headquarters. He is also a research professor of psychology at New York University and a partner in the Applied Research Group. His research interests are executive and management identification, development, and succession. He is coeditor (with W. Byham) of *Applying the Assessment Center Methods* and is coauthor (with M. Hakel, M. Sorcher, and M. Beer) of *Making It Happen: Designing Research with Implementation in Mind.* Moses received his B.A. degree in psychology (1961) from the City College of New York, his M.B.A. degree (1963) from the City University of New York, and his Ph.D. degree (1967) in psychology from Baylor University. He is also a fellow of the Society for Industrial and Organizational Psychology, a division of the American Psychological Association.

Edgar H. Schein is Sloan Fellows Professor of Management at M.I.T.'s Sloan School of Management. He received his B.A. degree (1947) in psychology from the University of Chicago, his M.A. degree (1949) in social psychology from Stanford University, and his Ph.D. degree (1952) from Harvard University's Department of Social Relations, also in social psychology. Schein's main research activities have been in the field of managerial career development and the process of socialization leading to the study of organizational culture. His recent publications include *Organizational Culture and Leadership* (1985) and *Organizational Psychology* (1965; 3rd ed., 1980).

Stephen A. Stumpf is associate professor of management and organizational behavior at New York University and director of the school's Management Simulation Projects Group. He received his B.S. degree (1971) from Rensselaer Polytechnic Institute in chemical engineering, his M.B.A. degree (1973) from the University of Rochester in behavioral science, and his Ph.D. degree (1978) from New York University in business administration. Stumpf's books include *Choosing a Career in Business* (1984) and *Managing Careers* (1982, with M. London).

Donald E. Super is professor emeritus of psychology and education at Teachers College, Columbia University. He has also served as director of the Division of Psychology and Education, chairman of the Department of Psychology, and director of the Career Pattern Study at Columbia. In addition, for more than three years he was honorary director and senior research fellow at the National Institute for Careers Education and Counselling and fellow of Wolfson College, Cambridge. He has since then been a research professor at the University of Florida during the academic year and has taught each summer at Virginia Polytechnic Institute and State University. He received the B.A. (1932) and M.A. (1936) degrees from Oxford, the Ph.D. degree (1940) from Columbia, and an honorary D.Sc. degree from the University of Lisbon. Super has published in both English and French, and his numerous works include textbooks on vocational testing and on the psychology of careers, and books on career maturity.

ℜℜℜℜℜℜℜℜ

Career Development in Organizations

ℜℜℜℜℜℜℜℜℜℜℜℜℜℜℜℜℜℜ

INTRODUCTION

ℜℜℜℜℜℜℜℜℜ

An Overview
of Current
Career Development
Theory, Research,
and Practice

Douglas T. Hall

Recently, I was asked by a large manufacturing firm to provide some information on the pros and cons of job posting as an element in a corporate career-planning program. The caller, a human resource specialist, was making the request in response to top management's interest in posting. Top management, in turn, was interested because employee surveys had uncovered a desire by employees for job posting as a means of providing information on career opportunities.

My initial reaction to the question about the value of job posting was that this same question was being asked ten or fifteen years ago. Haven't we moved beyond such questions? Upon further reflection, however, I realized that there was a significant difference in both who was asking the question and how it was being asked.

Note: I am grateful for the helpful comments and suggestions of Raymond Katzell, Kathy Kram, and Jeanne Brett in preparing this chapter.

1

The question (and interest) were now coming from top management, not from the human resource specialist. Years ago, however, I suspect that the main energy for a career-related activity such as job posting would have come from the human resource specialist, who would be looking to an expert resource to help unfreeze top management.

A second, more subtle difference emerged as we talked further. The human resource specialist described in great detail the career development activities that are already underway in that firm. For instance, a computerized individual self-assessment and career exploration program is in place, along with career workshops, both of which are available to all employees. All managers are taking part in training programs in career coaching and counseling skills, and a career planning discussion is being added to the performance appraisal process. Thus, in contrast to years ago, job posting would not be a rather tame first step in career development but rather one additional small piece (albeit a highly visible and quickly implemented one) of an existing, comprehensive career program.

A third difference from ten or fifteen years ago was that the caller was an expert on careers and career programs who personally felt little need for outside help. Ten years ago, there were few career specialists in corporate positions. However, the most important *similarity* to the early 1970s was that top management is still quite naive about career development. Then, as now, top management was in need of education regarding career management.

Let us move from this incident to a more general discussion of where the field of career development is today. We will start with a spectrum of career activities and then move on to the frontiers.

The Career Development Spectrum

The late Walter Storey, who did pioneering work at General Electric, described two important facets of the career development process. The first is the work of the *individual employee* who is attempting to plan his or her career in a personally satisfying and productive manner. The second relates to the activities of the *organization* that will effectively select, assess, assign, and develop employees to provide a pool of qualified people to meet future

Table 1. Current Concerns in Career Management and Career Planning.

Current concerns in career management

1. Strategic human resource planning
2. Succession planning
3. Assessment/Development of management potential
4. Training managers in career coaching/counseling skills
5. Alternative career paths (nontraditional)
6. New human resource movement systems
7. Legitimation of exit, downward movement
8. Concerns about baby boom cohort
9. Linking of career management systems to career-planning systems

Current concerns in career planning

1. More concern for *protean* (self-directed) careers
2. Midcareer coming earlier
3. More questioning, rejection of job moves (including promotions)
4. More honest self-assessment
5. More plateauing by choice
6. More two-career planning; more *family inputs* to career decisions
7. Desire for more mutual career planning with company
8. Need for more information on company career opportunities
9. Desire for more company assistance in implementing career plans (link to corporate career management system)

elements: top management's agreement on the basic mission of the organization and its derivation of clear, specific goals and objectives toward pursuing that mission; top management's communication of these missions, goals, and objectives to the rest of the organization; and close interaction between business planners and human resource planners so that the business plan and the human resource plan are realistically integrated. Detailed descriptions of strategic human resource planning in research and action are found in Fombrun, Tichy, and Devanna (1984) and Hall and Goodale (1986).

One of the "hottest" areas of concerns currently is *succession planning* (that is, human resource planning for the top positions in the organization). In this area, practice is ahead of theory and research. Because this process involves top management's identifying and grooming the next generation of leaders (top management's replacement), it is an activity about which the current leaders care deeply. There has not been a great deal of research

corporate needs. This individual-level approach is often called *career planning*, while the organization-level approach is termed *career management*. These two terms are defined as follows: *Career planning* is a deliberate process of (1) becoming aware of self, opportunities, constraints, choices, and consequences, (2) identifying career-related goals, and (3) programming work, education, and related developmental experiences to provide the direction, timing, and sequence of steps to attain a specific career goal. *Career management* is an ongoing process of preparing, implementing, and monitoring career plans undertaken by the individual alone or in concert with the organization's career systems (Storey, 1976).

As Thomas Gutteridge points out in Chapter Two, a balanced approach to organizational career development requires the use of both of these activities. The two facets complement and reinforce each other quite well. If individual employees have failed to plan for their own development, they may not be ready to respond to opportunities presented through organizational career management activities. (Or, as one observer stated, "Failing to plan is planning to fail.") Similarly, no amount of individual planning and preparation can be effective if organizational opportunities for career movement are not available.

One can think of these two activities as representing the end points of a spectrum of career development activities, as shown in Figure 1. The activities shown in the spectrum are not intended to represent an exhaustive list of career development activities; they merely illustrate different points on the continuum. At the extreme career-planning end of the spectrum are individual activities, such as self-directed career workbooks and tapes. The person receives a lot of information here and has high control. However, little of this information is communicated to the organization, which has less control over career planning. Something with a bit more of an organizational flavor to it would be company-sponsored career planning workshops.

At the opposite end of the spectrum (career management) is formal succession planning, which typically is done in secrecy by top management, with no involvement of the individual. Here the organization has high levels of information and control, while the

Figure 1. The Spectrum of Career Development Activities.

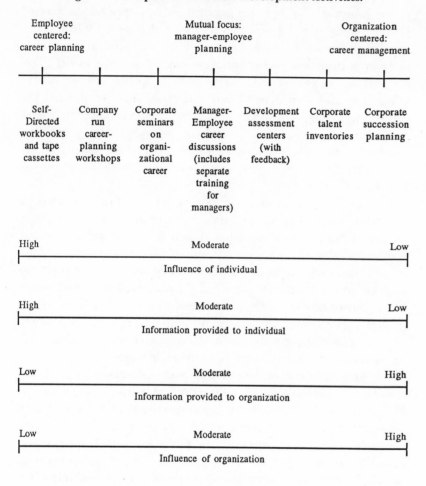

Note: This is a sample of program activities to illustrate different points of the continuum between career management and career planning. This is not a complete list of possible career development activities.

individual has correspondingly little of both. Moving a bit more to the individual career planning end, one finds corporate talent inventories, which are formal human resource information systems covering employee skills, experiences, and interests and utilizing some information provided by the individual.

In the middle of the career development spectrum are activities with equal involvement by the employee and the organization (usually represented by the employee's manager). Here there is shared influence and information. Perhaps the best examples of this mutual focus are career coaching and counseling discussions between boss and employee. The objective here is career planning for the employee, with the boss providing input on company realities and assistance in implementing career plans within the constraints of the corporate environment.

It is important to stress that an organization can engage in activities at any and all points in the career spectrum. The benefits of career planning and those of career management can be combined. As Chapter Two indicates, career development is now sufficiently established so that a rich set of career activities, representing the full range of the career spectrum, is now found in organizational practice.

Areas of Career Activity: Theory, Research, and Practice

At this point, let us use the career development spectrum to assess the current areas of activity for career researchers and practitioners. To simplify our discussion, we will look first at concerns related to the career management side of the spectrum. Then we will shift to concerns more on the career planning side. These concerns are summarized in Table 1.

Career Management Concerns. Probably the most important single development in theory, research, and practice related to careers in recent years has been the attention devoted to *strategic human resource planning,* the process of linking the organization's strategy for managing human resources to its basic business goals and objectives. While this sounds quite simple, it entails several in this area, perhaps in part because the topic is so sensitive in most organizations: "You're dealing with the family jewels here," as one executive put it. A useful conceptual scheme and survey of corporate practices has been provided by Joseph Carnazza (1982). Jeffrey Pfeffer and Gerald Salancik (1978) have theoretically examined issues of power and resource dependency in relation to succession planning. In most organizations, however, top management develops its own succession method so that it fits with its particular culture. In practice, the process is far simpler than the complicated human resource planning models found in the research literature (see Sorcher, 1985).

As a result of the succession planning process, there has been renewed interest in the *assessment and development of management potential.* One reason for this is that in today's leaner, flatter organizations, senior leadership is more critical than ever. Also, with fewer senior slots available, the consequences of a poor fit in any one position are quite serious. And with large numbers of talented, educated "baby boomers" from which to choose, there is more need for good methods of identifying high-potential candidates. In addition to assessment centers, which have become a well-accepted selection technology, researchers and practitioners are showing strong interest in management ratings and renewed interest in testing as a selection aid (see Schneider and Schmitt, forthcoming). A recent book by Sorcher (1985) is a useful guide in the areas of succession planning and identification of management potential.

Another area of interest that also contains a well-accepted technology is the *training of managers in career coaching and counseling skills.* Many organizations now offer one- or two-day management training programs that cover career concepts, coaching and listening skills, information on company career opportunities, and role plays. Such programs work best if the managers themselves have opportunities to receive career-planning assistance from top management (if not, they will be less motivated to help their subordinates.) Kram's (1985) research has identified key skills and resources needed to make this coaching effective.

There is also strong interest (but not much action) in the idea of *nontraditional career paths*. In today's flatter organizations, there is a need to increase the value attached to alternatives to promotion: lateral or rotational moves, nonmanagement career roles (for example, engineer, sales representative), temporary assignments, downward moves, and early and phased retirement. When such moves occur now, they tend to be on a case-by-case basis, not as part of a formal corporate career path.

Nontraditional career moves, better assessment, and coaching skills for managers would *facilitate the career development of women and minorities*. This continues to be a key concern in most organizations today, as we will see in several chapters.

As a means of implementing nontraditional moves, new types of *human resource movement systems* are being sought. Again, there seems to be more theoretical interest than action here (see Hall, 1984). Some organizations have created a formal role that is responsible for internal moves (such as the detailer in the U.S. Navy, the assignments officer in the U.S. Army, and the professional internal placement management in certain banks) (Morrison and Holzbach, 1980).

Because of this interest in nontraditional career movement, *exit and downward movement are becoming more acceptable*, and more research is being done in this area (see Latack, 1985). It is becoming clear that these "unpopular" forms of movement are active ways to free up the organization and the individual by opening up creative new options and directions of movement. The difficulty here is that the culture of the organization needs to change in order to attach value to these alternatives. Hall and Isabella (1985) report research findings and practical guidelines for changing norms attached to nontraditional career moves.

Along with concerns about the reduced supply of management positions is a related issue of demand: *concerns about the baby boom cohort*. These individuals are now well into their thirties (and thus hitting midcareer), and they represent a large, bright, well educated, and ambitious group. Will they become turned off when they experience limitations in rates of promotion? Are they deserting large organizations in favor of entrepreneurial ventures? Russell (1982) and Jones (1980) present research to explore the issues raised by the baby boom cohort. Hall and Richter's (1985) study found that the main issue here is not the number of baby boomers but their nature—a new set of values and behaviors that are affecting organizational cultures. Values such as autonomy, self-development, entrepreneurship, and balance between work life and family life are high priorities for this group. Few organizations seem to be systematically examining or preparing for these changes, however.

Ten years ago, I collaborated on a paper entitled "What's New in Career Management?" (Hall and Hall, 1976). In addition to covering what the title suggested, the paper also examined what was *not* happening in career management. At that time, a major deficiency was the *integration of career management systems and career-planning systems.* Now the story is quite different, as many organizations have worked to tie together such activities as succession planning, boss coaching, career-planning workshops, and greater career choice for the employee. This is still an interface that is difficult to manage in most organizations, but it is being studied and addressed in practice in many places, as Chapters Two and Six indicate.

Current Concerns in Career Planning. As we just illustrated, there is now more research and practical activity in linking organization-wide career programs to individually oriented activities. And what are some of these employee-focused activities? First, there is *more concern for the protean (or self-directed) career* (Hall, 1976). Especially since the recessions of 1979 and 1982, top managements have realized that the organization alone cannot possibly provide all of the career rewards an employee may seek. Thus, it is necessary to encourage employees to be proactive in assessing what they want most (values, needs, interests) and in planning ways to achieve those desires. Even very traditional, paternalistic organizations, such as Ford Motor Company, have advocated more employee participation in career planning (Horner, 1984). This change is one aspect of a "megatrend" that John Naisbett (1982) calls a shift from institutional help to self-help.

A number of specific changes in employee concerns are related to this protean shift. One reason employees have become more aware of the need to be protean is that *midcareer now comes earlier.* With flatter organizations and with thirty-ish baby boomers beginning to take up middle-level positions, people in their late twenties and early thirties are beginning to see their careers leveling off. Also, with more two-career couples, the concern for balance between work and family that we normally associate with midlife (the forties) is now turning up in people ten to fifteen years younger. Thus, people are beginning to see that if organizational opportunities are limited and the organization will not take care of their careers, employees will have to take care of themselves—that is, become more protean. Midcareer is a "hot" area for career researchers.

With the protean orientation, employees are more likely to *question and reject moves (even promotions).* This is often accompanied by *more honest self-assessment,* which results in a determination, say, that this promotion would not be a good fit for one's skills or that this geographic move would be terrible for one's spouse's career and for the family. In the past, there was more unquestioning acceptance of any move offered by the company, based on an assumption that "they know what is best for my career."

As a result of greater personal choice in career decisions, there is *more self-initiated plateauing.* When a person is settled into a satisfying job and his or her spouse and family are happy where they are, that person is more likely to turn down promotions that would mean either a more demanding job or a geographic relocation. Or perhaps as a result of good career self-assessment and planning, the individual may realize that, "I really love being an engineer. I want to grow as an engineer, but I do not want the hassles of management." Ann Howard and James Wilson (1982) have found empirical evidence of this reduced drive for upward mobility in the AT&T organization.

Part of what we have just been discussing reflects *more family inputs to career decisions and more two-career planning* (Hall and Hall, 1979). Many top executives are aware of this reality, but they do not know how to respond appropriately to it without intruding inappropriately on the employee's private life. (What they fail to realize is that they *already* are intruding on family and personal life through high job demands, relocation, travel, and other job pressures.) This is an emergent area of critical importance to organizations and individuals, where more creative human resource practices and research are sorely needed.

What most of these changes boil down to is *more mutual career planning* between the employee and the organization. To accomplish this, employees often report that their greatest career need is for *more information on company career opportunities*. It is impossible to plan without good information. And once he or she has developed a career plan, the employee needs assistance from the company in implementing that plan. Such information and planning is especially critical in facilitating career planning of women and minorities. Again, this requires that the individual career plan be linked in some way to the overall human resource planning process of the organization (the career management system). There is evidence that current activities in career theory, research, and practice are addressing this need.

Implementing Career Decisions: Linking Career Planning and Career Management

How can this important link between the individual's career planning and the organization's career management process be made? This section presents a model indicating the steps required to accomplish this person-organization integration (see Figure 2). The model focuses on mobility—that is, the placement process (transfers) that is a central factor in employee career management (Morrison and Holzbach, 1980).

Let us look at how this placement process works from the viewpoint of career management. It is assumed that several candidates are available for several jobs. The point of contact for individuals who become available for new assignments could be a career manager (assignment manager), who has access to each individual's complete file, including career progress reports, appraisals, and so on. The assignment manager has two roles. The primary one is to provide qualified candidates for organization jobs from an internal manpower pool. The second is to serve as a source of information to individuals within the organization. To an

Figure 2. Elements in the Career Management Process.

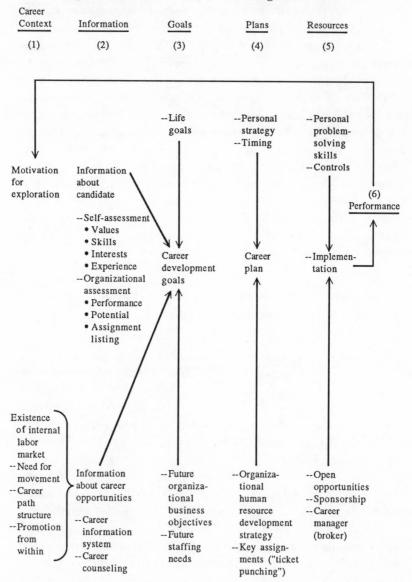

Note: Numbers refer to steps described in text.

extent, the assignment manager acts as a buffer between the individual and the organization. Through the career manager role, the career expectations and desires of individuals can be integrated with organizational requirements and constraints. The career manager role is described in detail by Morrison and Holzbach (1980).

While the career manager role is well established in military organizations (such as the detailer in the U.S. Navy and the assignments officer in the U.S. Army), it is still relatively unknown in other types of organizations. However, the basic activities of the role (providing candidates to managers and providing career information to employees) are being performed increasingly in private industry. Often the line personnel officers (such as the district personnel manager or director) will perform career management functions. For example, Continental Bank has a manager of internal placement who is essentially a career manager. More and more organizations are developing a succession planning or human resource planning process, with the directors of these functions often serving as career managers. And, in the absence of a formalized career manager position, line managers increasingly are charged with career management responsibilities for their subordinates.

So how does this placement process relate to individual career planning? The necessary meshing of individual and organizational needs can occur through several basic steps (see Figure 2). The first step is assessing the *career context*. The context represents basic prerequisites without which career development becomes an "uphill battle." At the individual level, the person must have motivation for career exploration, which initiates the process of career development. If the person is satisfied with his or her present position or is discouraged or for some other reason is not motivated to explore new career opportunities, the process stops right here. At the organizational level, there must exist an internal labor market through which internal candidates are trained, developed, and transfered to meet present and future staffing needs. Some critical elements of an internal labor market are top-level acceptance of the need for employee movement, a fairly clear career progression structure, and a policy of promotion from within.

Organizations with well-functioning internal labor markets (such as military organizations, AT&T, IBM, and Sears, Roebuck) tend to have more highly developed career management systems than do organizations that use the external labor market to meet staffing needs.

The second step is *information seeking.* Information about the candidate must be matched with information about career opportunities. Information about the person can be provided both through self-assessment (of one's values, skills, interests, experience, and other attributes) and through external assessment (performance appraisals, assessments of potential, formal assignment records, and so forth). A career counselor or a skilled manager can help the person by assisting the self-assessment process and by providing feedback on performance, potential, and past assignments.

One of the elements most often lacking in the career development process is information about career opportunities within the organization (Hall, 1976). Formal career or human resource information systems are being developed in a growing number of organizations, often providing employees direct access through personal computers. These formal systems are useful vehicles for permitting self-paced career exploration by employees. Career counseling or advice, provided by trained counseling staff or by trained managers, also can be an important adjunct to an information system, by helping the individual process the information and relate it to his or her own personal values, interests, skills, and experience. A career resource center often provides a physical space for both formal career information systems and counseling services. Such a resource center not only makes career exploration easier, but it also helps legitimize the process as well.

Once an employee has gathered information about him- or herself and about organizational opportunities, it is possible to begin the third step: setting realistic *goals* for career development. At the individual level, this requires that the person first think through his or her life goals, a process that probably will be aided by the self-assessment process just described. At the organizational level, in order for the career manager or counselor to help the person set realistic career goals, he or she must have some information about future business objectives and areas of the business that most likely. will be growing and providing good opportunities in the future. It also would be useful for him or her to have some idea of what the future staffing needs will be in the area in which the candidate is interested. For example, if the person is considering switching from manufacturing to marketing but marketing is forecasting a labor surplus for the next five years and thus has minimal need for new staff, this area would not be a promising one to pursue.

The fourth step, once the person's career goals have been crystallized, is the development of specific *plans* for pursuing these goals. At the individual level, the person must have acquired the ability to think strategically and to be able to apply strategy to him- or herself, not just to work projects. This also entails knowing what sort of timing is appropriate for various types of career moves.

At the organizational level, a strategy of human resource development is an important facilitator. Such a strategy could include elements such as creating the role of career manager, having maximum and minimum times for holding assignments, and the conscious use of lateral movement to develop varied skills (Hall, 1984). Related strategic human resource development would be a clear identification of key assignments through which a person must move ("ticket punching") in order to acquire the skills and experience needed for a desired career objective.

The fifth step in career management is helping the individual *implement* the career plan. It is particularly important to provide him or her with problem-solving and coping skills, which are instrumental in overcoming the inevitable difficulties that arise as one works on a plan. (Hall's Law is that Murphy's Law is intensified when it comes to implementing career plans.) Personal contacts with key managers, a peer support system, and networking also can be critical aids to successful career activity.

At the organizational level, the career opportunities the person identified as good-fit possibilities in step 2 (information seeking) must in fact be open. This does not mean that specific assignments must be open right now; rather, it means that there must be a realistic probability that they might be open (and open to this particular person) in the foreseeable future. Nothing dampens a person's motivation for further career exploration more severely than doing all the work of preparing for a career path that turns out to be blocked. This lack of congruence between individual career planning and organizational staffing needs represents a severe disincentive to future career planning. It is also important to have organizational support from people in positions of power. The career manager plays a powerful broker role in "selling" the candidate to frequently skeptical receiving managers (who might fear being victims of a "turkey trade"). Often managers can serve as informal sponsors in nominating and supporting a candidate for a desired position.

The sixth and final step in career development is *performance*. Once the person is in the desired position, he or she must perform well in order to be a candidate for further movement. Thus, good performance can be a feedback variable, triggering another cycle in the career growth process.

Chapters in This Volume

The frontier career activities described in the chapters of this book cover the full career development spectrum. The table of contents describes a sequence of chapters that allows the reader to view that spectrum in terms of major arenas of career development activity: cultural and organizational contexts, individual efforts, organizational programs, and current and future work. However, the chapters also afford the reader a view of the spectrum that focuses specifically on the individual and the organization; that is, on the micro and macro aspects I have discussed in this chapter. Figure 3 shows the relationship of the chapters to this spectrum.

On the micro, or individual, side, Donald Super's chapter (Chapter Three) explores the relationship between work and leisure, considering how the career relates to the employee's private life. Because leisure involvements affect employees' decisions about work and careers, this personal side of the employee's life has increasing relevance for employing organizations. More toward individual career planning, Frank Minor, in Chapter Six, describes

Figure 3. Chapters in this Volume in Relation to the Career Spectrum.

Employee-Centered: career planning		Mutual focus: manager-employee planning		Organization-Centered: career management	
• Super	• Minor	• London and Stumpf	• Kram	• Campbell and Moses	• Gutteridge
		• Hall			• Morrison and Hock

how computerized systems are helping individuals sort out personal values and interests and see how these personal profiles can fit with organizational opportunities. Such systems make individualized feedback and assistance with decision making available on a large-scale basis, getting away from the need for one-on-one career counseling.

Moving more toward the center of the spectrum, Manuel London and Stephen Stumpf (Chapter One) describe current trends in employee career values, as well as organizational programs that enhance various dimensions of career effectiveness. Chapter Four (Hall) examines personal and organizational factors that trigger changes for the employee in midcareer. These influences that disrupt a career routine result sometimes from personal life changes and sometimes from organizational changes.

Chapter Five, by Kathy Kram, looks at how individual development is affected by one facet of the organizational environment: work relationships. While interventions can be made in the work environment to promote developmental relationships, the dilemma is that if these activities become formal and organization driven (that is, if they move too far to the right on the career spectrum), they will lose the qualities of personal choice and commitment and thus will lose effectiveness.

Chapter Eight, by Richard Campbell and Joseph Moses, describes the experience of one innovative organization (AT&T) in developing successful career programs. These programs were organizationwide interventions in which the targets were generally the job assignment, the fit between employee and job, and the employee-boss relationship. Thus, both individual and organizational development outcomes were promoted.

Chapter Two, by Thomas Gutteridge, as we said earlier, describes the entire array of current organizational practices in the area of career development. Gutteridge also makes the important contribution of showing how career management activities can be integrated with career planning. Chapter Seven, by Robert Morrison and Roger Hock, looks at the organization in a more "macro" way, as representing an entire array of possible job assignments for the individual. They report an integrative, multidisciplinary model of how to study job mobility as a method of gradually "building in" new knowledge, skills, and abilities to the employee's repertoire of resources.

In Chapter Nine, a pioneer in the area of career development, Edgar Schein, assesses the general state of the field of careers, as represented by the chapters in this volume. It is not a totally positive assessment. For example, Schein sees much fragmentation in the field, with authors in one discipline being unaware of the relevant work of writers in other disciplines. We hope this volume will be a way to draw together different perspectives between two covers, if not within chapters. Schein concludes his chapter with useful ideas for future work in his call for more descriptive research.

Conclusion

The similar features of these chapters are that they all represent attempts to blend theory, research, and creative practice. These are not intended to be "annual review"-type chapters but rather more detailed explorations of new approaches to careers. We will continue in the next two chapters with an examination of the current cultural and organizational context of careers.

References

Carnazza, J. *Succession/Replacement Planning: Programs and Practices*. New York: Center for Research in Career Development, Columbia University Graduate School of Business, 1982.

Fombrun, C., Tichy, N. M., and Devanna, M. A. (eds.). *Strategic Human Resource Management.* New York: Wiley, 1984.

Hall, D. T. *Careers in Organizations.* Glenview, Ill.: Scott, Foresman, 1976.

Hall, D. T. "Human Resource Development and Organizational Effectiveness." In C. Fombrun, N. M. Tichy, and M. A. Devanna (eds.), *Strategic Human Resource Management.* New York: Wiley, 1984.

Hall, D. T., and Goodale, J. G. *Human Resource Management: Strategy, Design, and Implementation.* Glenview, Ill.: Scott, Foresman, 1986.

Hall, D. T., and Hall, F. S. "What's New in Career Management?" *Organizational Dynamics,* 1976, *5,* 17–33.

Hall, D. T., and Isabella, L. "Downward Moves and Career Development." *Organizational Dynamics,* 1985, *14,* 5–23.

Hall, D. T., and Richter, J. "The Baby Boom and Management: Is There Room at the Middle?" Unpublished working paper, Boston University School of Management, 1985.

Hall, F. S., and Hall, D. T. *The Two-Career Couple.* Reading, Mass.: Addison-Wesley, 1979.

Horner, P. "Career Planning at Ford Motor Company." Paper presented at annual meeting of the American Society for Personnel Administration, Chicago, Apr. 27, 1984.

Howard, A., and Wilson, J. A. "Leadership in a Declining Work Ethic." *California Management Review,* 1982, *24,* 19.

Jones, L. Y. *Great Expectations: America and the Baby Boom Generation.* New York: Random House, 1980.

Kram, K. E. *Mentoring at Work.* Glenview, Ill.: Scott, Foresman, 1985.

Latack, J. C. "Down or Out: Strategies for Managing Involuntary Career Movement." Symposium presented at annual meeting of the Academy of Management, San Diego, Calif., Aug. 13, 1985.

Morrison, R. F., and Holzbach, R. L. "The Career Manager Role." In C. B. Derr (ed.), *Work, Family and the Career.* New York: Praeger, 1980.

Naisbett, J. *Megatrends: Ten New Directions Transforming Our Lives.* New York: Warner Books, 1982.

Pfeffer, J., and Salancik, G. *The External Control of Organizations: A Resource Dependence Perspective.* New York: Harper & Row, 1978.

Russell, L. B. *The Baby Boom Generation and the Economy.*Washington, D.C.: Brookings Institution, 1982.

Schneider, B., and Schmitt, N. *Staffing Organizations.* (2nd ed.) Glenview, Ill.: Scott, Foresman, forthcoming.

Sorcher, M. *Predicting Executive Success: What it Takes to Make It into Senior Management.* New York: Wiley, 1985.

Storey, W. D. *Career Dimensions I, II, III, and IV.* Croton-on-Hudson, N.Y.: General Electric, 1976.

1

꒰ꩰ꒱꒰ꩰ꒱꒰ꩰ꒱꒰ꩰ꒱꒰ꩰ꒱꒰ꩰ꒱꒰ꩰ꒱꒰ꩰ꒱꒰ꩰ꒱

Individual
and Organizational
Career Development
in Changing Times

Manuel London

Stephen A. Stumpf

During the next twenty years, career development opportunities and programs will be affected by technological, organizational, and individual changes. New jobs and job displacements will result from new technology. Some organizations will experience pressure to decrease their size due to increased competition. Most organizations will need to be adaptable and employ a flexible work force. In addition, changes in family responsibilities and personal values will affect work patterns. Confronted with change and uncertainty, individuals will need to be adaptive, able to handle ambiguity, and resilient in the face of career barriers.

Technological, Organizational, and Human Systems Interface

Technological, organizational, and individual changes affect each other and influence careers through organizational policies and programs, competencies and other characteristics of individuals and groups, and career alternatives. Some futurists have called recent massive changes the "third industrial revolution" (Finkelstein and Newman, 1984) or the "third wave" (Toffler, 1980). Some of the technological change centers on computers, which influence information collection and communication. However, technological change goes beyond developments in computer science to include developments in engineering, the sciences, and health and financial services.

Organizational structures are also changing to enhance organizational effectiveness and efficiency. Changes include fewer levels of organizational hierarchy to be more cost effective, international spheres of operation, and a greater need for group efforts. (See Campbell and Moses' case analysis of AT&T in Chapter Eight.) Some changes are more social, economic, or political in nature. Human values are changing as family structures are altered and people find new ways to meet their needs and new needs to meet. The increased number of dual-career couples means that there is less likely to be a single breadwinner in the family. Today, balancing work and family is a dominant concern.

Technological, organizational, and societal changes influence how organizations treat people, the types of people organizations hire and develop, and the career opportunities available. For instance, the composition of the work force and demographic characteristics determine the numbers and types of people vying for entry-level positions. Technological change creates new jobs as well as job displacements suggesting the need for retraining. Organizational uncertainty and economic pressures create the need for innovative, entrepreneurial behavior, decentralized work structures, and increased responsibility to client or user demands. Technological and information system developments affect how and where people work and the need for coordination and collaboration with others. In the future, it will not be effective to optimize a technical system and then make the best residual fit of the social system to the technical system; both systems need to be designed together (Davis, 1983–1984).

Changing Career Opportunities

Changes in Social Values. Technological change is coinciding with changes in social values. People want more opportunities for development, autonomy, flexibility, and meaning-ful work experiences (Hammett, 1984). They want to partici-pate fully in the work environment; they react adversely to rigid hierarchies and the lack of involvement in decisions affecting them. Organizational structures and management styles must develop to implement technological advances in ways that are appropriate to changing human values (Maccoby, 1984; Robertson, 1982).

Changes in the work force have meant that career progres-sion is not as linear or predictable as it was in the past. For example, there is little that is linear or predictable in a career sense for the woman who reenters the work force after raising a family, for the person who makes a midcareer occupational change, for the individual who shifts from employer to employer, or for the person who retires early. Consider the thousands of fifty-year-old managers who are offered a financial incentive to leave their company before retirement age. If they enter the open job market after being with one company most of their careers, they may have to make an occupational shift without the planning or thought that normally goes into such a change.

Changes in Management Style. Market and economic conditions have created new demands on management in many industries. For example, consider the merger of a large, profitable bureaucratic industrial distribution company in Canada with a large, unprofitable Canadian steel fabrication company with slim managerial ranks and few resources (Hurst, 1984). The resulting company was York Russel, Inc. The executives of the industrial distributor were accustomed to working with facts and solid markets; the managers of the steel fabrication company were not. Both managements found that they had to achieve a balance between what they called "hard" management and "soft" management. The hard approach focused on tasks that were static, clear, content and fact oriented, and scientifically based, whereas the soft approach focused on tasks that were more fluid, ambiguous, process oriented, perceptual, and artistically based. Each manager needed an appreciation for multiple roles, including being action oriented and knowledgeable, managing detail, taking creative risks, challenging existing policies, and integrating people and ideas to give the management team a sense of direction and shared experience.

Technological and organizational changes often redefine productivity and development from an individual to a group or team phenomenon. In the twenty-first century, we will speak of a team's or organization's ability to apply skills and experiences to new possibilities in a way that is innovative and that adds value (Finkelstein and Newman, 1984). Productivity will require finding, building, and combining know-how in flexible, effective ways. Development will include working as part of a team, learning new skills so as to be able to switch functions with members of the team, receiving frequent and prompt feedback, being rewarded for one's contribution to the team, and sharing rewards based on the outputs of the team.

The organization structure of the future will not be a neat array of boxes structured in a pyramid. Firms experiencing rapidly changing and uncertain environments, such as high-technology and financial services firms, demonstrate that there is no one best way to organize. Flexibility is key. Individuals must be able to adopt different roles, move from group to group, establish broad interpersonal and technical skills, be innovative in dealing with ambiguity, and know when to act independently and when to act cooperatively.

The Need for New Competencies. The changes in human values and managerial styles noted above suggest that new competencies will be required for individual and organizational effectiveness. A world of uncertainty and complexity requires accepting the fact that we seldom deliberately change things from A to B, acknowledging uncertainty, and seeing the world as "both/and" (connected) rather than "either/or" (separate) (Michael, 1983). In such a world, collaboration, involvement, participation, and trust are preconditions for learning. Being resilient and adaptable, managing ambiguity, and being innovative in our career and family management are going to be the foundation for a meaningful career. Insight into ourselves and our environments is needed if we are to respond to change effectively.

A Summary of Trends

Taking into account technological, organizational, and human/societal changes, employees in the 1990s will face:

1. more and different kinds of specialists with different values, career insights, and technical languages
2. more people working away from the traditional office setting
3. more flexible approaches to work (such as flexible hours, job sharing, and part-time employment)
4. decreased loyalty to companies (people will change jobs and careers more often)
5. formal organizational structures giving way to project teams, task forces, matrix structures, and interdependent units
6. an increasing need to train and retrain people at different career stages in order to maintain job security
7. changes in how people relate to each other (for instance, communication via computer lacks nonverbal cues and displays no emotions)
8. more collaborative and cooperative work, including involvement in decision making
9. pressure to increase job satisfaction by changing job content

Career Development Programs: A Perspective for the 1990s

Developing Career Motivation

We have argued that technological, organizational, and human system changes are driving organizational policies and management styles, competency requirements, and career options. Given these variables and their relationships, we now consider employees' career motivation and what it suggests organizations should do to develop employees.

Career motivation includes being resilient in the face of change, having insight into one's self and the environment, and identifying with one's job, organization, and/or profession as career goals (London, 1983, 1985). These elements of career motivation are defined as follows:

Career Resilience. This is the extent to which we keep our spirits up when things do not work out as we would have liked. This includes how resistant we are to career barriers or disruptions affecting our work. People who are high in career resilience see themselves as competent individuals who are able to control their responses to what happens to them. They get a sense of accomplishment from what they do and are able to take risks. They know when and how to cooperate with others and when to act independently. They respond to obstacles and undesired events by reframing their ideas and repositioning their energies to allow them to move ahead anyway.

Career Insight. This refers to the extent to which people are realistic about themselves and their careers and how accurately they relate these perceptions to their career goals. People who are high in career insight try to understand themselves in light of their environments. They look for feedback about how well they are doing. They set specific career goals and formulate how they can achieve these goals. They tend to know how to capitalize on their strengths and overcome or avoid situations requiring strengths they do not have.

Career Identity. Our career identity is the extent to which we define ourselves by our work. People who are high in career identity are involved in their jobs, their careers, and their professions. They are likely to feel loyalty to their employers. Career identity reflects the direction of people's career goals—whether or not they want to advance in the company, be in positions of leadership and high status, and earn more money, and whether they are content to wait for this to happen or strive to accomplish these goals as soon as possible.

Manager Development Guidelines

Our research and a review of the management literature suggests a set of situational variables that influence the individual characteristics of career motivation (London, 1985). These situational conditions are based on widely accepted concepts in the areas of job design, leadership style, goal setting, performance appraisal, and feedback. These conditions are summarized in Table l in the form of manager development guidelines. The guidelines suggest that career development programs need to extend beyond goal setting and career planning to include the nature of supervision (for example, the feedback given), the nature of the job (for example, the level of challenge), and organizational conditions (for example, opportunities for advancement and recognition).

Several new and innovative career development programs that are suggestive of trends for the 1990s support the career development guidelines in Table 1 and enhance the different elements of career motivation. These programs are discussed as follows under the career motivation element to which they contribute most in our opinion.

**Table 1. Manager Development Guidelines for
Enhancing Career Motivation.**

Career motivation dimensions	Manager development guidelines
Career resilience	
Belief in oneself	Positive reinforcement for jobs well done
Need for achievement	Opportunities for achievement
Willingness to take risks	Rewards for innovation without undue punishment for failure
Career insight	
Having clear career goals	Support for career development
Knowing one's strengths and weaknesses	Feedback
Career identity	
Job, organization, and professional involvement	Job challenge and encouragement of involvement
Need for advancement and recognition and wanting to lead	Rewards and opportunities

I. Building Career Resilience

The need for people to have greater career resilience stems from several trends: the increased amount of retraining needed for people to keep up with technological changes, changes in the ways people relate to each other given the computer and communications explosion, and pressures to maintain or increase job satisfaction by changing job content. The kinds of career development programs that will enhance career resilience are those that identify and develop the key competencies required by the job, establish learning guides to direct employees' efforts, and help employees deal with increased uncertainty in the work environment.

A. Competency Models. One approach to helping managers face today's environment of rapid change and competitive pressure is to identify the key competencies that managers need in order to be successful. Earlier we suggested that tolerance of uncertainty and ambiguity, flexibility, and automony will be increasingly needed in the future. Organizations need to conduct studies to identify the key competencies required in their specific environments. Such research should compare successful managers to less successful managers, and the results should be used for the selection and development of future managers.

One company identified five major outputs expected of successful managers: (1) setting performance goals, (2) designing challenging jobs and effective work groups, (3) generating a positive work climate, (4) fostering contacts with other departments to facilitate business objectives, and (5) accomplishing the mission of the work group and the organization as a whole. The company emphasized that it was not specifying how managers should accomplish these outcomes or what abilities they needed in order to accomplish them. The particular activities chosen to accomplish the outcomes were each manager's responsibility; the company recognized that there were different ways to attain the same outcome. Managers in the company formulated their goals in terms of outputs and specified criteria for determining whether the outputs would be successfully accomplished. At the end of each year, supervisors evaluated subordinates based on whether the outcomes had been accomplished.

B. Learning Guides. Training is a way for companies to inform managers about organizational expectations and to provide support in meeting those expectations. IBM, for example, requires its managers to have forty hours of training a year, some of which is general management training in elements of effective supervision. Another company offers traditional classroom training but finds that many managers do not avail themselves of such training because they do not see the tie to immediate business needs. This organization published a set of learning guides to help managers understand how they should set goals, counsel subordinates about career opportunities, evaluate performance, and give feedback. One guidebook outlined methods and examples of how to design meaningful jobs and encourage collaboration in work groups.

C. Dealing with Ambiguity. As stated earlier, new competencies are required in a world of uncertainty, complexity, and change. We must understand that we can affect our environment— but not necessarily in exactly the way we intend (Michael, 1983). People react to ambiguity in different ways. Some see ambiguity as challenging; others see it as negative. The challenge of the future is to get managers to understand what situations make them most effective in doing their jobs.

Business simulations offer one way to assess and develop a person's ability to handle ambiguity effectively. Several exercises now exist that ask a group of managers to manage a simulated organization (Petre, 1984). Trained staff observe the participants, evaluate the decisions (or lack thereof), and provide group and individual feedback on more than a dozen managerial skills. The Center for Creative Leadership in Greensboro, North Carolina, designed a simulation based on a fictitious glass manufacturing company called Looking Glass, Inc.; IBM designed a high-technology firm called the Simmons Simulator; and New York University's School of Business designed two financial services companies—Metrobank and Investcorp. Each of these simulations has been used by a large number of organizations to address management skills in a live environment. The simulations allow managers to experiment with new behaviors without the fear of being evaluated as they would be on the job. The content of the simulations can be varied to create ambiguous environments in

which initiative and creativity count and by-the-book behaviors are
of little value.

II. Programs That Build Career Insight

The need to increase people's career insight is driven by the
increasing number and kind of job opportunities, flexibility as to
one's choice of workplace (home or office) and approach to work
(flexible hours, job sharing, part-time employment and so on), and
opportunities to change employers if dissatisfied. Support for the
development of career insight can come from the boss in the form
of encouragement for goal setting, information about career
opportunities, and feedback on job performance and potential for
advancement. Employees' understanding of their skills, needs, and
ambitions in relation to career opportunities can come from other
sources as well—peers, subordinates, and actually doing the job.
Also, companies may offer programs aimed at helping employees
understand themselves and the opportunities available to them
within the organization. These include motivation awareness
training, computer-based planning systems, development journals,
and assessment centers for evaluating managerial skills and career-
related personality characteristics, needs, and interests. It also
includes training for new careers. These career development
programs are discussed as follows:

A. Motivation Awareness. Motivation awareness training
has been developed in one company for new managers and for high-
potential managers on a fast advancement track (London, 1985).
The objective of this half-day program is to help managers increase
their awareness of their career motivation and understand the
viewpoints of their peers and supervisors. Participants begin by
watching a videotape of managers like themselves describing how
they get a sense of achievement from their work, deal with new
assignments, take actions with uncertain outcomes, depend on
others, balance work and nonwork activities, form career goals,
obtain feedback, and vie for promotions. The participants then
discuss how their responses compare with those on the tape. Next
they watch a videotape of interviews with supervisors describing
perceptions of new managers (or fast-track managers), problems

and barriers to supervising, and how the supervisors encourage work involvement, provide opportunities and rewards to subordinates, give career information and feedback, and encourage innovation. The participants then discuss their own supervisors as barriers to or facilitators of their career development and what they can do about it. Finally, the participants establish priorities for their development, such as obtaining more feedback. They write action steps to accomplish these priorities and share them in a group session, soliciting feedback from each other.

B. *Development Journals.* A development journal is a record or set of notes made to help one track one's development needs over time. This technique asks managers to record their job experiences and important related events (such as training programs) and then reflect on these experiences and examine linkages among them. The process may be facilitated by materials given to participants periodically. Such materials might include forms for keeping track of events, information about career opportunities, and self-assessment measures focusing on expectations, needs, interests, or values. Participants score themselves and can see their profiles immediately. Learning guides are provided to help them interpret their scores. The managers are asked to return the results anonymously so that the scores can be averaged and a summary of the group results returned to help them compare their results with those of others. Some of the self-assessment instruments ask for evaluations on the same performance dimensions the bosses use to evaluate them. Some measures are repeated over time so that the managers can see how their responses have changed.

C. *Computer-Based Career-Planning Programs.* IBM developed a computer-based career-planning program for the company's internal use (see Chapter Seven). Run on a personal computer, the program asks employees what they are doing to enhance their development; if they are not doing much, the program informs them in blunt language that their opportunities at IBM are likely to be limited. One purpose of the program is to match job description information with employees' needs and interests. The program challenges employees' responses to be sure that they understand the implications of the results. For example, an individual may indicate interest in a particular job but not with jobs that usually follow that position in the career path. This would suggest that the employee would be in a dead-end position.

The computer program takes about three hours to complete, and employees are encouraged to repeat it whenever they wish. One potential disadvantage is that employees may not be accurate in judging their abilities, and this could lead to inaccurate expectations. To avoid this, IBM encourages employees to discuss the results with their bosses. While the program does not reveal information about current vacancies, bosses have access to this information and can help employees make a job move when it is in the interest of both the business and the individual. The computer program is not necessarily geared to helping employees advance in the corporate hierarchy. Rather, the focus is on skill and motivation awareness, objectives for broadening one's knowledge of the business, and investigating opportunities for new job experiences at the same level.

Another similar microcomputer program assists individuals in developing career insight. Five modules help employees: (1) analyze their present career satisfaction and understand the career changes they may face, (2) assess themselves on interests, skills, and values, (3) gather information about career opportunities, (4) help identify decision-making styles and improve decision-making skills related to career moves, and (5) identify realistic goals and establish an action plan to increase the likelihood of success.

D. Career Motivation Assessment. London and Bray (1984; see also London, 1985) designed a two-day assessment center that focused on individual characteristics associated with career motivation. The career motivation assessment used in-depth interviews, behavioral exercises, personality and projective tests, and several questionnaires and essays. The material on each participant was reviewed by the assessors, who rated each participant on the dimensions of career motivation (career resilience, career insight, career identity, and related variables). Selected results were then fed back to the participants.

The career motivation assessment can provide input for career planning, but its intention is broader. Focusing on personal variables, such as belief in oneself, need for achievement, and risk-taking tendency (elements of career resilience), the assessment center can provide the individual and the career counselor with information that is helpful in matching the individual to jobs and that suggests ways to improve interpersonal relationships, take initiative, seek more rewarding assignments, and so on.

The assessment process also offers information on career insight, including not only the nature of one's career goals but also one's sensitivity to the social and political environment at work and the accuracy of one's self-perception. Information about career identity is helpful in understanding one's needs in comparison to others in the company and in relation to organizational conditions and opportunities. The career motivation assessment is most valuable to individuals who feel that they lack career direction, self-confidence, and/or a sense of their own strengths and weaknesses.

E. Retraining. Retraining will be increasingly important in the future. Millions of people will be "deskilled" as their jobs become archaic and their skills obsolete (Nussbaum, 1983). The U.S. Navy deals with this issue by requiring officers to develop a subspecialty, usually a staff position such as personnel or the management of computer programmers. Officers transfer every few years between line positions and positions in their subspecialties. The subspecialty is often unrelated to the specialty area, which is usually technical.

Most workers do not have the opportunity to develop a second skill on which to fall back in case of displacement by new technology. Gary Hart, while campaigning for the 1984 Democratic Presidential nomination, suggested that individuals and organizations be required to pay into an Individual Training Accounts Fund (Hart, 1983). This fund would cover retraining and moving costs for displaced employees and spread the burden of transitional adjustments.

III. Programs That Build Career Identity

A sense of career identity is necessary in order to give employees some stability within an uncertain work environment. The fact that traditional organizational structures are giving way to project teams, task forces, matrix structures, and other temporary systems undermines people's ability to define themselves by their

work. The decreasing loyalty to an employer that typically results
and the increasing need to seek retraining further reduce one's
feeling of career identity. Yet a strong career identity seems to be
necessary for individual and organizational effectiveness.

Career identity reflects the current direction of our career
goals, such as striving for advancement, wanting recognition, and
desiring to make more money. Today's young managers, on the
average, are less desirous of being leaders and followers than were
young managers in the past. They do not want to be part of a
hierarchy but just want to be left alone to pursue their own goals.
Also, they are less certain that a management career is for them
(Howard and Bray, 1981). Results from a variety of companies show
changing values toward more balanced life-styles with less
emphasis on work (Opinion Research Corporation, 1980). For
example, dual-career couples, already making high combined
salaries, worry as much about juggling child-care responsibilities
and leisure interests as they do about their careers. And they may
be unwilling to relocate for a new job, even if it involves a
promotion.

A. Specialized Development Programs. Research indicates
that the organization's support for career development and
opportunities for advancement and for transfer into more
responsible assignments at the same level influence a young
manager's expectations. One study found that managers in a high-
potential development program were more motivated to advance in
the corporate hierarchy than were managers in another company
that did not provide special treatment or concern for development
and in which there were few opportunities for advancement and
movement to more challenging assignments (London and Bray,
1984). The philosophy in the former company is that young
managers are resources for the future, while the latter company
believes that the function of all managers is limited to meeting
current business needs. One possible explanation for the differences
in motivation level between the two companies is that the
development-oriented company may have attracted and selected
more motivated people than the other company. However, no
company differences in the backgrounds of the participants suggest
this, and the researchers proposed that if the managers from

the nondevelopment-oriented company were transfered to the development-oriented company, their motivation levels would increase.

   B. *A Development Ethic.* Career identity can be influenced by job opportunities and the career information available to employees. In the development-oriented company just mentioned, managers at all levels were attuned to providing developmental assignments, counseling subordinates on career opportunities, and giving performance feedback. Assessment centers, career-planning programs, and promotion and transfer policies supported this effort. Employees knew that advancement was necessary in order to obtain more challenging assignments. Many signals in the company made career development and positive expectations for the future salient to the younger managers.

   In many organizations, managers espouse the idea that they develop their subordinates so the subordinates can perform better and advance in the company. However, managers often pay little attention to actually developing subordinates, because it is not directly related to the immediate needs of the business and the objectives of the department. Some companies have tried to overcome this by evaluating supervisors on the extent to which they develop their subordinates. Consequently, developing subordinates becomes a legitimate performance goal, is part of the annual performance appraisal, and is one factor contributing to merit pay increases. Doing this requires that training, learning guides, and upper-level management commitment support the process.

IV. *Career Motivation Programs Targeted to Different Career Stages*

   The following section examines career motivation at three career stages: early career, midcareer, and late career. Several career motivation programs are discussed as they relate to the differing needs of people at different stages in their careers.

   A. *Early Career.* Early job experiences are important to later success (Berlew and Hall, 1966; Stumpf and Hartman, 1984). The early job environment motivates the employee and gives the employee opportunities that lead to better opportunities. Pro-

motion is a tournament: You have to be promoted from first
level to second level to be eligible for third level, and since
organizations are pyramidal in structure, opportunities become
fewer as one climbs the corporate ladder (Rosenbaum, 1979).
Therefore, early successes are important to later career success.

New Manager Orientation. Socialization into the organization informs the new employee about what is expected at a time
when the employee wants to be accepted and so is susceptible to
influence. Formal orientation programs usually provide information about organizational systems and policies, such as benefit
programs, the performance appraisal and reward systems, and so
forth. At Dow Jones and Company, a group of about twenty new
managers from different departments are brought together for the
orientation. These new managers spend one day sharing information about their jobs and how they interface with other departments. For example, the discussions highlight the relationships among circulation services, production, customer service, and
so on. New managers thus gain a better understanding of how the
organization operates. In the process, they meet people from other
departments who can help them do their jobs. This encourages
building networks and relationships, which thereby improves
organizational effectiveness and enhances career identity.

Another type of orientation is the motivation awareness
program discussed earlier. The goal here is to encourage new
managers to think about their own needs and interests in relation
to career opportunities and barriers in the work environment.

Alternative Early Career Tracks. Companies have different
philosophies regarding how to treat new employees, particularly
those hired into management. One philosophy, often used by major
banks, is to hire bright college graduates and put them into a "sink-
or-swim" training program. The first year of such a program bears
some similarity to a fraternity or sorority hazing, with new
managers required to work long hours, digest volumes of material,
change jobs every few months to learn how different departments
operate, and produce exceptional results. Those who do well seem
to identify with the company and are advanced rapidly. Those who
do not often look elsewhere for employment.

An alternative is to begin by hiring an employee for a specific job to meet a current business need, not for a general managerial position. Using this system, the first eight months to a year on the job constitutes a period of acclimation, during which the newcomer has a chance to demonstrate good performance and potential for advancement. The most successful new managers are then placed on a fast-track program to prepare them for rapid advancement. Those who do not show potential and those who do not succeed on the fast track are placed on a standard career track. All jobs on the standard career track provide opportunities for challenge and advancement supported by career planning and development activities, but these opportunities occur at a slower pace than they do for high-potential managers (London and Stumpf, 1982; London, 1984). As such, career motivation in terms of resilience, insight, and identity are likely to be enhanced.

The choice of development programs and policies an organization uses depends on what the managers of the organization must know in order to get things done. A manager may be required to know how different parts of the organization operate and/or know several areas in-depth. The desirability of a fast-track program depends on the rate of growth and change in the organization and the number of promotion opportunities likely to be available in the future.

In general, the number of people involved in a fast-track program should be adjusted on the basis of projections of opportunities in middle and higher levels of management. However, an organization may continue to hire into a fast-track program even when opportunities are declining, in order to infuse new blood. This may create unrealistic expectations and a problem of turnover of talented individuals not resilient in the face of likely disappointments. One company faced with this situation has instituted a "vitality" program by offering economic incentives so that long-tenure middle managers can retire early. This makes room for younger employees to be advanced rapidly into middle management.

A difficulty with training managers to be generalists by moving them into a succession of different jobs is that they have trouble accomplishing truly substantive efforts, and as such they may not be viewed as credible by their coworkers. A good briefing about each new job is necessary to spell out what is expected. It also helps to have someone to whom the person can go to discuss a problem without risk, thereby fostering learning and career resilience.

B. *Midcareer.* Today the notion of a midcareer crisis is well known. This is the feeling of anxiety that occurs as we begin to wonder if we will accomplish all we hope to or if our goals are the right ones to begin with. Factors precipitating midcareer crisis include physical events, such as a change in appearance, sexual problems, or a breakdown in health—each one forcing us to realize our mortality. Marital strife, problems with children, or children leaving home (the "empty nest syndrome") are other causes (Kets de Vries, 1978). People who have adapted well to change in their lives in the past are likely to act constructively in response to these changes and the associated feeling of anxiety (Vaillant, 1977; DuBois, 1981). Others who are less effective at solving problems and making adjustments are likely to deny the realities of aging, be passive, distort reality, behave defensively, lower their aspirations, or become depressed and give up.

A pervasive problem in corporations today is the plight of midcareer managers who are plateaued in middle management positions. Longitudinal research has shown that plateaued managers adapt rather quickly to the lack of advancement opportunities, experiencing little trauma by lowering their expectations and developing nonwork facets of their lives (Bray and Howard, 1980). For instance, men in midcareer enjoy older children more and invest more in parenting as their children age. Happily, this coincides with people's career plateaus when they are less concerned about career advancement (DuBois, 1981).

A difficulty that is occurring now and that will become even stronger in the future is the declining need for middle managers. As stated at the outset, organizations are cutting the number of middle-management positions in an effort to become more cost effective. As computers come into greater use, middle managers become less necessary as processors and interpreters of information. Consequently, retraining is necessary not just for occupational workers displaced by production technology but also for middle managers displaced by information and analysis technology. On the one hand, this situation creates the possibility for increased unemployment for midcareer managers. On the other hand, it creates opportunities for increased career insight and resilience at a time in their lives when middle-aged workers are rethinking their goals as they come to terms with the match between their dreams and reality.

Considerable research will be necessary on effective ways of retraining. Perhaps new college curricula and new means of financial support will be necessary. It may become more acceptable for midcareer individuals to stop work and obtain another college degree or vocational training. Midcareer training may become accepted and even fashionable, creating an entirely new realm of education. Business organizations may increasingly offer financial incentives and paid outplacement services, as many do now, to encourage early retirement in efforts to reduce management surplus. These incentives could be geared less to those close to retirement or to those who can find new employment in their fields and more to individuals who can benefit from retraining for a midcareer change.

Retraining should be valuable in keeping plateaued managers motivated. Counseling also may help midcareer managers focus on their values, clarify their goals, and generate new goals, recognizing that they may stay at the same level in the organization for the rest of their careers. Still other strategies for enhancing career motivation in midcareer include lateral transfers to new types of work, meaningful job assignments, increased responsibility, serving on special task forces, serving as an internal consultant to help work groups, and being a mentor (Bardwick, 1983; London, 1985). Slower rates of advancement may become acceptable as young managers learn about fewer advancement prospects and develop accurate expectations. This also may mean altering the reward system to provide opportunities for merit increases and/or advances in pay grade to account for differences in responsibility within the same level of management.

C. Late Career. Late career is generally a time for maintaining established career patterns and eventually disengaging from the work force. Young elders (fifty-five to seventy-five years old) have a higher level of education, are healthier, and enjoy a longer life

expectancy than ever before. Many young elders are "knowledge
workers" (that is, they are in technical, professional, managerial,
and administrative capacities) and are accustomed to intellectually
challenging work. These young elders are valuable resources to
society, whether they are employed or retired. Mary Kouri (1984), a
career development counselor and gerontologist, argues for a
reengagement of young elders. She recommends that organizations
provide support for gradual, phased retirement. This may be
accomplished through providing extended periods away from work
for one to five years before retirement or gradually reducing the
number of hours worked per day or days worked per week. Older
employees can be valuable mentors, helping younger employees
learn how to adapt to change. Programs for helping younger
workers understand and take advantage of older employees'
experience and to keep older employees abreast of organizational
changes will probably be necessary. Preretirement-aged employees
can be valuable representatives of the organization in the
community. Unlikely to be transfered, they are entrenched in their
communities and contribute to the organization's reputation as an
employer.

Issues For Women and Minorities

While women and minorities are advancing in corporate
hierarchies, they are still underrepresented in middle management,
and they are almost absent from boardrooms and positions of
corporate leadership. Campbell and Moses, in their case study of
AT&T in Chapter Eight, discuss the actions taken by the company
to hire and develop more women as managers. Women face difficult
challenges in managing multiple roles and making role transitions.
Many young women today are delaying starting a family until their
careers are established. While some are willing to forgo a family for
career success, others feel that they can do both. Some women
change their career goals in their thirties as they begin to view life
as involving more than career advancement.

Women who start a family early, perhaps after holding a job
for a few years, often reenter the work force after their children are
in school (Yohalem, 1979). This necessitates sizeable adjustments.

Educated women returning to work in their thirties feel that they have many years ahead for a meaningful career (DuBois, 1981). Unfortunately, corporations often act as if it is too late for these women to gain the experience needed for rapid advancement beyond middle management. As a result, the women may find that their job experiences are not as exciting and fulfilling as they had hoped they would be. Effective working relationships may be difficult for women to establish in organizations because they have to overcome stereotypes. Developing mentor relationships with higher-level managers also may be difficult for women, further blocking the possibility of career advancement (Kram, 1985). Women are subject to discrimination in selection for entry-level jobs, lower salaries, and not being treated equally by peers (that is, not receiving sufficient information to do the job or being isolated from coworkers) (Terborg, 1977).

The difficulties of managing multiple roles, making role transitions, and possible sex discrimination on the job contribute to women experiencing less career motivation. The development of career resilience, career insight, and career identity takes on even greater importance for both women and their organizations.

Blacks also face problems of adjustment and unfulfilled expectations. Confronted by discrimination and low advancement prospects, many talented blacks have been leaving corporations to start their own businesses where they have more control over their careers (Hymowitz, 1984). Unfortunately, large corporations are losing sight of the fact that equal employment opportunity efforts are necessary to achieve real nondiscriminatory policies (Fernandez, 1981). In addition to recruiting blacks with executive potential, all organizations must provide the support necessary for them to achieve their potential.

Trends and Future Directions: A Summary

We have suggested that changes in technical, organizational, and human/societal systems influence not only each other but also organizational policies and programs, styles of management, competency requirements, and career alternatives. These latter changes are likely to influence career development programs and are hypothesized to affect individuals' career motivation. Table 2 summarizes the trends, their implications for organizations and individuals, and areas for development and research. Our predictions and recommendations for research and practice are discussed as follows:

1. While there is some disagreement in the literature on the effects of new technology and economic conditions on employment prospects, we believe that the widespread introduction of computers and labor-saving equipment (such as robots) will result in fewer positions for managerial as well as production workers. Jobs in the service sectors are likely to become more available. Pressures to reduce costs and the decreased need for managers to analyze and process raw information will eliminate many middle-management positions and decrease promotional opportunities for new managers. The challenge to be met is to provide the retraining required to shift the workforce into more knowledge worker occupations. Midcareer changes should become more frequent and more acceptable as the rate of technological change increases the role of technical and managerial obsolescence.

Career research should examine how employees effectively adjust to periods of transition and stability at different career stages. Both major career changes and adjustments in attitudes and ambitions as career paths are blocked should be considered. Research also needs to investigate ways to help individuals search for suitable alternatives and make career changes without feeling "locked in" by financial obligations. Psychologists will develop midcareer counseling programs and clinical methods to help people adjust to career changes. Also, we must learn more about adult learning processes and apply the latest developments in instructional technology.

2. With more people working away from the traditional office setting and adopting more flexible approaches to work (such as flextime, job sharing, and part-time employment), organizational structures should become more flexible and complex. The adoption of matrix structures suggests that people should have more than one boss and that one's reporting relationship should

Table 2. Career Development Research and Practice in the 1990s.

Trends	Organizational implications	Individual implications	Areas for programs and research
Technological advances Increased competition Economic pressures Uncertain conditions Need to be innovative Competition for talent Changing roles and values Heterogeneity of work force in skills and ambitions Changes in how and where work is done Acceptability of career changes Security of two-career family	Pressure to increase productivity and reduce costs Fewer traditional opportunities in management Changed meaning of development—from development for advancement to development for more autonomy or a different type of job Career barriers due to organizational change (decline) Change in management style—encouraging employee participation in decisions, rewarding innovation, managing interactions New and more flexible work schedules and organization designs Recognizing impact of organization decisions on employees Experimenting with new personnel and information systems based on employees' needs Productivity improvement programs	New Goals Different ways of achieving job satisfaction and motivation Reevaluating balance between work and family Critical stages of susceptibilities to influence Periods of transition and stability Need to be resilient—handling ambiguity and career barriers Need to know oneself and understand the work environment Career identity changes over time Need to learn new management behaviors Learning to take risks Willingness to change Precarious loyalty to the organization Feelings of discontent and being locked in	Focus on individual and organizational development and change Identifying skills needed for future productivity Identifying future job opportunities and areas for retraining Implementing midcareer counseling programs Facilitating employee movement between and within organizations Studying adult learning Using latest advances in instructional technology Helping employees through transitions Developing simulations and assessments for employee development and for coping with changing conditions Developing new performance criteria recognizing changing expectations Facilitating changes in management style Contributing to quality of work life and employee involvement programs and their evaluation Making personnel programs flexible and person-centered (programs that can be tailored to individual needs) Designing flexible group- and organization-centered structures Facilitating work team development

change depending on one's project. The job of the manager should entail boundary spanning, designing more temporary work systems, and managing interactions as opposed to directing the work activity of subordinates.

With the growth in number and kind of specialists with different values, career insights, and technical languages, there should be an associated growth in the breadth of criteria used to evaluate workers. While profitability and market share will continue to be organizational goals, quality of work life and employee well-being should become important goals in their own right, not just for their contributions to decreased costs. These goals will become real for the work force as organizations effectively train and reward supervisors for how well they develop their subordinates.

Career research needs to include the larger number of criteria for organizational success and focus on the relative effectiveness of various flexible and temporary alternative organizational structures. Psychologists will be called on to help in custom designing flexible group and organization structures. Methods to facilitate work team development will be important as teams form to accomplish specific tasks and then disband. People will need help in maintaining and increasing their productivity as they move from project to project and from group to group.

3. As formal, hierarchical organizational structures give way to more project teams, task forces, and matrix structures, career opportunities will be less standardized and less structured along well-defined career paths. Advancement should take place less in terms of movement up the corporate hierarchy and more in terms of increased responsibility and earning power. Career success needs to be redefined to include alternatives to promotion, such as indexes of competence, power, and status.

Career research is needed to help define general competency areas that guide people in making career transitions. Just as career paths serve as a road map for career movement in a fairly structured organization, positions requiring the same general competencies, although they may be in different departments or disciplines, should become the schematic for managing career transitions. For instance, research skills in the social sciences may be applicable to marketing, personnel, public relations, and program evaluation in a variety of business areas. Psychologists may be asked to facilitate movement of employees between and within organizations by applying selection and placement methods to midcareer employees and establishing new staffing systems, perhaps using national job banks to let people know what types of jobs are available. Work will be necessary to evaluate demographic data and skills inventories and compare them to job requirements in different industries. Such ongoing research will identify career opportunities and the types of retraining that will be necessary to take advantage of them.

4. As the need for retraining increases and as pressures mount to seek job satisfaction through changing job content or the job itself, employees need to develop greater career resilience. They need to be able to quickly bounce back after a shock to their ego systems. This suggests that career resilience should become more important to career success than career planning per se. Being resilient—handling career barriers and ambiguity effectively— should be crucial for individual and organizational success in the 1990s. Organizational career programs should be geared to providing general support for employee development, not just providing training directed toward hierarchical advancement.

Career research should examine how career resilience develops and changes over time. We need to have a better understanding of what job experiences contribute to "seasoning"— that is, experiences that prepare managers to succeed in changing and uncertain work environments. Psychologists should help organizations develop policies and train supervisors in management strategies that reinforce employees' self-confidence and encourage achievement and innovation.

5. The greater opportunities for specialization, the higher levels of uncertainty associated with the many changes taking place, and the increased need for periodic retraining suggest that those who develop strong career insights will be better able to manage their careers. People need to take a broad look at themselves, learning how to integrate their work with other aspects of their lives. It should become socially and professionally acceptable to

make major occupational changes in response to changing work opportunities and values.

Career development efforts should help individuals understand their strengths and weaknesses, needs and interests, and the social/political work environment. Management simulations and assessments should be offered to diagnose and develop managerial strengths rather than simply to evaluate employees for promotion potential. Employees should receive information about themselves from several sources—superiors, peers, subordinates, trained assessors—and this information should be used to determine training needs and career opportunities.

Career research needs to take a developmental perspective by examining how people and organizations change and affect each other over time. People go through many critical stages during their careers—at which time they are particularly susceptible to influence and need to adjust to major role transitions. Research needs to identify these stages and transitions and help organizations evaluate their efforts to provide support for employees at critical times.

6. Increased uncertainty in the work environment and changing roles for family members will drive many people to reevaluate the balance between work and nonwork activities. For many, identification with work as the major component of their self-concept will be altered. Their lowered career identity could result in less commitment to work, less loyalty to the employing organization, and lower motivation to advance. Organizations should recognize that their decisions affect individuals' nonwork lives and that many employees are not willing to sacrifice family and leisure interests for their jobs.

From the employee's perspective, the increased heterogeneity of the work force in terms of goals and values should provide a wider variety of career options. Some individuals will prefer being specialists—and may change their specialties several times during their careers. Others will seek traditional careers as workers or managers with the goal of advancement within the emerging organizational hierarchy. The economic security from a two-income family situation should reduce the organization's power to inflict its will on employees; however, it also may lock dual-career families into a higher standard of living that they may choose not to give up.

Research is needed to examine how career identity is changing over time. To the extent that career identity is less today than years ago, the links between individuals and organizations are weakened. The impact of new career management systems on career and organizational commitment needs to be addressed in light of such changes. Therefore, evaluation research is needed on such management systems as alternative work schedules, flextime, child-care options, preretirement planning, and career and life counseling.

References

Bardwick, J. M. "Plateauing and Productivity." *Sloan Management Review*, 1983, *24*, 3, 67-73.

Berlew, D. E., and Hall, D. T. "The Socialization of Managers: Effects of Expectations on Performance." *Administrative Science Quarterly*, 1966, *11*, 207-223.

Bray, D. W., and Howard, A. "Career Success and Life Satisfactions of Middle-Aged Managers." In L. A. Bond and J. C. Rosen (eds.), *Competence and Coping During Adulthood*. Hanover, N.H.: University Press of New England, 1980.

Cummings, L. L., and Schwab, D. P. *Performance in Organizations: Determinants and Appraisal*. Glenview, Ill: Scott, Foresman, 1973.

Davis, L. E. "Workers and Technology: The Necessary Joint Basis for Organizational Effectiveness." *National Productivity Review*, 1983-1984, *3* (1), 7-14.

DuBois, L. "Career and Family in Mid-Life Men and Women." Unpublished doctoral dissertation, Department of Psychology, Adelphi University, 1981.

Fernandez, J. P. *Racism and Sexism in Corporate Life*. Lexington, Mass.: Lexington Books, 1981.

Finkelstein, J., and Newman, D. "The Third Industrial Revolution: A Special Challenge to Managers." *Organizational Dynamics*, 1984, *13* (1), 53-65.

Goldstein, A. P., and Sorcher, M. *Changing Supervisory Behavior.* Elmsford, N.Y.: Pergamon Press, 1976.

Hammett, J. R. "The Changing Work Environment: High Technology and the Baby Boomers Challenge Management to Adapt." *Employment Relations Today,* 1984, *11* (3), 297–304.

Hart, G., "Investing in People for the Information Age." *The Futurist,* 1983, *17* (1), 10–14.

Hornstein, H. A., and MacKenzie, F. T. "Consultraining: Merging Management Education with Organization Development." *Training and Development Journal,* 1984, *38* (1), 52–56.

Howard, A., and Bray, D. W. "Today's Young Managers: They Can Do It, But Will They?" *The Wharton Magazine,* 1981, 5 (4), 23–28.

Hurst, D. K. "Of Boxes, Bubbles, and Effective Management." *Harvard Business Review,* 1984, *84* (3), 78–88.

Hymowitz, C. "Taking A Chance: Many Blacks Jump Off the Corporate Ladder to Be Entrepreneurs." *The Wall Street Journal,* Aug. 21, 1984, pp. 1, 16.

Jones, E. W., Jr., "What It's Like to Be a Black Manager?" *Harvard Business Review,* 1973, 5 (4), 108–116.

Kets de Vries, M.F.R. "The Midcareer Conundrum." *Organizational Dynamics,* 1978, 7 (2), 45–62.

Kiesler, S., Siegel, J., and McGuire, T. W. "Social Psychological Aspects of Computer-Mediated Communication." *American Psychologist,* 1984, *39* (10), 1123–1134.

Kouri, M. K. "From Retirement to Re-Engagement: Young Elders Forge New Futures." *The Futurist,* June 1984, pp. 35–42.

Kram, K. E. *Mentoring at Work.* Glenview, Ill.: Scott, Foresman, 1985.

London, M. "Toward a Theory of Career Motivation." *Academy of Management Review,* 1983, *8* (4), 620–630.

London, M. "Development for New Managers." *Journal of Management Development,* 1984, *2* (4), 3–14.

London, M. *Developing Managers: A Guide to Motivating and Preparing People for Successful Managerial Careers.* San Francisco: Jossey-Bass, 1985.

London, M., and Bray, D. W. "Measuring and Developing Young Managers' Career Motivation." *Journal of Management Development,* 1984, *3* (3), 3-25.

London, M., and Stumpf, S. A. *Managing Careers.* Reading, Mass.: Addison-Wesley, 1982.

Maccoby, M. "A New Way of Managing." *IEEE Spectrum* (Institute of Electrical and Electronics Engineers), June 1984, pp. 69-72.

Michael, D. N. "Competence and Compassion in an Age of Uncertainty." *World Future Society Bulletin,* 1983, *17* (1), 1-6.

Nussbaum, B. "Reskilling Workers." *The New York Times,* June 12, 1983, p. E19.

Opinion Research Corporation. *Strategic Planning for Human Resources: 1980 and Beyond.* Princeton, N.J.: Opinion Research Corporation, 1980.

Peter, H. W. "Developing Managers for Social Change." *Journal of Management Development,* 1984, *3* (1), 16-27.

Petre, P. "Games That Teach You to Manage." *Fortune,* 1984, *110* (9), 65-72.

Robertson, J. *Management for the XXI Century: Education and Development.* (The American Assembly of Collegiate Schools of Business and the European Foundation for Management Development, sponsors.) Hingham, Mass.: Kluwer Boston, 1982.

Rosenbaum, J. E. "Tournament Mobility: Career Patterns in a Corporation." *Administrative Science Quarterly,* 1979, *24,* 220-241.

Stumpf, S. A., and Hartman, K. "Individual Exploration to Organizational Commitment or Withdrawal." *Academy of Management Journal,* 1984, *27,* 308-329.

Terborg, J. R. "Women in Management: A Research Review." *Journal of Applied Psychology,* 1977, *62,* 647-664.

Toffler, A. *The Third Wave.* New York: Random House, 1980.

Vaillant, G. E. *Adaptation to Life.* Boston: Little, Brown, 1977.

Yohalem, A. *The Careers of Professional Women: Commitment and Conflict.* Montclair, N.J.: Allenheld, Osmun, 1979.

2

ꙅꙅꙅꙅꙅꙅꙅꙅ

Organizational
Career Development
Systems:
The State
of the Practice

Thomas G. Gutteridge

In many respects, the 1970s can be aptly characterized as the "human resources decade." During this period, much was written about the growing need for organizations to manage their people resources more effectively, and the personnel function in many institutions came of age, moving from a transactions-oriented, paper-pushing, reactive department toward a forward-looking controller of human resources (see Foulkes, 1975; Meyer, 1976). One focus of this increased organizational concern for people has been forecasting and establishing plans for fulfilling the firm's overall employment needs. In other institutions, the primary emphasis has been on identifying employee career interests and matching these aspirations with specific organizational opportunities. Generally, however, there has been limited consensus concerning what constitutes a comprehensive human resource management activity, as well as much confusion regarding the distinctions between such related processes as human resource planning, succession planning, career development, career planning, career counseling, and the like.

Human Resource Management: A Conceptual Model

One reason for the frequent confusion between human resource planning and career development is the failure to recognize that these processes are complements rather than substitutes or synonyms. As illustrated in Figure 1, career development and human resource planning are both subelements of a comprehensive human resource management system. As this latter term is generally used, human resource management is seen as a proactive, strategic, integrative approach to the improved use of organizational human resources. Of course, in some organizations, human resource management is nothing more than a new label attached to the traditional, compartmentalized operations of the personnel department. As set forth in Burack and Gutteridge (1978), however, human resources management differs from personnel administration in at least the following ways:

1. Human resource costs are viewed as an investment rather than simply an uncontrollable expense.
2. Human resource management adopts a proactive rather than a reactive approach with respect to resolving various human resource issues and problems.
3. Human resource management is characterized by a change in role perspective—moving from an emphasis on the completion of personnel transactions toward a future-oriented approach in which the personnel department acts as a controller (steward) of the organizational human resources.
4. Human resource management emphasizes the linkage between human resource planning and such related functions as strategic planning, economic/market forecasting, investment/ facilities planning, and so on.
5. Human resource management reinforces the necessary interconnection of human resource planning with such personnel subfunctions as recruiting and selection, training, compensation and benefits, organizational planning, and career management.

Figure 1. Human Resource Management: A Conceptual Model.

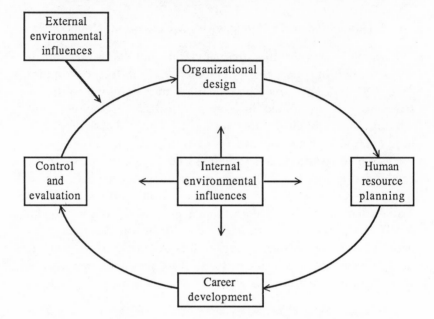

Human resource management: A systematic effort to ensure an effective interface between an organization's human resources and its internal and external environment. (An "effective interface" is one that maximizes organizational and individual goal attainment subject to the constraints imposed by each one on the other.)

Organizational design: The process through which organizational structures or patterns are created and the resultant employee role prescriptions are established.

Human resource planning: The process by which the need for and internal availability of human resources for some future time period is estimated. It also includes the personnel action plans required to fulfill the net manpower requirements and to achieve the organization's manpower objectives.

Career development: The outcomes of actions on career plans as viewed from both individual and organizational perspectives.

Control and evaluation: A system and set of procedures designed to assess the effectiveness of the other human resource management processes in terms of their impact on both the organization and the individual.

In a general sense, then, the principal objective of human resource management is to ensure that the organizational work force is effectively managed so as to both achieve institutional goals and provide adequate opportunities for employee growth and development. As indicated in Figure 1, human resource management is comprised of four distinct yet interrelated subsystems: organizational design, human resource (manpower) planning, career development, and control and evaluation. And, as indicated, all of these subprocesses are influenced by a variety of internal and external environmental pressures.

The organizational design component is concerned with such issues as appropriate organizational structure, desired reporting relationships, functional responsibilities, and the like. The control and evaluation phase is necessary so that corrective action can be taken as needed when the results accomplished deviate from the planned objectives. The primary issue here is what constitutes the basic difference between career development and human resource planning as illustrated in Figure 1. To answer this question, we need to define each of these concepts separately.

Even the term *career* connotes a number of different meanings; this definitional problem is further complicated when it is combined with other words to form such phrases as career development, career planning, career management, and career system. To some, the word *career* suggests career advancement and upward mobility. To others, it is a term used to describe those in high-status occupations, such as doctors and lawyers. Douglas T. Hall (1976) and others, however, have argued persuasively that a career is simply a lifelong process comprised of the sequence of activities and related attitudes/behaviors that take place as a person's work life unfolds. By this definition, therefore, all employees are considered to have a career. A career development task force, established under the auspices of the American Society for Training and Development and chaired by Walter Storey, has built upon Hall's definition of career by constructing a working model of organizational career development (see Storey, 1979). As depicted in Figure 2, within an organizational context career development represents the outcomes created by the integration of individual career-planning activities with institutional career

Figure 2. A Working Model of Organizational Career Development.

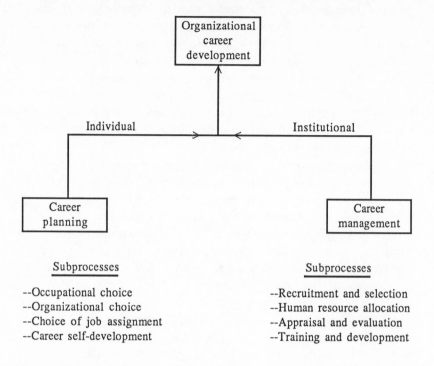

Career: The sequence of a person's work-related activities and behaviors and associated attitudes, values, and aspirations over the span of one's life.

Organizational career development: The outcomes emanating from the interaction of individual career-planning and institutional career management processes.

Career planning: A deliberate process for (1) becoming aware of self, opportunities, constraints, choices, and consequences, (2) identifying career-related goals, and (3) programming of work, education, and related developmental experiences to provide the direction, timing, and sequence of steps to attain a specific career goal.

Career management: An ongoing process of preparing, implementing, and monitoring career plans undertaken by the individual alone or in concert with the organization's career system.

management processes. These outcomes may be described in individual terms, such as better self-understanding and the identification of desired career goals, as well as in terms of organizational results, such as reduced turnover of valued employees and better communication of career opportunities to employees.

Career development thus is comprised of two separate but interrelated functions: career planning, which is an individual process, and career management, which is an institutional process. In turn, career planning consists of those activities in which individuals must engage in order to make informed choices as to occupation, organization, job assignment, and self-development. This includes such activities as self-assessment, the evaluation of available career opportunities, and the preparation of a career strategy with an implementation plan, all of which are key in order for employees to enhance their personal career development. Career management refers to specific human resource activities, such as job rotation, potential appraisal, career counseling, and training and education that are designed to help match employee interests and capabilities with organizational opportunities.

As indicated in Figure 2, career development is designed to be a joint process. In some circumstances, however, employees develop career plans even when they are unable to integrate these plans with appropriate institutional career management processes. Similarly, in some organizations a career management plan is prepared without reference to the employees' career interests—that is, promotion and transfer decisions are based solely on the institution's perceived human resource requirements without regard to the employee's career interests.

In keeping with these definitions, conventional management development programs are a subset of the career management process, which, in turn, is only one-half of the career development process. Typically, most management development programs consist of a combination of selected job assignments together with some training and educational experiences, and they are designed to strengthen the managerial capabilities of a selected group of high-potential employees embarked on a fast-track career path. Only rarely have organizations expanded this management

development effort into an integrated and systematic career
development program that is responsive to both the career
aspirations of a diverse employee group (professional, technical,
and managerial employees) and the firm's own staffing needs.

Career development is not synonymous with manpower
planning. Rather, as reflected in Figure 3, human resource
planning and career development are intended to fulfill different
objectives. Therefore, having one in place does not negate the need
for the other. As indicated in Figure 3, the basic objective of human
resource planning is to enable organizations to anticipate their
future human resource needs by forecasting the expected demand
for labor, inventorying the available internal supply, and
identifying the difference between what is needed and what is likely
to be available. The outputs from this human resource forecast are
then used to formulate the personnel action plans required to fulfill
the net human resource requirements. In turn, these personnel
action plans are an input to the career management process, where
they are integrated with employee goals in establishing specific
organizational career activities. It should be noted that, in addition
to being linked with career management programs, employee career
plans also can serve as a useful input in the forecast of internal
supply.

From the above description, it should be clear that, although
they may utilize some of the same tools and techniques (such as
skills inventories, promotability forecasts, and succession
planning), human resource planning and career development are
not identical processes. Human resource planning is intended to
identify and provide ways to fulfill the organization's aggregate
employment needs, whereas career development focuses on the
development of individual employees and improving the match
between individual career interests and specific institutional career
opportunities.

Pressures for Change

Increased organizational interest in employee career
development is by no means accidental. Rather, career development
is a response to a diverse set of external and internal institutional

Figure 3. Interface Between Career Development and Human Resource Planning.

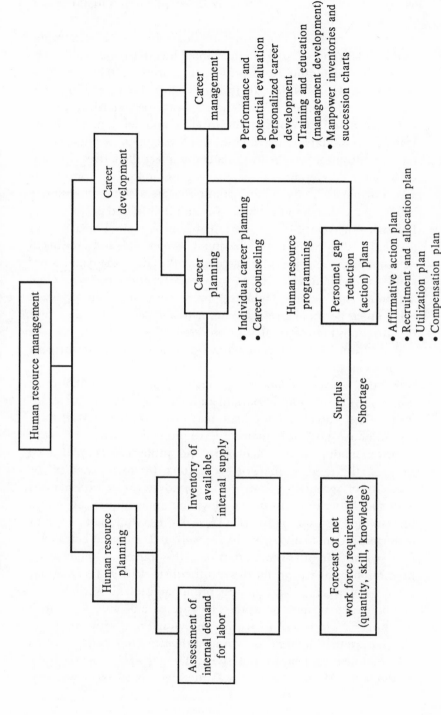

pressures as well as to expressed employee interest. For example, employees throughout the organizational hierarchy and at all career stages are demanding more from their employers than simply a paycheck and job stability. Increasingly, they also are seeking such psychological rewards as challenging work, personal fulfillment, self-respect, and the opportunity to grow and develop. Similarly, many professional and managerial employees are.now questioning their organization's right to unilaterally affect their lives through such career development decisions as geographical reassignments and job transfers. Also, many employees are seeking to obtain a better balance between their work life, family life, and personal life. For still other employees, career planning is viewed as a way of alleviating the problem of professional obsolescence and a means to maximize their prospects for career growth. Given these and other similar individual concerns, it can be readily understood why more and more employees are adopting an active rather than a passive role in their personal career development and demanding that their organizations help facilitate this process.

Although expressed employee interest is a significant motivating factor in the establishment of institutional career programs, Walker and Gutteridge (1979, p. 29) concluded that three other issues were more important influences in program development. First, career development may be viewed as an effective response to a series of human resource problems, such as excessive turnover among valued managers and professionals, plateaued workers, the need to increase work force productivity, and the necessity of reconciling unrealistic employee career expectations with stabilizing or declining employment opportunities. A second institutional pressure is the increased desire on the part of senior management in many firms to develop and promote employees from within. In many organizations, this increased reliance on promotion from within has been difficult to achieve because of a perceived shortage of high-quality promotable talent. A final factor has been management's expressed desire to aid employee career planning as a means of increasing individual commitment and to help ensure that the right person is in the right job, both of which are assumed to bear a positive relationship to work force productivity. All in all, therefore, Gutteridge and Walker concluded that most organizations adopt career development programs primarily in response to pragmatic human resource concerns and because they believe it will help ensure a continued supply of qualified, talented personnel.

While these factors suggest widespread organizational support for career development programs as a concept, there is a wide gap between the ideal and the reality of current practices. Although other chapters in this book deal with these barriers to change in greater depth than is possible here, it is important to note that these potential obstacles also can be subdivided into individual versus organizational categories. For instance, not all employees will enthusiastically endorse career development programs: Some will perceive that career development is primarily or exclusively an organizational responsibility, while others will conclude that their career progress is simply a matter of luck or of being in the right place at the right time. Still others will argue that there is no sense in career planning, since one cannot foresee the future. Finally, some individuals will find the self-assessment process inherent in career planning threatening and/or may be reluctant to make the changes required to implement a career strategy.

In most organizations, there are also a number of institutional practices and beliefs that mitigate against the successful implementation of a career development program (for example, cream rises to the top, no one ever helped me, we know what is best for our employees, and so on). In addition to these negative attitudes, there are also likely to be concerns that career development will be too expensive, that it will place an unreasonable strain on other personnel systems, or that it will create unrealistic employee expectations. Also, many supervisors may be unwilling to assume the responsibilities often demanded of them in organizational career development programs. Another possible institutional barrier is the credibility gap that may exist because employees view career development as simply another fad in a long line of "new personnel programs." A final barrier is the danger inherent in any organizational change that top management will push for immediate results from the career development program and will scrap it if the results are not forthcoming in short order. Walker and Gutteridge, among others, have concluded that five

years or more may be required to successfully implement a
comprehensive career development program (1979, p. 4).

In sum, probably the single greatest institutional problem in
implementing an effective career development program is cultural
inertia. Career development represents something more than
business as usual for both employees and the organization. If this
new philosophy is simply grafted onto a traditional system that
deemphasizes individual responsibility, the result is likely to be a
career system that is more lip service than results. However, these
institutional barriers need not negate the positive pressures for
change. The challenge is to design and implement an operational
career development system that accomplishes specific system
objectives while simultaneously responding to identified individual
and institutional barriers.

Career Development System Components

As previously discussed, career development programs must
incorporate individual as well as institutional elements. Thus,
while specific career tools and techniques will vary from one
organization to another, there is a series of generic elements that
must be incorporated into any comprehensive career system. These
elements include: (1) individual self-assessment data concerning
employee attitudes, interests, skills/abilities/competencies, values,
and the like, (2) organizational data concerning such factors as
available career opportunities and associated skill requirements,
projected organizational employment needs, the organizational
value system, and availability of various career tools, (3) systems for
inputting data from individual to organization and from
organization to individual, (4) systems to ensure meaningful
dialogue and feedback between the individual and the organization
concerning the match between employee career needs and
organizational employment opportunities, and (5) developmental
systems that provide opportunities for personal and professional
growth in line with individual career strategy.

Given these systems requirements, Table 1 profiles some of
the more common tools and techniques incorporated within
organizational career development programs. As illustrated in

Table 1, some career development techniques, such as career workshops and workbooks, are primarily oriented toward the individual and are designed to assist them in establishing a career strategy. Other approaches, such as succession planning and career ladders, focus primarily on the identification and fulfillment of organizational career requirements, referred to in this chapter as the career management function. Finally, career development also includes a matching function that emphasizes the integration of

Table 1. Organizational Career Development Tools.

A. Self-assessment tools
   1. Career-planning workshops
   2. Career workbooks
   3. Preretirement workshops
B. Individual counseling
   1. Personnel staff
   2. Professional counselor
      a. Internal
      b. External
   3. Outplacement
   4. Supervisor or line manager
C. Internal labor market information/placement exchanges
   1. Job posting
   2. Skills inventories
   3. Career ladders/career path planning
   4. Career resource center
   5. Other career communication formats
D. Organizational potential assessment processes
   1. Assessment centers
   2. Promotability forecasts
   3. Replacement/succession planning
   4. Psychological testing
E. Developmental programs
   1. Job rotation
   2. In-House human resource development programs
   3. External seminars/workshops
   4. Tuition reimbursement/educational assistance
   5. Supervisor training in career counseling
   6. Dual-career programs
   7. Mentoring systems

employee career plans with institutional human resource needs via such tools as job posting and skills inventories.

Before proceeding with a description of the career tools listed in Table 1, it should be noted that career development programs have been applied at all levels of the organization, ranging from hourly workers through nonexempt salaried employees to top management executives. Marriott Corporation, for example, has a job advancement program designed to provide hourly employees with career ladders leading to positions of increasing skill, responsibility, and pay and eventually into management (Hostage, 1975). Similarly, the municipality of Anchorage, Alaska, has established some mini career ladders to assist hourly employees in making the transition to paraprofessional technical positions. The Mattel Corporation offers a career-planning seminar for executive secretaries designed to help them assess their transferable skills, identify career goals, and establish implementation strategies (Gutteridge and Otte, 1983). Citicorp has established a career development program to help college-trained workers employed in clerical positions prepare for exempt-level jobs. At the executive level, much of the organizational career development activity is carried out under the rubric of succession planning. For example, the corporate director of management development at S. C. Johnson and Sons, Inc., holds an annual career development discussion with the company's senior executives. The focus of this discussion is the career interests of these executives and how their goals match with the organization's needs for executive talent. In general, even though most organizational career development programs are open to all employees, the primary focus is on professional, managerial, and technical employees. This is probably a reflection of both the perceived high value of such employees to the organization and their substantial level of organizational commitment.

It also should be noted that some career development programs have been designed primarily in response to the particular needs of special-interest employee groups, such as women, minorities, high-potential managers and plateaued professionals. Columbia Broadcasting System (CBS), for example, has a director of career development for women and another for minority affairs. The majority of CBS's career activities, such as career counseling and career development seminars, are directed toward the particular needs of their women and minority employees. CBS has established a women's advisory council as well as a Blacks in Corporate Life program to deal with the career issues of these employee groups. Gulf Oil Corporation designed a career development program for women in cooperation with Chatham College. This program, which is now also available to men, provides three areas of career-planning support for participants: skills assessment, individual advising, and a career-planning workshop. The goal is to assist employees with at least one year of college course work to plan a personal career path combining academic studies with career opportunities at Gulf Oil. The career program established by the NASA Goddard Space Flight Center is centered around career transition points and utilizes such tools as a career resource center, career-planning workshops and a career development work experience program to enable employees to try out alternative career options. As a final example, Transamerica Corporation has a corporation-wide managerial resources planning program that involves the identification of high-potential employees with the ability to move into one or more key managerial positions. Once these high-potential employees are identified, they are involved in a rotational development program in which they move through a series of positional assignments supplemented by external training.

In addition to the question of which employee groups will be served by which career development tools and techniques, there is also an issue in terms of the organizational scope of coverage. That is, will the program encompass the entire enterprise or only specified segments, such as a particular function or major division? Typically, career development programs are established first in a limited subset of organizational units rather than on a company-wide basis (that is, the program may be started first at company headquarters or at a particular division). Then, over time, as the career program demonstrates its effectiveness, it may be expanded company-wide and made available to a wide variety of employee groups and organizational levels. It should also be noted that, in keeping with the emphasis on individual responsibility for career development articulated in this chapter, most organizational career development programs are voluntary—that is, employees are not required to participate, although they may be encouraged to do so. Thus, the level of employee participation in various career development activities typically varies, ranging from a low of about 30 to 40 percent of the eligible employee population who may enroll in a group career-planning workshop up to the almost 100 percent participation characteristic of such programs as supervisor/subordinate career discussions and succession planning.

Self-Assessment Tools. All three of the self-assessment tools discussed here—career-planning workshops, career workbooks, and preretirement workshops—have a common objective: to provide employees with a comprehensive, systematic way of identifying and working toward their individual career preferences within the institutional career structure. Thus, these techniques should be viewed primarily as a means to an end rather than an end in themselves in that the output from these tools are inputs into other career systems. Typically, career-planning workshops use a structured, interactive group format to educate employee participants on how to prepare and implement an individual career strategy. This objective is accomplished by means of experiential exercises and other structured activities that require workshop participants to formulate, share, and discuss with each other personal data concerning strengths and weaknesses, values, career goals, and related information. Fundamentally, this workshop experience involves identifying and discussing with other group participants individual answers to such questions as: Who am I? Where am I now? Where do I want to be? How can I get there? As an example, the career development program at Massachusetts Mutual Life Insurance Company includes a three-hour orientation to career planning designed to give employees a general understanding of the Massachusetts Mutual Career Program. A second, more extensive three-day workshop (one and one-half days per week for two weeks) entitled Life/Work Planning is geared to individuals who are unsure of what they want from their careers and, therefore, can benefit from a systematic exposure to self-analysis and decision-making and planning techniques in a career context.

The workbook format is intended to fulfill the same basic objectives as a group career workshop, but it does so in an individual, self-directed fashion rather than on a participative, interactive basis. Thus, a typical workbook, such as that developed by Arizona Bank, General Electric, Merck, and Xerox, uses a series of exercises and reference materials to guide employees through the individual career-planning process. However, the workbook is designed to be completed by the individual alone and thus is self-paced.

In this computer age, it should be no surprise that a microcomputer-based interactive system has been designed to guide employees through a structured career-planning process. This system, entitled *DISCOVER,* is marketed by the American College Testing Program and uses a series of interactive exercises and organizationally specific data to lead employees through a five-step career planning process: (1) understanding career development and change, (2) assessing yourself, (3) gathering information, (4) making decisions, and (5) taking action. (For further information, contact The American College Testing Program, Educational Services Division, P.O. Box 168, Iowa City, Iowa 52243.) One final form of career-planning program is the preretirement workshop, which focuses on the life/career concerns of employees nearing retirement age, such as health, financial condition, and the forthcoming transition from work to retirement status.

As suggested, the intended output from all three self-assessment tools is a process as well as a product. Ideally, a career workshop or workbook teaches employees an approach for developing an individual career strategy, and these career-planning skills can then be applied over the individual's entire life/career span. In addition, however, most career workshops and workbooks encourage employees to develop a specific career strategy that then can be integrated with other elements of an organizational career system, ultimately leading to the actual development of an individual's career as well as providing individual inputs relative to the organization's career needs.

According to the survey conducted by Gutteridge and Otte (1983, p. 31), career workshops and workbooks are often among the first techniques implemented by organizations when they decide to establish a career development program. In part, this emphasis reflects organizational agreement that career development is fundamentally an individual process that it can facilitate but should not control. This focus also acknowledges that many employees are not familiar with career-planning methodology and thus require initial assistance in preparing a career strategy. The development of an individual career strategy by employees is also an important precondition to their effective participation in other organizational career programs, such as job posting or career path planning. Career workshops and workbooks are also a popular organizational tool because they provide a highly visible means of communicating to employees the institutional commitment being made to the career development process.

Individual Counseling. The career counseling techniques discussed in this section are also individually focused in that they involve discussions between institutional representatives and employees regarding various kinds of career issues. However, career counseling means different things to different people. On the one hand, career counseling may be something very informal, such as a brief discussion between a personnel representative and an employee concerning possible enrollment in a management development program. On the other hand, career counseling may refer to an annual discussion between supervisors and subordinates concerning the match between employee career goals and organizational career requirements. Or, in some organizations, career counseling may involve a series of one-hour sessions over a period of several months in which a full-time staff counselor assists the employee in preparing and implementing an individual career plan.

Career counseling can involve several different types of organizational resource persons. Not surprisingly, the most common form of employee career counseling is that provided by personnel staff members on a part-time basis. In a small but growing number of organizations, such as Coca-Cola, Disneyland, and Syntex, career counseling is provided by professionally trained, specialized staff counselors. These staff counselors, usually with training at the master's or doctoral level, typically also are assigned responsibility for developing and implementing the organization's career development program, in addition to their counseling activities. Given the counselor's primary concern with the match between the individual and the organization, only a minority of organizations refer employees to external counselors for career-planning assistance. In instances where this occurs, the primary focus seems to be on helping employees assess their career potential and teaching them an approach for developing a career strategy.

Outplacement counseling is another organizational career development approach. However, rather than focusing on continuing employees, outplacement counseling is designed to assist terminated employees in making the transition to a new organization. Primarily as a consequence of the depressed economic climate, the past decade has seen increased demand for outplacement services. Ironically, the growth of outplacement counseling often has resulted in organizations providing better career-planning services to individuals leaving their employ than to those employees on which the organization is building for the future.

One of the most controversial aspects of individual counseling is the appropriate role of supervisors. In most organizations, the employee's immediate superior is an important link in the career development process; however, the available literature suggests that the supervisor-subordinate career discussion process is fraught with difficulties. As Walker and Gutteridge have articulated (1979), career planning means an increased burden for supervisors, which many of them are ill equipped to handle. Further, many supervisors believe that career counseling is not part of their job and, if it is, it is a responsibility for which they are not properly rewarded. Given these problems, if supervisors are to be effectively involved in the organizational career development process, it is imperative that their roles be clearly defined, that they be provided training that properly prepares them for these roles, that their career development responsibilities be incorporated into the organizational reward system, and that the supervisors themselves be provided an opportunity to discuss their own career objectives with their superiors and organizational personnel representatives. Xerox Corporation is one institution in which these ideals have been incorporated into an effective organization-wide supervisor/subordinate career discussion process.

Overall, career counseling is one career development tool that seems to be provided in one form or another for all employee groups, with the possible exception of senior management. While the diversity of career-counseling approaches and the typical lack of structure make it difficult to define exactly what does and does not constitute career counseling, it is clear that, in most organizations, counseling-type interventions are required to facilitate the career development process.

Once employees have been encouraged to assume greater responsibility for managing their own careers and have been provided a process through which to develop an individual career strategy, there is a need to match these individual inputs with the organizational opportunity structure. In those organizations in which career counselors serve as brokers or referral agents, this matching process can be accomplished through one-on-one discussions. In most organizations, however, there is a need to improve existing systems or to develop new ones in order to provide employees with organizational career information and to assist them in implementing their career plans. In addition, organizations need to establish various career systems if they are to ensure that institutional job opportunities are filled with qualified, motivated individuals. Some of the tools we have discussed fulfill both the informational and placement dimensions of career management, while others focus primarily on one or the other.

Information/Placement Exchanges. Job posting and skills inventories are two examples of career management tools with a dual information/placement focus. Job posting, which is a tool commonly used for internal staffing, is a valuable method for communicating important career information to employees, such as the precise skills and abilities required for a variety of job vacancies. Further, it can be a useful mechanism for stimulating career discussions between the company and the employee, and it can provide a partial guide to the need for specialized training and development programs. Of course, job posting is not a career development panacea. Since it is dependent upon individual self-selection, its coverage of the desired segment of the organizational work force is partially incomplete. Also, there is frequently considerable management resistance to the concept of open competition for job vacancies, which often leads to the counterproductive listing of "bagged" jobs. These are positions that are posted even though the supervisor has already selected someone to fill them. While job posting is still most prevalent as a nonexempt staffing tool, a growing number of firms, such as McGraw-Hill and General Motors, are deciding that job posting can be a powerful motivating force for individual career development as well as an effective approach to internal staffing for exempt salaried jobs. Thus, they are expanding the job-posting system to include job positions up through middle management.

Another human resource system, which organizations such as CBS and Merck have utilized for career development purposes, is the skills inventory, sometimes known as a career information system. Basically a skills inventory is a comprehensive record of the education, work history, qualifications, accomplishments, and, less frequently, career objectives of individual employees. In most organizations, the coverage of the skills inventory system is restricted to exempt managerial employees, and, historically, the system has been used primarily to identify likely candidates for internal placement. Typically, employee participation in the system is voluntary, and the individual is responsible for providing the requisite input data. In terms of its career development applications, a skills inventory can help pinpoint shortages of critical skills required by the organization as well as highlight the need for specific types of programs necessary to provide a skilled work force. In addition, the technology exists to incorporate future-oriented career development data, such as work preferences and work goals, individual self-assessment information, developmental plans, and target assignments, into a skills inventory. These career data then can be matched against available organizational development information, such as promotion opportunities, transfer assignments, management development programs, task force activities, and the like.

In some organizations, such as Aetna and McGraw-Hill, detailed career ladders or career path charts are used to document possible patterns of job movement (both laterally and vertically) that an employee might follow within the organizational hierarchy. Typically, these career paths are developed on the basis of historical career data and/or a consensus of subjective managerial judgments as to what constitutes logical lines of career progression within particular functional areas or operational units. Although some organizations have developed career ladders for hourly employees and nonexempt workers, there is a tendency to orient career path handbooks primarily toward professional, managerial, and technical employees. McGraw-Hill, for example, has conducted a careful analysis of its internal career structure and published booklets describing traditional career paths in terms of the types of jobs available in various units or departments and the most likely routes for advancement in these areas.

While career ladders may help organizations respond to employee questions concerning likely career progression, they possess some inherent limitations. First, career ladders typically give too much weight to the way careers have evolved in the past. In most organizations, future career needs are likely to shift in response to a variety of environmental pressures, thereby undermining the relevance of identified career tracks. Similarly, past career progression patterns may be misleading to the extent that they resulted from unusual combinations of individual qualifications, organizational needs, and serendipity. Another problem with these anecdotal career-pathing methods is their frequent failure to consider lateral moves and cross-functional assignments. Career paths also fail to incorporate the dynamics of individual career choice and overemphasize lockstep progression at the expense of the need for individual career planning.

Some organizations maintain a career resource center as the focal point for distributing materials and information relating to career development. In these instances, the career information center serves as a mini library and is typically stocked with a variety of company materials, reference books, learning guides and self-study tapes. One organization, the United States General Accounting Office, has designed a very sophisticated career resource center in which employees can complete a career-planning process by rotating through a series of four stations: (1) understanding self, (2) understanding environment, (3) taking action, and (4) life management. (See Gutteridge and Otte, 1983.) Each station has a series of structured exercises and informational materials designed to help the individual develop one particular aspect of a career-planning strategy.

In addition to publishing career path handbooks and establishing career resource centers, many companies utilize a variety of brochures, manuals, flyers, and other printed materials to communicate a diverse array of career data to employees concerning the availability of such career development services as tuition assistance, developmental programs, and the like.

Potential Assessment Processes. Organizations have long had programs for assessing employee career potential. Typically, these processes primarily have focused on quantifying the promotability of professional, managerial, and technical employees rather than on their development. In recent years, however, there has been a growing tendency among organizations to integrate these potential assessment processes into a comprehensive career development framework by combining the assessment and developmental components.

Assessment centers, for example, traditionally have been used to evaluate the capability of employees to assume supervisory and managerial responsibilities at a higher level. In an assessment center, the participant completes a variety of situational exercises, both individually and in a group setting, under the observation of a corporate assessor. These corporate assessors, usually high-level managers, constitute an evaluation panel; based on the behavior of participants in the assessment center, they draw conclusions about their management potential and developmental needs. Traditionally, the assessment center decisions were reported in the form of go/no-go recommendations concerning the participant's suitability for higher-level responsibility. In a developmental context, however, these assessment center reports provide detailed feedback on the strengths and weaknesses of individual participants. These inputs then can be used to construct individual career development plans and/or to design a training program for an entire group of managerial candidates. In addition, the personal insights obtained by employees from participating in the assessment center exercise, coupled with the performance feedback provided by the assessor staff, are other sources of developmental opportunities. Finally, an assessment center also can serve to increase the participants' understanding of the tasks, role behaviors, and other requirements of various organizational positions. Lawrence Livermore National Laboratories is one example of a company that is using assessment centers for developmental purposes.

The idea of utilizing promotability forecasts to isolate those individuals with exceptionally high career potential and provide them special developmental experiences has intuitive appeal. It limits the number of persons whose career progress has to be closely observed, focuses maximum attention on the most promising candidates, and undoubtedly reduces the administrative costs of any career development program. This approach, however, has some obvious disadvantages. At best, the early identification of managerial potential is an imprecise prediction. Further, there is a danger that the promotability forecast will become a self-fulfilling prophecy and this "crown prince" philosophy of career development will alienate those capable employees not included. Finally, many organizations fail to follow up their promotability forecast with any type of developmental action, and they do not ask employees identified as "high potential" for input concerning their career development aspirations. This latter failure can be both embarrassing and counterproductive if the employee's career aspirations do not match the organization's plans for him or her.

In a parallel process to promotability forecasts, a number of organizations require managers to identify the most likely successors to incumbents, including themselves, for key executive positions. Ideally, the succession-planning process can be used to identify organizational areas in which there is a shortage or surplus of promotable talent, document alternative career paths, pinpoint promotional barriers, and minimize the need for external recruitment of experienced managers. Again, however, there are some inherent problems with succession planning. First, the common practice is for the incumbent or the incumbent's boss to select likely replacements; however, this appraisal of senior managerial potential is better accomplished on the basis of the collective judgment of multiple assessors than on that of a single individual. Second, in most organizations, managers are not informed of their inclusion on a replacement chart. This absence of employee input to the succession-planning process can become critical if an identified successor refuses an assignment because it does not match his or her own personal career goals. Finally, organizations must be careful to anticipate future staffing needs and not simply replicate present job requirements when establishing succession plans.

Typically, in most organizations the potential appraisal process encompasses all professional, managerial, and technical employees up through middle management, while the succession-planning process is restricted to senior management positions. Some of the approaches for increasing the developmental orientation of these tools include: (1) Use assessment of management potential and/or successor status as the stimulus for a career development discussion with the employee. (2) Integrate the assessment evaluation with a variety of developmental activities designed to enhance the employee's ability to handle higher-level responsibilities. (3) Recognize and respond to the fact that these systems will not encompass the career development needs of all valued employees.

One final approach to potential assessment, the use of psychological testing, is an important technique for executive selection, although it has been discontinued by some organizations. In moving from a selection emphasis to a developmental orientation, there is an important role for diagnostic tests and inventories in helping employees assess their particular interests, aptitudes, values, and so on. In using such instruments, however, great care should be taken to stress that the results are tentative guides rather than rigid, inflexible predictors of an employee's career characteristics. Further, especially if sophisticated personality instruments and value clarification exercises are used, the interpretation of test results must be completed by trained career development specialists.

Developmental Programs. If one objective of individual career planning is the preparation of a viable career strategy, a second one is the actual implementation of that plan. Most organizations already have in place a variety of procedures to actively stimulate employee growth and development. Researchers and practitioners alike agree that the employee's current job is the most important source of career development. As defined in this chapter, career development does not necessarily imply vertical mobility. And, for many employees, career development is best accomplished by restructuring their present job so that it provides challenging goals that are stretching, meaningful, and psychologically fulfilling. Job rotation, the use of cross-functional or lateral transfers, is another technique for introducing variety and growth into an employee's career. While this approach traditionally has been used in the development of new professional employees, Hall (1976) and others have argued that job rotation may be especially meaningful for senior personnel who have become stale, functionally overspecialized, and obsolete.

There are also a variety of in-house and external training/ education activities, including tuition reimbursement for degree-granting programs, which can provide opportunities for employee development. Other activities that can support employee development include supervisory coaching and feedback, mentor/protege relationships, and programs that stimulate intellectual exchanges with peers and colleagues. As already indicated, it is also important to train supervisors for their role in the career development process. Such training is likely to be developmental for the supervisors involved, as well as being a positive factor in the career development of subordinates. Finally, some organizations have established special programs to identify better ways of managing the conflicts introduced by the growing number of "dual-career families".

While there are a wide number and variety of available career development interventions, it is apparent that this career development methodology far exceeds the utilization of these techniques by United States organizations. In part, many of the career development activities discussed here are relatively new in application and are not yet widely utilized. Also, in many companies in which career development programs do exist, they are still largely an informal, experimental, and fragmented activity. Further, in spite of the general universal acceptance of the efficacy of career development programs, there is relatively little empirical evidence to substantiate this positive evaluation. Typically, the underlying assumption of organizations is that practical benefits will accrue to the company as well as to its employees through the implementation of a career development system. All too often, however, the organizational value of these career development activities is accepted as a matter of faith and little or no formal evaluation is conducted to evaluate the cost and benefits from system installation. As with any organization development intervention, however, the evaluation of program effectiveness should be closely tied to the objectives the program has been designed to accomplish: improved employee retention, increased employee loyalty and career orientation, increased motivation and current job performance, more focused development activities, and so forth. The final section of this chapter will have more to say about the evaluation of program effectiveness.

Probably the best way to understand how real-world organizations combine the tools and techniques just discussed into a comprehensive career system is to outline the career development programs existent in a few sample organizations. Therefore, following the concluding section of this chapter, case studies from three different organizations are provided. Rather than being selected as illustrations of either good or bad approaches to program implementation, these cases are intended to highlight the diversity of possible approaches.

Program Implementation Strategies

It should be readily apparent from the preceding discussion that, while there is considerable interest in employer-assisted career development programs, many such programs lack a rationale and have been established without regard to an overall plan. Consequently, career development exists on the periphery of many organizations rather than being part of the human resource mainstream. As shown by Gutteridge and Otte (1983), the primary key to making career development effective is an institutional commitment to using specific practices to satisfy the need of particular employee groups and resolve identified human resource issues rather than establishing a general program driven by a desire to implement particular career development techniques. That is, organizational career development programs should be issue and objective oriented rather than technique driven. Table 2 summarizes

Table 2. Indicators of Career Program Effectiveness.

A. Goal attainment

Achievement of prespecified individual and organizational objectives on qualitative as well as quantitative dimensions.

Individual	*Organization*
1. Exercise greater self-determination	1. Improve career communications between employees and supervisors
2. Achieve greater self-awareness	2. Improve individual/organization career match
3. Acquire necessary organizational career information	3. Enhance organization's image
4. Enhance personal growth and development	4. Respond to Equal Employment Opportunity/Affirmative Action (EEO/AA) pressures
5. Improve goal-setting capability	5. Identify pool of management talent

B. Actions/events completed
1. Employee use of career tools (participation in career workshops, enrollments in training courses)
2. Career discussions conducted
3. Employee career plans implemented
4. Career actions taken (promotions, cross-functional moves)
5. Management successors identified

C. Changes in performance indexes
1. Reduced turnover rates
2. Lower employee absenteeism
3. Improved employee morale
4. Improved employee performance ratings
5. Reduced time to fill job openings
6. Increased promotion from within

D. Attitudes/Perceptions
1. Evaluation of career tools and practices (participant reaction to career workshop, supervisor's evaluation of job-posting system)
2. Perceived benefits of career system
3. Employees express career feelings (responses to career attitude survey)
4. Evaluation of employee career-planning skills
5. Adequacy of organizational career information

some of the possible individual and organizational indicators of program effectiveness.

As mentioned earlier, career development is not a panacea. Indeed, there is a history of abandoned career development programs and programs that have had limited effectiveness—minimal employee participation, little evidence of actual employee career development, and so on. In my experience, some of the factors that have led to these negative organizational experiences include:

1. The career development effort was technique driven ("let's implement a career-planning workshop") rather than responsive to desired programmatic objectives. Thus, while much activity (such as employee participation in career-planning workshops) may have occurred, there was limited impact on overall employee career development.

2. The program was designed and implemented by a charismatic employee development specialist but was not integrated into the organization's value system. Thus, because the career system is person dependent, when the career resource leader departs the organization or moves on to another assignment, the career development program dies for lack of leadership.

3. The career system was viewed as a personnel department activity and thus peripheral to the priorities of line managers, often leading to a lack of employee participation.

4. There was a deterioration in the organization's business indicators, and the career development program was eliminated as part of the effort to cut back on unnecessary expenses.

5. Career development was viewed by managers and employees alike as a philosophical or academic exercise that bore little relationship to the bottom-line organizational objectives.

6. The career development program was designed as a stand-alone activity and therefore was not linked to other human resource processes, such as performance appraisal, jobposting, management succession planning, and training and development.

While there is no magic formula for success in implementing career development programs, the author has developed a program planning model he believes maximizes the probability of a successful, long-term career system. Table 3 is an adaptation of a basic organizational change approach that requires responses to the following questions: (1) Where does the organization want to be in the human resource (career) area? (2) Where is the organization now in terms of its current human resource (career) condition? (3) How does the organization get from where it is now to where it wants to be? and (4) How did the organization do in achieving its desired human resource (career) outcomes?

An earlier version of this planning model was used by the municipality of Anchorage, Alaska, in implementing a career system in the Anchorage Water and Wastewater Utility. (See Ideus, 1985.) Evaluation of this project revealed changes in employee attitudes, as measured by a before-and-after employee career survey, and improvements in objective indexes, (turnover rates and levels of internal hires and promotions).

Table 3. Career Development Program Planning Model.

1. Identify problems, pressures, needs, opportunities
2. Identify success indicators
   - Employees (career plan prepared, career discussion held)
   - Managers (better employee performance ratings, less time required to fill job openings)
   - Top management (improved employee morale, lower turnover)
   - Human resource development staff (greater employee use of existing development programs, positive internal evaluation of career systems)
3. Evaluate existing processes, tools, and techniques
4. Program design
5. Develop implementation strategy
   - Resource requirements (human and budgetary)
   - Support elements and barriers
   - Approaches for enhancing organizational commitment
   - Time priorities and sequencing
   - Communication of program effectiveness to organization
   - Evaluation strategy
6. Introduce and evaluate pilot
7. Begin full-scale implementation/ongoing evaluation

Career-Planning Model. As previously discussed, the initial step in the program-planning model recognizes that career development systems should be issue or objective driven rather than technique oriented. Thus, the organization should first conduct a needs assessment to ascertain what it wishes to accomplish via a career development program. As indicated, these outcomes or objectives may relate to individual issues as well as to institutional concerns. The second step is to translate these pressures into success indicators as defined by potential participants (employees), line managers, and senior executives, as well as by the human resource development staff. This identification of success indicators is important not only as a guideline to required career development tools but also as a baseline for the eventual evaluation of program success.

As discussed, career development is not some radically new process. Instead, in most organizations it represents a blend of some relatively new tools with existing, more traditional developmental practices. These tools are integrated in the context of an organizational philosophy that emphasizes the balance between individual career objectives and institutional human resource requirements. Therefore, an important third step in the establishment of an institutional career system is the evaluation of the availability and effectiveness of existing human resource tools that can be integrated into a total program.

The fourth step (program design) in the program-planning model brings together the previous three steps. In this stage, we must analyze the range of career development interventions to ascertain which are most likely to help us accomplish our desired objectives and resolve our specific career issues. The needed career development tools then can be compared against the existing systems to determine which interventions must be developed from scratch versus those that can be adapted from already available techniques. In addition to deciding which career development tools to incorporate in the career development system, this program design phase also should consider which employee target groups will be the initial focus of the career system. This decision will usually be dictated by the needs analysis conducted in step one.

Once the career system tentatively has been designed, consideration must be given to how best to implement it. This fifth phase involves a series of subquestions relating to such issues as (1) resource requirements, (2) anticipated barriers to and support elements for program implementation, (3) available approaches for increasing commitment of senior management, supervisory personnel, and employees to the system, (4) desired sequencing of career development processes and employee target groups, (5) how best to communicate system successes to the organization, and (6) program evaluation strategy.

The sixth step in the planning model involves the actual implementation of the career system on a pilot basis. The pilot evaluation considers such issues as how well the career development system is meeting its objectives; changes in various performance indexes, such as retention, average promotion times, time to fill job openings, and so on; participant reactions to specific tools and techniques; supervisor reception of and support for the program; cost elements; and related variables. Based on the conclusions from this evaluation, in the seventh step, the career development system is refined and then implemented on a full-scale level. Of course, program evaluation is continued on an ongoing basis as the system is further developed. And, as indicated, over time this system is enlarged to include additional tools and techniques, a broader segment of employee work groups, and a variety of different geographical locations.

This model provides a conceptual framework for planning organizational career development activities in a systematic manner. Not all of the ideas presented will apply in every organizational setting. Also, organizations already may have completed some of the steps outlined in the program guide. Nevertheless, the approach suggested can be a vehicle for evaluating the comprehensiveness of an already-existing career development system and, as modified to best fit the specific needs of an organization, it can help ensure that broad "motherhood" commitments to career development can be translated effectively into specific actions that are controlled as they are implemented. Also, this approach can help ensure that the resulting career development system is credible to organizational decision makers as well as to participants, and it can help obtain the commitment of key organizational leaders.

Conclusions and Recommendations

As suggested throughout this section, career development is one program in which what is good for the organization is also good for the individual. Not only does career development have the potential to link together various human resource strategies to achieve organizational objectives, but it also provides a vehicle whereby employees can identify their career goals and establish ways of moving toward those objectives within the institutional environment. The challenge is how best to transform the general interest in career development into a well-conceived program that is responsive to the specific needs of both the employee and the institution. As one final note, this chapter summarizes a series of brief recommendations that experience suggests are positively related to program success.

1. Start small and design a specific program in response to particular institutional and employee needs. Expand the program on a gradual basis, identifying priorities and desired time sequencing.
2. Design the system to interface with other ongoing personnel processes, such as performance appraisal, human resource planning, and training and development programs.
3. Obtain top management support via policy, physical presence, and budgetary provisions.
4. Encourage line management "ownership" of career development activities and utilize personnel as third-party change agents.
5. Establish indicators of program effectiveness and measure and communicate the results.
6. Promote voluntary employee participation in the program.
7. Provide a balance of individual and organizational interventions.
8. Prepare and train employees and managers for changes likely to occur as a result of system implementation.
9. Be patient and provide time for problem solving.

The following three mini case studies describe the implementation of career development systems by some typical United States corporations.

Case Study 1: Disneyland.

Corporate Background

Disneyland, a division of Walt Disney Productions, Inc., is a multifaceted family entertainment and recreational facility. Although Disneyland recently opened a facility in Tokyo, Japan, this case study relates to the Anaheim, California, facility. Disneyland's employment ranges from 4,000 employees to a seasonal peak of 8,000 in the summer. The average hourly employment is 4,500 individuals, including carpenters and plumbers. The salaried employment averages 500 individuals employed in such capacities as entertainers, sales clerks, ride operators, and beverage hosts and hostesses.

Program Origin

The Disneyland career development program began in 1976 and is administratively located in the employee relations division. The career planning department is staffed by a manager who reports to the director of the employee relations division, who in turn reports to a Disneyland vice-president. Other program staff include a counselor, two career development representatives, and two clerical personnel. In establishing the career program, the primary objectives were: (1) to develop a reservoir of human resource talent to staff anticipated future expansion and offset attrition, (2) to help minimize mismatches between what the employee wants and what the company needs and offers in terms of employment opportunities, (3) to assist individuals in their future career development, including better preparing them for promotion and increased responsibility, and (4) to help employees develop and increase their self-awareness and to better understand their own personal abilities and limitations.

Program Description

Included in Disneyland's career system are several services:

Disneyland Intern Program. This six-month developmental program was established in 1968 and brought under the career-planning umbrella in 1976. The program's primary goal is to establish a core of qualified, high-potential management personnel through a formalized education and development program. A minimum of one year of service with a Walt Disney Productions subsidiary as well as favorable supervisory recommendation is required for participation. The program is offered twice a year, and approximately thirty individuals are included in each offering. Employees selected for the program enter an ongoing six-month developmental program involving weekly classes as well as in-depth, on-the-job training. Upon completion of this program, employees are considered for Disneyland managerial openings as they occur.

Employee Career Counseling. Disneyland has a full-time, professional career counselor who provides counseling services to employees on request. This program is frequently combined with a career-planning workshop, as described below. Employees are encouraged to sign up for the career planning orientation as well as to meet with the career counselor. The first meeting with the counselor lasts one hour, during which time the employee is encouraged to discuss his or her educational objectives, desired career directions, and possible career changes. The employee may return for additional career counseling as often as desired. This career counseling is usually voluntary, although there are some supervisory referrals. The only restriction in the career-counseling program is that participants must have been employed at Disneyland for at least three full-time equivalent months.

Career Planning Workshops. Disneyland offers a series of workshops designed to help employees determine their career objectives through the development of an individual career plan. One such workshop, the career orientation, is a bimonthly program, using a group setting, in which employees learn about the many aspects of the career-planning process and are provided an overview of the services available through the career planning department. Workshops dealing with goal setting, decision making, job satisfaction, and worker effectiveness are offered each month by the career planning department. Classes in resume preparation and job interviewing techniques provide helpful suggestions and key facts employees should know in preparing for internal job interviews. These classes last about an hour and a half, and the class attendance is limited to fifteen. In addition, videotapes of interview simulations are available for employees currently involved in an internal job search.

Career Resource Library. Disneyland established a career library in 1976. This library includes functional organization charts, job descriptions for all salary positions, descriptions of training programs, college catalogs, and the Occupational Outlook Handbook, as well as books on occupational trends, career planning, retirement planning, and so on.

Job Posting. Disneyland has a job-posting system and fills approximately 85 percent of its salaried openings through its promotion-from-within policy. As positions become available, they are posted through organizational flyers. A weekly job listing indicating the open positions that can be filled internally is included in the Disneyland employee newsletter.

Skills Inventory. Disneyland has a computerized skills inventory system that contains data on all employees who have used the services of the career planning department. This information includes the employee's educational level, work experience, EEO category, current work classification and experience factors, desired career interests, relocation preferences, and job classifications. This system is updated annually, and it is the first place researched when a salaried opening occurs. When an opening occurs, a listing is produced from the skills inventory of those individuals who have been previously recommended by management for such positions and/or have expressed an interest in the available functional area. Those employees identified by the skills inventory are interviewed by the company when the position opens.

Career Forum. Disneyland schedules monthly presentations for interested employees. These forums feature company representatives who provide an in-depth look at career opportunities within their area of expertise. General career information is also provided for those individuals interested in external job opportunities. Disneyland's career planning department also assists its seasonal employees with limited external career placement by inviting representatives of major firms to recruit qualified candidates from the Disneyland staff.

Future Directions

Disneyland employs a large number of part-time employees who are full-time college students. The career development program was established, at least in part, in response to the career concerns of these part-time employees, who felt overqualified and underutilized. Consequently, they applied for any available salaried career positions, regardless of whether their interest or qualifications met the job requirements. The career program was viewed as a means of providing employees an opportunity to realistically assess their potential in terms of the match with the Disneyland requirements. At present, line managers are not involved in the career development process. In the near future, Disneyland hopes to expand its career-development services by providing a career-development workshop for supervisors, increasing the availability of career-counseling services and implementing a preretirement planning program. It is hoped that the Disneyland career-planning system also will be expanded to its Tokyo subsidiary as well as to other Disney corporate subsidiaries.

Case Study 2: Municipality of Anchorage, Alaska.

Organizational Background

The focus of this case study is a career development project established at the Anchorage Water and Wastewater Utility (AWWU). AWWU is one of three major utilities owned and operated by the municipality of Anchorage. Located in south central Alaska, the municipality of Anchorage has a rapidly growing population approximating 250,000 individuals. The municipality of Anchorage, as an organization, employs approximately 3,500 individuals. The services provided by the municipality include a full range of local governmental programs, an aviation and port facility, as well as three utilities (electric, telephone, and water and wastewater). The municipality is divided into four major functional areas: (1) public services, (2) public safety, (3) administration, and (4) public utilities. Each of the four areas is headed by an executive manager, who reports to the mayor. Each of the utilities is headed by a general manager responsible for administration, operations, physical facilities, and related organizational activities. The municipality has a department of human resources (DHR), whose director reports to the executive manager for general administration. The DHR administrates such standard personnel functions as labor relations, affirmative action, and human resource development. Within the DHR, the training and development division is responsible for employee development, organizational development, and training activities. The career development project described in this case study was an activity of the training and development division.

Program Origin

The career development program of the municipality of Anchorage was established in January 1982, when the training and development division hired a career development specialist. The decision to hire such a specialist coincided with the election of a new mayor who during his campaign had promised to improve the quality of work life for Anchorage employees and who also was committed to improving the productivity of the municipality's human resources. While his announced goal was the establishment of a municipal-wide career development program, the mayor agreed to commence this process by establishing a career development pilot. Several criteria were used in establishing the pilot: (1) support and demonstrated commitment on the part of senior management, (2) organizational stability, (3) a broad base of occupational areas, (4) a medium-sized employee population, and (5) the presence of unionized and nonunionized employee groups.

The AWWU fulfilled all of these criteria and was selected as the primary pilot program. An employee task force was developed within the utility to assist in program design and implementation. This task force, together with the DHR staff, developed a career philosophy that was formally endorsed by the mayor as the municipality's career development philosophy. It states: "The municipality of Anchorage will have the ability to reach its highest potential when its employees, at all levels, are reaching their potential. This potential can be best met through a joint effort between the employee and the municipality. Career development will assist us in that effort through endeavors that will assist employees in career and life planning and in outlining careers within the municipality and by managing employee aspirations, potential, and capabilities in an effort to provide a quality environment and quality service to the current and future citizens of Anchorage."

In establishing the AWWU career program, the primary objectives were to:

1. obtain positive change in the overall organizational career development climate and employee career attitudes,
2. increase employees' knowledge regarding the organizational opportunity structure, future organizational directions, and the way in which the system works,
3. develop alternative ways of coping with identified employee career blockages,
4. provide employees with increased knowledge of training and educational opportunities,
5. increase the willingness of individuals to participate in self-development activities,
6. enhance individual development with respect to both current jobs and potential future positions,
7. integrate career development with the performance appraisal process,
8. ensure the continuation of AWWU career development programs beyond the eighteen-month pilot period, and
9. ensure adequate backup talent for key managerial positions.

Program Description

The AWWU career development program is open to all
employees and includes the following activities:

Career-Planning Workshops. The utility used external
consultants to design and staff a two-day group career-planning
workshop. This workshop takes employees through a series of
exercises designed to help them identify their valued skills, goals,
and career plans.

Supervisor/Subordinate Career Discussion Training. This
three-day workshop is designed to help supervisors understand their
role in the career development process. During the workshops,
supervisors examine the nature of the career-planning process, the
differing roles of supervisors and employees in this process, and
approaches for discussing career issues with their subordinates. One
important feature of this program is the role playing by supervisors
and subordinates in conducting the career conversations that occur
during the third day.

Career-Planning Booklets. A series of career-planning
booklets was developed as an added resource. This set includes a
career-planning guide designed to help employees focus on their
desired career goals on an individual basis, an action-planning
guide designed to help employees translate their career objectives
into specific action plans, and a guide for supervisors on how to
conduct employee career discussions.

Career Resource Center. The municipality has established a
career resource center, which contains a variety of tools to assist
employees in thinking through their career goals and objectives.
This center includes reference books, cassette tapes, and independent study materials.

Job Posting. In addition to improving the timely distribution of job announcements, the municipality began announcing
open and upcoming positions in the company newsletter in a
special section entitled "Career Opportunities."

Career Information Dissemination. Career development
bulletin boards were established at five major employee centers to

post such information as organizational training calendars, job-posting information, career resource center information, and other relevant data.

Career Blockage Identification. This problem involved the task force analyzing problems related to employee career mobility, ascertaining the extent of the problem, and proposing alternative solutions.

Career Counseling. Individual counseling is offered on a limited basis by the DHR staff and is supplemented by an external career-counseling organization that is part of the Anchorage community college system.

Employee Career Orientation Program. The municipality developed an employee orientation program that includes a pictorial slide description of the organization and a career development packet describing the AWWU career program.

Future Directions

The AWWU career program has completed its eighteen-month pilot phase and is now implemented in the utility as a regular program. The success of the AWWU career program was evaluated using a before and after employee career attitude survey, as well as available personnel data. Specific findings included a 16 percent decrease in AWWU turnover, over 68 percent participation by employees in AWWU career programs, and increases in the level of internal promotions and voluntary transfers, as well as increased participation by employees in organizational training and education programs. Also, there was found to be an increased willingness on the part of employees to assume personal responsibility for their own career development and a generally more favorable attitude of employees toward AWWU career programs and practices.

In addition to AWWU, the municipality also established two other career pilots. One, the health department, was only moderately successful due to the absence of top-management support and insufficient program resources. The third, the

Anchorage Telephone Utility (ATU), involved a consent decree that dictated the establishment of certain career activities. Although the forced environment made the program implementation somewhat more difficult, the ATU career system is slowly being implemented. The next challenge for the municipality of Anchorage is expanding the successful AWWU program municipality-wide. Also, the career development staff is seeking to integrate the career programs with a new human resource planning process being established by the municipality.

Case Study 3: Xerox Corporation.

Organizational Background

Xerox Corporation is a diversified office products manufacturer headquartered in Stamford, Connecticut. Xerox employs over 60,000 individuals in various locations in the United States, of whom about 80 percent are salaried and 20 percent hourly.

Program Origin

Xerox's career systems were established in 1975 and are now available company-wide throughout the United States. The basic objective of Xerox's career program is to create employee awareness of career needs, organizational opportunities, and the developmental steps required to implement career plans. These objectives translate into the following goals for the career development process: (1) establish and communicate its career development philosophy, (2) sell employees on the importance of career planning, (3) teach employees how to go about planning their careers, (4) provide employees with information about jobs and the systems of advancement at Xerox, (5) provide employees with personal assistance to help resolve career conflicts, and (6) accomplish the above objectives in over 150 separate geographical locations.

Xerox's career development program was established initially in response to employee interest, as well as EEO/ affirmative action pressures and top-management interest.

Originally, Xerox's career development programs had a strong focus on minorities and women. Over time, the program has been expanded to include the full range of nonexempt (administrative, clerical) as well as exempt, (professional, managerial, technical) employees. At present, the program has only a limited application to executives; however, there is some directed development that will help potential senior managers. The primary organizational responsibility for Xerox's career programs rests with line managers, who are assisted by consultants and coordinators from the personnel staff. Participation in Xerox's career development program generally is voluntary, except for high-potential development and succession planning. There are three basic elements in Xerox's career model. These include: self-evaluation (of needs, wants, strengths, experience, and training), career choice information (information about career paths, selection standards, job requirements, business outlook, and realistic options), and development action planning (formal education, company training programs, job moves, books, films, and mentors).

Program Description

The tools used by Xerox to implement the elements of its career model include: (1) for self-evaluation—career-planning workbook, career action planning text, career-planning workshops; (2) for career choice knowledge—career videotape library, career counseling, open job posting, replacement planning system, career path handbooks; and (3) for developmental action planning— training program building block, audiocassette training packages, and so on. Among these career-planning tools, several merit special attention:

Career-planning workbook. This self-paced workbook is entitled, *Failure to Plan Is Planning to Fail.* The workbook includes five chapters (general information, self-analysis, job goals, reality testing, and contingency and growth planning) and was designed to: (1) help Xerox employees formalize their thoughts about career planning, what it is, and why it is vital, and (2) provide employees with a personal planning document that they can keep and update.

Career Information. The Xerox career information center serves as the focal point for all resources and information related to career planning. The thrust of the center is to consolidate existing material and develop new career resources that can be readily available to Xerox employees. The information center includes a series of tapes addressing such topics as: (1) reasons for career planning, (2) how to do career planning, (3) special issues for minorities and women, and (4) interviews with senior functional officers. In addition to the videotapes, the career information center also has books and other reference sources.

Managers' Career-Planning Handbook. There are several versions of this handbook, one of which was developed by Xerox of Canada. At Xerox, each manager is expected to hold an annual career discussion with his or her subordinates. The basic function of the workbook is to assist the manager in effectively performing this career-counseling role.

Section 1 of the Xerox Canada handbook introduces the rationale underlying career development, the responsibilities and roles of employees versus the manager, and an overview of the career-planning process. Section 2 provides career-counseling guidelines for managers on how to plan for a formal career guidance session, how to hold a career discussion, how to acquire interviewing skills, how to help employees establish a career development action plan, how to follow up on a career-planning discussion, and so on. Appendix A in the handbook provides suggestions on how to manage and control a career discussion, an employee guide and blank form for completing the Xerox career development action plan, and some guidelines on how to deal with employee career-planning questions. Appendix B is a strategy guide for managers on how to conduct a career discussion with employees who represent different career capabilities. For example, it discusses adequate performers with potential, fast trackers, and those with limited potential. Appendix C provides sample open-ended questions for the manager's use.

Career-Planning Workshops. These workshops are offered on a demand basis and provide information about career-planning tools and teach behavioral models. The workshop is one day in length and follows the workbook format. In addition, it includes exercises on lifeline career planning and organizational politics.

Future Directions

Xerox considers its career workshops and career workbooks to be among the most effective career tools it uses. Although the career workshop reaches only a small population, it is considered to be very effective in stimulating individual career planning and opportunity identification. The career workbook is also considered to be effective because it encourages employees to realistically evaluate their career objectives. The job-posting system is considered to be a valuable career management tool because it is stimulating internal moves. The career information system is only modestly effective, however, because it is hard to keep the video materials up-to-date and the tapes have lost their credibility. Similarly, the managers' career-planning handbook is only considered adequate. At Xerox, as in many organizations, implementing an effective supervisor/subordinate career discussion process remains an elusive objective. In the years to come, Xerox hopes to better integrate its career development activity with the human resource planning function. Also, it plans to better address the career issues of selected target groups, such as handicapped employees. All in all, however, the Xerox career-planning system is considered to be a success in terms of encouraging employees' responsibility for their own career development and integrating individual career objectives with organizational employment opportunities.

References

Burack, E. H., and Gutteridge, T. G. "Institutional Manpower Planning: Rhetoric Versus Reality." *California Management Review*, 1978, *20* (2), 15.

Foulkes, F. K. "The Expanding Role of the Personnel Function." *Harvard Business Review*, 1975, *53* (2), 71-84.

Gutteridge, T. G., and Otte, F. L. *Organizational Career Development: State of the Practice.* Washington, D.C.: American Society for Training and Development, 1983.

Hall, D. T. *Careers in Organizations.* Glenview, Ill.: Scott, Foresman, 1976.

Hostage, G. T. "Quality Control in a Service Business." *Harvard Business Review,* 1975, *53,* 98–106.

Ideus, K. "Career Development Project: A Case Study." Unpublished master's thesis, Department of Education, Alaska Pacific University, 1985.

Meyer, H. E. "Personnel Directors Are the New Corporate Heroes." *Fortune,* 1976, *93* (2), 84–88, 140.

Storey, W. D. (ed.). *A Guide for Career Development Inquiry: State-of-the-Art Report on Career Development.* ASTD Research Series Paper No. 2. Madison, Wis.: American Society for Training and Development, 1979.

Walker, J. W., and Gutteridge, T. G. *Career Planning Practices.* AMA Survey Report. New York: AMACOM, 1979.

3

ҖѬҖѬҖѬҖѬ

Life
Career Roles:
Self-Realization
in Work and Leisure

Donald E. Super

The title of this chapter suggests that work and leisure are two quite distinct constructs—that they constitute two separate worlds. Such is not the case, as psychological studies carried out nearly fifty years ago (Super, 1940a, 1940b, 1941; Super and Carlson, 1942) have shown. It is more valid, and more helpful in practice, to think of work and leisure as being sections of a rotating stage in a large theater in which one section is set for the playing of leisure roles, another set for the work role or roles, another for study, another for homemaking, and another for community service. These stages are interconnected so that during the course of a given day, a given week, or a given month a person may move from one stage setting to another, playing, as his or her life situation calls for it, a diversity of roles—at breakfast a homemaker, later in the day a worker, later still perhaps a leisurite, and later again a homemaker. Sometime during the week he or she may add the role of citizen in attending a Parent/Teacher Association, Council of Social Agencies, or library committee meeting. Most men and women do play a combination of work, leisure, study, home and family, and civic roles.

Life Career Roles

That this is the case has been the keystone of my approach to careers, what I have called a life-span, life-space, formulation. To those two dimensions I added, without so naming it, a life-depth dimension in my Life Career Rainbow (Super, 1980, 1984). Figure 1 portrays seven major roles that most people play during the course of their life cycles and shows the differing amounts of participation and commitment to each of these roles at the various life stages.

This figure and this concept are familiar to many who are engaged in career development work as well as to a significant number who have used materials such as those that, with colleagues, I have developed for courses and workshops (Bowlsbey, 1984; Super and Bowlsbey, 1979). Conceptually, the diagram helps show the numerous and intricate relationships between the various life career roles, while practically it helps adolescents and adults examine their past, present, and future careers and think about how they are using their talents and their opportunities for self-fulfillment.

A career can, in its fullest and, I believe, its most appropriate sense, be viewed as the sequence and combination of roles that a person plays during the course of a lifetime. It has three dimensions: (1) time—its length or span or life cycle, (2) its breadth or scope—the amount of the potential life space it uses, and (3) its depth—the degree of involvement in each of the roles played. All three dimensions are shown in Figure 1.

The *span* of the career—the duration of the role—is a function partly of the age, health, and performance of the individual and partly of the situation in which he or she functions. Thus, the role of pupil or student, and with it the career of student, begins at about age five or six and is continuous (apart from school vacations) until sometime between the ages of sixteen and twenty-six. The role of student may at times be resumed at various later stages as the individual seeks or is forced into further education, refresher training, retraining for a new job, or better preparation for a civic or leisure role. It ends only when the individual stops studying both formally and informally, whether for employment,

Figure 1. The Life Career Rainbow: Seven Life Roles in Schematic Space.

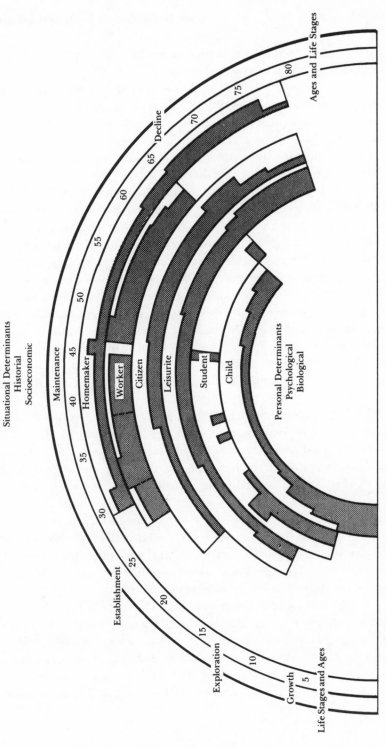

Source: Brown, Brooks, and Associates, 1985. Used by permission.

for community service, for homemaking, or for leisure—now often in the late seventies or eighties.

In contrast, the career as paid or profit-making worker, the occupational career, generally begins rather late in adolescence as the educational career either wanes with school leaving or intensifies with higher education or occupational training. Academic training in a trade or profession may be viewed as preoccupational and thus as part of the occupational career; it also can be viewed as part of the student role, as educational and even as exploratory (witness the large percentage of first-year engineering students in state universities who drop out of engineering in order to transfer to business administration or to go directly to some other kind of work). Entry into the occupation or even holding the first job for a certain amount of time may perhaps better be viewed as the beginning of the occupational career. Most researchers appear to favor entry as the real beginning. It is true, however, that for some the occupational career begins with part-time or summer work while still in school or college, especially in the case of farm children and students in cooperative education. The transition from school to work is not always an abrupt one, for sometimes the two roles merge.

The occupational career may be said to terminate with retirement, now mandatory only at age seventy but in fact often voluntary in the mid-sixties. But retirement, like entry, is for many a slow transition involving tapering off before or after official retirement and, in some instances, continuing to work in a more focused or specialized way or on a part-time basis. This is particularly likely to be the case when people have special knowledge or skills, as in the higher-level professions, such as those of physicist, psychologist, lawyer, historian, and writer. The roles of worker and of pensioner thus also often merge during the retirement transition in a postoccupational career.

The *scope* of a career may be seen in the number of roles played, in the number of roles that have substantial amounts of shading or coloring in the Life Career Rainbow. These roles sometimes are played in sequence, as in the case of student and worker roles, and sometimes simultaneously, as in the roles of worker and leisurite, homemaker and worker, and some students who are also engaged in paid employment. Thus, at the peak of a career one person may play only two roles, those of homemaker and of worker, devoting all waking hours to parenting, housekeeping, and paid employment, while another person may at that same age and life stage occupy the positions and meet the role expectations of worker, homemaker, student, leisurite, and citizen. In each case, one may observe signs of role conflict and stress if the roles demand all or more than the person can give; however, one may also observe in each type of case a high degree of self-fulfillment if the individual is up to the demands and if his or her values are being attained in playing those roles. The life space may be richly filled, or it may seem barren and empty if the roles are not satisfying. The number of roles played, the time devoted to each, the ability to play them, the amount of affect invested in each role, and the way they are played are major determinants of job satisfaction, life satisfaction, and stress.

The choice of roles may not be as great as the Life Career Rainbow suggests, but with changing values, economies, and legislation, men and women today generally are more free to make role choices rather than to accept socially imposed roles than they were 100, 50, or even 20 years ago.

The *depth* of commitment to each role is shown, in some color renditions of the Life Career Rainbow, by the depth of the color in each arc or role. Thus, if the worker role is colored blue, the eager new employee determined to do well in his or her job will have a deep blue arc in starting employment; but, if he or she becomes disillusioned with the job after some experience in it, as happens not infrequently, the blue will fade and become paler. Being promoted or transfering to a more self-expressive job, the color will again become darker, deeper, richer. Even when shading is used, changes in the darkness of the shading can reflect affective commitment. And, in any case, shading can show another important aspect of depth—that is, the degree of participation or the amount of time devoted to the role. Thus, in Figure 1 the new employee is shown to be devoting a very large part of his or her waking hours to work; then, not long before his or her marriage, the time spent on work decreases as first courtship and then taking on the homemaker role make inroads into the evenings and weekends that had been given to working at home on job assignments.

An application of this conceptualization of roles and of the relative importance of roles has been developed by the Work Importance Study (Super, 1982). It is the Salience Inventory (Super and Nevill, 1985a), which measures the relative participation, commitment, and value expectations of youth and adults, yielding scores for each of the five major life career roles commonly played by men and women of those ages. It is used both in surveys of students and workers at all occupational levels and in counseling men and women considering entering the world of work or experiencing what appear to be career crises. More detail on these applications appears later in this chapter.

Our Changing Economy, Our Changing Society

Society has always changed and is still changing. What is new are the nature of the changes and the rate of change. In the industrial economies of the nineteenth century, working hours were essentially the waking hours, for people worked as many as sixteen hours per day, six days per week, for fifty-two weeks per year. These hours held for men, women, and children in unskilled, semiskilled, skilled, and lower-level white-collar jobs. The conditions in which they worked, whether in the textile mills, the coal mines, or the cotton or corn fields, are hard to believe today. We live and work now in what is often called a *postindustrial economy,* a name that historians of the future certainly will not use, for it is a nondescriptor. Historians have done better in naming earlier economic eras, giving them names that tell us something about their nature: the guild system, the mercantile system, the domestic system, and the factory system. These are terms that tell us more than does the term *industrial revolution,* for in each of the periods named above industry was revolutionized. The pace was slower, and the nature of the change was different, but change there was. The use of a negative to describe the nature of the changes now taking place suggests uncertainty as to what it is that is emerging as our factory system changes. But our society seems to be at once more technological and more humanistic: If we are wise and fortunate, it may be known in the future as *technohumanistic.*

Some writers fear that technology may crush our budding, sometimes overly sentimental, humanism. Others hope that technology will instead free people to be more truly human. We have come to see that work, in the sense of paid employment, is not as satisfying to everyone as the work ethic would have it (Kanungo, 1982; O'Toole, 1973), that other roles, such as leisure, are not as enriching as we would like them to be, and that homemaking is not as satisfying as the nineteenth-century ethic made it out to be. Our greater abundance of leisure, the greater abundance that organized labor seeks in its efforts to further reduce the working day and the working week, is too often squandered on spectator sports and on noisy, often ugly and violent, musical and dramatic entertainment.

What Is Leisure?

Many different definitions of leisure have been suggested by behavioral scientists. Parker and Smith (1976), after reviewing these definitions, suggest that the concepts of *spare time* and *uncommitted time* are not precise enough and prefer the term *discretionary time* if one qualifier is to be used. They offer, by way of greater clarity and elaboration, the following formulation (p. 45): "Time and activity are dimensions which are both present in all categories of life space (utilization). . . . Between compulsory activities (in order to live or to earn a living) and freely chosen ones, some activities have the character of obligations. This applies to both work and nonwork activities. . . . Leisure implies relative freedom of choice, and it is possible to work during one's leisure time." In an attempt to further refine the concept, Susan Sears (in McDaniels, 1984b, p. 35) offers the following definition: "*Leisure*—relatively self-determined activities and experiences that are available due to discretionary income, time and social behavior; the activity may be physical, intellectual, volunteer, creative, or some combination of all four."

The term *volunteer* seems redundant, as it denotes self-determination and discretion or choice. The term *activities* is helpful, but taken as a synonym for experiences, it is too limiting in combination with the adjectives at the end of the definition—idling, lying in a hammock and daydreaming, is not a physical, intellectual, volunteer, or creative experience. Perhaps the phrase should be modified to read "self-determined activities and inactivity."

In an attempt to provide a more complete definition, a number of conceptualizations of leisure are explored here, drawing on both a priori reasoning and empirical research. Several recent American studies summarized by McDaniels (1984b) point up the fact that newspaper reading and television watching head up the list of daily leisure activities. The content of what is read is not so much self-fulfilling as self-stultifying. Some of the other findings are more encouraging: Spending time with the family is an activity engaged in by some 80 percent of those interviewed; although this tells us little about how the time is used, it suggests desirable social interaction and relationships. Seeking companionship was the second most common goal reported, followed by relaxing, learning new things, thinking and reflecting, and keeping informed about local, national, and international events. Participating in voluntary community activities, next in importance, was reported by nearly 50 percent of the carefully selected sample.

The operational definition of leisure implicit in the list is worth examining. Reading and watching television are activities, and so is spending time with one's family or friends. Classifying the survey's list according to Maslow's needs, they appear to be, in this order, belongingness and love, physiological needs, information and understanding, and safety and self-esteem. The need for beauty does not appear as such but may be comprehended in some of the objectives and activities named (the categories overlap and confuse needs with the activities in which needs may be met).

Common dictionary definitions reflect the confusion of popular usage. The short Merriam-Webster defines leisure as "time free from work or duties . . . relaxation, rest, repose." These are treated as synonyms for leisure, even though they conflict with some of the components of the definition (time free from work) and do not fully comprehend what it includes (domestic chores, child care, and community service). Time free from work may be devoted to work that is unpaid, such as service as a hospital volunteer, improving one's home or garden, the education of one's children, and cultivating one's own mind. Was Sir Isaac Newton, lord of a manor and fellow of Cambridge University when fellowships were generally sinecures, working when, dozing under a tree in his orchard, the legendary apple chose a trajectory that led him to formulate a law of physics? Did Montesquieu, also lord of a small manor, write on political philosophy for financial gain at a time when publication was expensive and readers were scarce? Leisure often involves work, although not in the sense of paid employment, business, calling, travail, grind, or drudgery. Newton, Montesquieu, John Locke, and many like them may have found that their leisure pursuit of knowledge, aided by putting their thoughts on paper and sharing them with others, was relaxing in comparison with other things they were called upon to do, such as making planting and marketing decisions, dealing with incompetent or greedy tenants or subordinates, keeping records, and paying their family debts to local merchants.

The "pursuit of leisure" is a common phrase, and pursuit is not always relaxing. It, too, requires effort. Amateur tennis, chess, crewel work, and sketching are leisure activities, but they are work in that they all require the systematic expenditure of effort for the attainment of an objective. Many people do them for purposes other than earning a living, and if they required much in the way of travail or drudgery, they would be given up.

The Nature of Leisure

We clearly need a definition of leisure, and, fortunately, we now have a small but significant body of knowledge from which to derive one. It is the psychological and sociological studies of leisure in relation to paid work that have done most to throw light on the nature of leisure. At first these studies did little more than note changes in the nature of children's play activities with age (Lehman and Witty, 1927). But in the mid 1930s, I began a study of the relationships of avocations to vocations (Super, 1940a). This study was published at a time when, because of World War II, psychologists were directing their energies toward the psychology of work and survival. It was therefore undiscovered when, a generation later, psychologists and sociologists interested in the subject searched the literature and assumed they were cultivating ground hitherto tilled only by historians and philosophers.

In this early study, amateur musicians, amateur photographers, model railroad builders and operators, and stamp collectors were administered the Strong Vocational Interest Blank (now the Strong-Campbell Interest Inventory) together with demographic and job and life satisfaction questionnaires. The first three groups of hobbyists were found to be engaging in their hobbies in one of three ways: as *extensions* of their occupations, as *compensation* for their occupations, or as activities *unrelated* to their occupations. Only stamp collecting showed no relationship to any occupation or to any family of occupations, despite the artistic, social science, or business components that one might hypothesize as underlying that interest. But model railroaders tended to be of three types: professional engineers or machinists who found in their hobby opportunity to continue the pursuit of an enduring interest and the use of valued skills in a situation that was less constrained than their jobs; people employed in engineering types of jobs who found in their hobby greater outlets for a greater range of interests and abilities than their work permitted; and people employed in unrelated occupations, such as accounting, life insurance, and printing, who found in their avocation opportunities to use skills and pursue interests for which their employment afforded no outlets.

The hobbyists who were best satisfied with their occupations and jobs were those who had hobbies rather like their occupations. These same hobbyists were also happiest with their home lives and with life in general. The "theory of balance"—the notion that one's hobby should be different from one's work—was very popular with sociologists and mental hygienists unaccustomed to counting during the years between the two world wars, but was clearly too simple to be valid. A more valid theory, this study showed, might be called a "theory of self-expression" or a "theory of self-fulfillment," for more important than having a hobby that is different from one's paid job is doing something—whether in one's job or outside of it—that one enjoys doing and does well. The avocation may be *similar* to one's work when the work is satisfying, or it may be *different* if the individual in question has abilities and interests that do not find expression in his or her work, or it may be *neutral* when the work is satisfying but other interests and abilities do not find expression in the occupation.

This classification of leisure pursuits has since been confirmed by sociologists who are interested not so much in mental health as in social behavior. Thus Champoux (1981) found in a recent study of employed people in general that leisure interests and activities could be classified as *supportive* to, *extensions* of, and *compensations* for the occupation engaged in, while still others are *neutral*. Champoux's data, methods, and generation were different from those of the early study, but the findings are clearly similar. Both studies show that a hobby such as model engineering might help an engineer's work by enabling him or her to keep or to develop knowledge and skills that are not used at work but that would be helpful in expanding or changing a work role; it might also help him or her in making contacts leading to more interesting or more profitable employment. It might help a person, too, to make a major occupational change. For example, take the case of an unemployed printer who was an active member of a model railroad club in New York City. He had developed real skill in working on the signal system of his club's railroad, in both designing and installing. A fellow member suggested that he apply for a subway system signal specialist's job, as candidates then were in short supply. He was soon hired, to the satisfaction of all concerned.

It has been found, too, that leisure activities can *conflict* with occupational activities, as they can take time and energy away from the job. A subcategory therefore should be added to the classifications cited or treated as a new category to supplement the category called supportive. Thus, a sales representative might spend time in painting that another person might spend locating and cultivating prospects, and a lawyer might spend time in stamp collecting that is needed for studying new developments in law related to his or her practice. At the same time, it should be noted that a leisure pursuit in this sense can be conflicting, supportive (finding sales prospects while playing golf), or neutral (fishing when one's work is under control even though one feels no need to get away from the job).

There are other ways of looking at leisure than through its relation to a current occupation. It is of interest to some educators (for example, McDaniels, 1984b) as *preparation for work* prior to entry into the labor force or even after entry, as in the case of the model railroader-printer cited previously. Thus, a student interested in social work might do volunteer work in a neighborhood center for orientation and for the development of knowledge and skills, or an engineer working for a power company might become active in an environmental protection group with an eye toward developing abilities needed in managing the company's impact on its environment and its relations with its public. Reviews of life experiences in developing dossiers with women homemakers interested in entering the labor force and with men facing career crises in their jobs have proved the usefulness of leisure activities for both exploration and training. Those interested in leisure as recreation may be offended by this work ethic view of leisure, but recognizing its value in orientation and in training does not, in itself, involve a rejection of its contributions to nonoccupational careers.

Another view of leisure that seeks to exploit it for social objectives is that of leisure activities as *supplements to* or *compensation for* work; this view plays up one of the characteristics isolated in the more scientific studies cited above. In an era when work is often repetitive, mechanized, and fragmented, many observers believe that those who do it feel constrained and unfulfilled (Ginzberg, 1979; Kanungo, 1982; Terkel, 1972). Such workers do not get to see any real resultant product or outcome of their work: Putting nuts on bolts in an assembly line, operating a press to stamp out seemingly meaningless pieces of plastic or metal, or tapping the wheels of locomotives may fall into this category in the minds of those who do such work. Some observers consider it essential to the self-fulfillment and happiness of these workers—and to their mental health—that they find opportunities in their leisure to use their unused abilities, to express their interests, to see the results of their efforts in some meaningful form, and thus to have a sense of worth and identity through their activities. This might be considered a refined version of the theory of balance, but it is in reality a theory of self-expression.

Finally, leisure might be seen as a *substitute for work* in an economy that does not provide employment for all its potential workers. Numerous studies, some dating from the Great Depression of the 1930s (Super, 1942) and others conducted during the depressed years of the 1970s and 1980s (Jahoda, 1982; Kaufman, 1982; Watts, 1983), document and illuminate the impact of unemployment on erstwhile and would-be wage earners and on their families. In a society that values work and that uses occupation as a source of identity as well as of support, not having a job is a stigma that symbolizes a loss of role, purpose, and meaning. This is so whether work is viewed by the individual as a means of self-fulfillment, a source of social support, a way of structuring time, a source of prestige and self-esteem, or simply as a means of making a living.

Leisure activities may be seen as a substitute for work in retirement, for they may be income producing, they may be a source of self-fulfillment and social support, and they do structure time and provide a source of respect and self-esteem. Winston Churchill's paintings, John Stuart Mill's writings, King Christian of Sweden's tennis playing, Lewis Carroll's children's stories, and Sir Roger Bannister's four-minute mile—these are all examples of the playing of leisure roles in ways that not only structured time while using abilities not used in their occupations (of prime minister, civil servant, chief of state, mathematician, and physician, respectively) but also brought prestige and feelings of worth and self-fulfillment to the hobbyist-workers named.

Given the many differing but overlapping definitions of leisure, can one propose a better? The following characteristics appear to be important in varying combinations and degrees:

1. Leisure involves the use of time.
2. Leisure time is time free from the need to play other roles, such as those of worker, student, homemaker, and citizen.
3. It may, as in playing tennis, require the expenditure of effort, but it may, as in idling in a hammock, require no effort.
4. Leisure pursuits are engaged in to meet some personal need, attain some value or values, and sometimes to use some ability or abilities.

5. They may thus have a clear goal, such as producing a painting, or have an ill-defined goal, such as relaxing.
6. They may be classified as extensions of, compensations for, or even as unrelated substantively to the occupation pursued.
7. They may support, conflict with, or be neutral to one's other roles, such as that of worker, in their use of time and effort.
8. They may have preparatory or replacement value for occupations in preemployment, unemployment, and retirement.

Individual differences in defining leisure, it is suggested, are matters of perception, distorted in one way or another by personal needs and situations. Having a uniform scientific definition, such as the above, is viewed as important to a better understanding, and therefore to better studies, of leisure. Given individual differences in the perception of leisure, one may expect to find changes in individual definitions with time and experience. We need studies of these questions.

Leisure in a Postindustrial Society

Given the perspective on leisure we have just discussed, what role may we expect it to play in a postindustrial, perhaps technohumanistic society? In this society, Spenner (1985) suggests, occupations are being both upgraded and downgraded both in the substantive complexity of the work and in the degree of autonomy or control exercised by individuals. The nature of the trend appears to vary with the industry and occupation studied and the methods of study (aggregations of data and case studies). Reviewing these studies, Spenner finds little or no change in the substantive complexity of work since 1900 and only slight upgrading of occupations since World War II, while autonomy has not been studied sufficiently in aggregate studies to permit the drawing of conclusions. Neither do the case studies of occupations and industries allow the drawing of firm conclusions, the sampling of occupations and industries being highly selective. Spenner concludes that the rate of change is slow for the labor force taken as a whole. Even today, change appears to be evolutionary, despite some dramatic examples of revolutionary change. But the computer revolution may be changing this conclusion.

In passing, it is worth noting in this context of industrial and organizational psychology that two of the best background references for this chapter, and especially for this section of the chapter, were written by sociologists (Spenner, 1985; Parker and Smith, 1976). In Spenner's eighty-two-item bibliography, only two references have authors listed in the American Psychological Association Directory, and they are both "junior" authors. Parker and Smith's work, a chapter in an edited collection, is equally lacking in psychological references (in this instance, studies of leisure). With the extensive work done on skills by such psychologists as Marvin Dunnette, Edwin Fleishman, Edwin Ghiselli, and Ernest McCormick, this suggests that behavioral scientists may have major blindspots, paralleled by our general failure to take into account work such as that, dating in both instances from the early or mid 1970s, by sociologists.

Spenner's work suggests a fivefold classification of occupational statuses that may be useful in considering the future of leisure in a postindustrial society: (1) upgraded occupations and workers, (2) downgraded occupations and workers, (3) static occupations and workers (little or no change in substantive complexity), (4) unemployed members of the labor force (displaced and neverplaced), and (5) retired members of the labor force. These categories, derived but not borrowed from Spenner, may be examined with an eye to their implications for leisure use and leisure counseling.

Upgraded Workers. These workers—and those about to be upgraded—should find leisure activities useful in orientation to their new or prospective work, in anticipatory socialization. The unemployed printer who was a model railroader, for example, began to develop a concept of himself as a signal expert before he ever contemplated work of that type. The school boy or girl who becomes enamored of a computer may use it as a tool or as a toy; only after spending some time with it may he or she come to see computer science as a field of study, research and development, or applications for earning a living. The orientation, as Jordaan (1963) pointed out, may be intentional or unintentional; the role of career development and counseling programs is to help make it intentional. Leisure activities also can be preparatory; that is, they can provide opportunities for the development of knowledge and skills and for familiarization with resources that facilitate movement from one specialty to another, from one occupation to another. The printer discussed above learned his new trade as a hobbyist without realizing that that was what he was doing. The "hacker" who in playing with a home computer develops skills and "bulletin board" knowledge is preparing, knowingly or otherwise, for an occupation. So, too, is the manager who, intrigued by the possibilities of the computer provided at work, not only learns to use it as intended but develops new data bases and new programs that give one mastery over data needed in an emerging specialty, data that are not yet as well controlled by peers and competitors. This training may be job related, but it may involve other applications as well.

Downgraded Workers. These workers also may find in leisure activities ways to compensate for what is happening in their jobs. They, too, may find orientation and training possibilities in leisure activities. These may lead to a reversal of the trend in the individual's career, for they may lead to new occupations or jobs in which upgrading is taking place. Their leisure activities may, perhaps more frequently, lead to life enrichment when job enrichment fails, through the use of abilities, the pursuit of interests, and the attainment of values that are no longer available in the job. Thus the engineer who finds new work too restricted by the breaking up of "jobs" may find in model railroading or in a home electronics laboratory opportunities for self-expression that the job no longer provides (extension), or he or she may find in an unrelated hobby (compensation) the opportunity for self-expression—as an amateur regional planner on the regional planning board or as a volunteer social worker in a recreation center with crafts as the medium for making contact with children, young people, the unemployed, or the retired.

Static Workers. Even in some occupations in which upgrading and downgrading are taking place, some workers remain static: custom tailors are a well-known example. And some occupations remain static; that is, few if any of their members are affected by change. For some workers, the lack of change is a blessing: enjoying doing their work as they always have, they find security in the lack of change. For some the lack of change causes boredom, discontent, or burnout. Failing to find satisfaction in their job, they wish for other opportunities. If they are mobile and if the economy is fluid and open, they may find the variety that they desire or better opportunities to use their abilities and attain their values. But if their opportunities for change are limited for personal or for societal reasons, they must stay where they are and suffer the lack of self-fulfillment. Here is where leisure does play for some, and holds the promise of playing for far more workers, the role of major psychological source of role satisfaction. The increased attention being paid today to leisure education and leisure counseling, and the proliferation of community and company leisure programs, make it possible to find, in activities such as softball, bowling, archery, drama, music, sketching and painting, and volunteer social work, opportunities for physical activity, social prestige, creativity, altruism, and the attainment of values that are less easily found in semiautomatic, routine, anonymous, jobs.

Unemployed Workers. It is often difficult for unemployed workers to think of leisure as a substitute for employment, for having been denied the esteemed role of breadwinner, having been denied the occupational title that provides identity for most adults in modern economics, leisure activities to them seem meaningless and leisure roles trivial. The protestant work ethic thus has created and preserved a problem for society: Work is salvation; nonwork is perdition. If, however, work comes to be seen as perdition, as in the case of the alienated, who see no place for themselves in the economy (Kanungo, 1982), social values and norms may change. Education, social work, and personnel work in business and industry need to help develop a value system in which the emphasis is on self-fulfillment in socially desirable ways. These include both the self-expressive and the society-maintaining occupations and the other major social roles of the Life Career Rainbow: leisurite, homemaker, citizen, and student. If the constructive use of abilities, the pursuit of desirable values, and engagement in constructive activites that provide outlets for enduring interests were valued in any and every role, then self-fulfillment and excelling in leisure roles would be respected by others and would be a source of self-esteem. Leisure would then compensate for non-self-fulfillment in work.

Retired Workers. Retirees often take on their new roles with feelings of rejection and resentment at having been "put on the scrap heap," although this is by no means the universal reaction to retirement. When workers taper off, gradually reducing the temporal, physical, and emotional demands of work, retirement often comes gracefully and pleasantly. When they move from one regular adult job to another tailored to their needs and capacities, they may feel a new freedom and have a second blooming. These last two types of retirement are particularly common in the professions, whether an individual is employed by someone else or works independently. It is managerial, clerical, and blue-collar workers who are most likely to feel "redundant," finished, although if retirement provisions are adequate and the workers have other leisure interests and involvements that give them roles and outlets, retirement may be a liberating event and experience. For all, if there is continuity in meaningful life activities from work to retirement, the newfound leisure may lead to continuing or even greater self-fulfillment (Steer, 1970).

Multiple Roles for Self-Fulfillment

The current concern for underemployment and unemployment, with their emphasis on work and its material rewards, too often leads to a neglect of other, nonmaterial human needs and values. But attention also must be paid to the other major life career roles of leisure, community service, study for its own sake or for the improvement of appreciation and performance in nonwork roles, and homemaking. Each of these roles provides opportunities for the use of many abilities, outlets for many interests, and opportunities to attain many different values. In many of them, one can be creative, interact with others, be physically active, and sometimes even attain economic security, even though work is now the prime source of the latter and the principal source of prestige and self-esteem. Economic security has been attained by inheriting wealth or by marrying it, and it is now frequently found in unemployment insurance for relatively short periods in the United States and in

Social Security pensions in retirement. Even when unemployment insurance or old-age pensions provide material security, as in some countries, this meeting of material needs has been found to be insufficient for self-esteem and public recognition. People do not live by free bread alone. Herein lies the potential of the leisure role.

Redefining the Concept of Career Development

Management today is inclined to look askance at career development activities that may channel talents, energies, time, and people into activities that are not directly related to corporate objectives of increasing productivity, sales, and profits. It is frequently the experience of career development specialists working with business and industry that aspects or components of employee career development programs that might so channel employees, either within the company or outside of it in their leisure or in outplacement, are opposed and blocked. This was, to cite just my own experience as a part-time consultant and full-time university professor, true in eight out of eleven instances during a nine-year period ending in 1975: Only three corporations were willing to risk developing career development programs that might lead employees away from their corporate career ladders.

In a constantly changing technology, however, the leisure pursuit, the avocationally developed talent of today, may prove to be crucial vocationally tomorrow. In an economy in which some occupations are being downgraded, the avocational outlet may be central in the life satisfactions of a worker whose job has become largely a means of supporting a leisure and family life-style. Newton's thoughts about the trajectory and force of the apple falling in his orchard were perhaps extracurricular at the time, but they were economically productive in due course. The steam toy invented by an ancient Greek named Hero was just a toy until Papin, Newcomen, Watt, Stephenson, and Fulton put the toy to work in the mines, on rails, and on rivers. It is not for trivial reasons that some of the major corporations in the United States and in Great Britain provide time off with pay for managers and engineers to pursue, at some of our leading universities, self-selected courses of study that are unrelated to their work.

Implications for Program Development

This is where education, guidance, and personnel programs must find ways of changing roles and perspectives on roles. The Life Career Rainbow is being used in some curriculums and career development programs as a basis for examining the adequacy of what is being done to help young people and adults prepare for and cope with their careers. The schema helps focus attention on the variety of roles people play and on the interaction and interelationships of these roles. It helps point up how abilities and interests not used in one role (the job) may be used in other roles (such as leisure), leading to better satisfied and more adaptable workers at whatever level of employment.

Five steps are important in planning and instituting a corporate career development program based on this contemporary conceptualization of the relationships between work and leisure in an evolving economy with a changing work force. These are: (1) Identify all of the abilities, values, and interests of the work force, even those that seem irrelevant to the present needs of the company; (2) Survey the available and potential outlets for these qualities in the company and in the greater community; (3) Help individual employees know and understand their talents and their potential, together with the possible outlets for them; (4) Plan corporate and individual programs for the cultivation and use of talents and opportunities, going beyond the usual focus on current manpower needs to include leisure potentials in an individual and in the greater community; (5) Encourage and facilitate the carrying out of these personal, corporate, and community programs.

The first step, identification, has already been tried, sometimes with success and sometimes with failure, in a number of corporations, but the focus generally has been on talents needed for corporate development. Leisure skills and interests that have already been developed tend to be slighted both in their collection and in their storage in personnel folders and in computer files. When values are surveyed, the data are usually anonymous and aggregrated, not used to find out what individuals may seek in their work and other roles. The definitions used need to be revised and broadened, and instruments such as the Adult Career Concerns

Inventory (Super, Thompson, and Lindeman, 1985), the Values Scale (Super and Nevill, 1985b), the Strong-Campbell Interest Inventory (Hansen, 1985), leisure assessment approaches described by Peevy (1984) and Edwards (1984), and the Salience Inventory (Super and Nevill, 1985a) (which assesses the relative importance of the major life career roles, including work and leisure) can be used to supplement and objectify the interview in assessment.

The second step, the survey of outlets, has often been undertaken with a focus on manpower needs; the methods are therefore familiar. But such a survey has much less often looked beyond the company, and when it has it has been for the outplacement of redundant employees. It has not often been done to identify leisure outlets that the company might want to publicize with an eye to both corporate and individual development, for matching people with opportunities for greater self-development away from work.

The third step, counseling with individuals, has often been described (Crites, 1981) in conjunction with career development programs, both educational and organizational, with the focus on the individual. Leisure counseling has been dealt with by Peevy (1984), Edwards (1984), and Loesch and Wheeler (1982); Hall (1976), Knowdell (1984), and Stumpf (1984) have focused on career development problems, programs, and processes in organizations.

The fourth step, planning corporate programs and individual programs for the cultivation and use of talents, is familiar insofar as manpower for the company is concerned. The same principles apply to leisure programs; the difference lies in the focus on the whole person and on the totality of the environment in which the individual functions and might function.

The fifth step is putting the corporate program into action and, through it, helping individuals put their own programs into effect. It is here that a combination of counseling insights, knowledge of resources, and administrative ability are put to the test. As has often been pointed out, it is too easy to "test 'em and tell 'em," to have "three interviews and a cloud of dust," and to "kiss the counselee goodbye at the door." Follow-up work keeps the career development manager or counselor in contact with both the human and the institutional resources with which he or she works.

Conclusion

In the last analysis, our vision of the future of work and leisure is a clouded one, and what we think may be its nature may turn out to be wrong. The futurists propose conflicting scenarios, and sociologists who analyze current trends tend to disagree as to what the trends are, as Spenner (1985) has shown—this despite the clear picture that labor economists such as Goldstein (1984) present in summarizing the studies done from that perspective.

If computerized automation leads to an economy in which a small number of highly trained people are needed, together with a larger number of skilled support workers, there will be a large, less able leisure class that is not needed in the work force. Leisure will then become our major social role, and society will survive or fail on the basis of how it handles the development of the leisure role.

If, on the other hand, we develop into a society in which large numbers of people have no alternative but to work at society-maintaining jobs, leisure will be important for the outlets that it provides for self-realization in the maintainers of that society. The minority employed in self-fulfilling occupations will still often need to develop their leisure roles, partly for their own well-rounded development and partly as a means of keeping in touch with the society maintainers and the society-maintained—the unemployed and the retired.

References

Bowlsbey, J. A. *Discover.* Iowa City, Iowa: American College Testing, 1984.

Brown, D., Brooks, L., and Associates. *Career Choice and Development: Applying Contemporary Theories to Practice.* San Francisco: Jossey-Bass, 1984.

Champoux, J. E. "A Sociological Perspective on Work Involvement." *International Review of Applied Psychology,* 1981, *30,* 65–86.

Crites, J. O. *Career Counseling.* New York: McGraw-Hill, 1981.

Dunnette, M. D. (ed.). *Handbook of Industrial and Organizational Psychology.* Skokie, Ill.: Rand McNally, 1976.

Edwards, P. B. "Leisure Counseling: The Practice." *Journal of Career Development*, 1984, *11*, 90–100.

Ginzberg, E. *Good Jobs, Bad Jobs, No Jobs.* Cambridge, Mass.: Harvard University Press, 1979.

Goldstein, H. "The Changing Structure of Work." *Occupational Trends and Implications.* In N. C. Gysbers, and Associates, *Designing Careers: Counseling to Enhance Education, Work, and Leisure.* San Francisco: Jossey-Bass, 1984.

Gysbers, N. C., and Associates. *Designing Careers: Counseling to Enhance Education, Work, and Leisure.* San Francisco: Jossey-Bass, 1984.

Hall, D. T. *Careers in Organizations.* Santa Monica, Calif.: Goodyear, 1976.

Hansen, J. I. *The Strong-Campbell Interest Inventory.* Palo Alto, Calif.: Consulting Psychologists Press, 1985.

Jahoda, M. *Employment and Unemployment: A Sociopsychological Perspective.* New York: Cambridge University Press, 1982.

Jordaan, J. P. "Exploratory Behavior." In D. E. Super (ed.), *Career Development: Self-Concept Theory.* New York: College Entrance Examination Board, 1963.

Kanungo, R. N. *Work Alienation.* New York: Praeger, 1982.

Kaufman, H. G. *Professionals in Search of Work.* New York: Wiley, 1982.

Knowdell, R. L. "Career Planning and Development Programs in the Workplace." In N. C. Gysbers, and Associates, *Designing Careers: Counseling to Enhance Education, Work, and Leisure.* San Francisco: Jossey-Bass, 1984.

Lehman, H. C., and Witty, P. A. *The Psychology of Children's Play Activities.* New York: Barnes & Noble, 1927.

Loesch, L. C., and Wheeler, P. T. *Principles of Leisure Counseling.* Minneapolis, Minn.: Educational Media, 1982.

McDaniels, C. "The Role of Leisure in Career Counseling." *Journal of Career Development*, 1984a, *11*, 64–70.

McDaniels, C. "The Work-Leisure Connection." *Vocational Guidance Quarterly*, 1984b, *33*, 35–44.

O'Toole, J. *Work in America.* Report of a special task force to the Secretary of Health, Education and Welfare. Washington, D.C.: U.S. Department of Health, Education and Welfare, 1973.

Parker, S. R., and Smith, M. A., "Work and Leisure." In R. Dubin (ed.), *Handbook of Work, Organization, and Society.* Skokie, Ill.: Rand McNally, 1976.

Peevy, E. S. "Leisure Counseling: Some Emerging Approaches." *Journal of Career Development,* 1984, *11,* 81–89.

Spenner, K. I. "The Upgrading and Downgrading of Occupations: Issues, Evidence, and Implications for Education." *Review of Educational Research,* 1985, *55,* 125–154.

Steer, R. A. "Satisfaction with Retirement and Similarity of Self-Ratings of Past Occupation to Present Activities." Unpublished doctoral dissertation, Teachers College, Columbia University, 1970.

Stumpf, S. A. "Adult Career Development: Individual and Organizational Factors." In N. C. Gysbers, and Associates, *Designing Careers: Counseling to Enhance Education, Work, and Leisure.* San Francisco: Jossey-Bass, 1984.

Super, D. E. *Avocational Interest Patterns: A Study in the Psychology of Avocations.* Stanford, Calif.: Stanford University Press, 1940a.

Super, D. E. "The Educational Value of Stamp Collecting." *Journal of Educational Psychology,* 1940b, *31,* 68–70.

Super, D. E. "Avocations and Vocational Adjustment." *Character and Personality,* 1941, *10,* 51–61.

Super, D. E. *The Dynamics of Vocational Adjustment.* New York: Harper & Row, 1942.

Super, D. E. "A Life-Span, Life-Space Approach to Career Development." *Journal of Vocational Behavior,* 1980, *13,* 282–298.

Super, D. E. "The Relative Importance of Work." *The Counseling Psychologist,* 1982, *10,* 95–103.

Super, D. E. "Career Life and Development." In D. Brown, L. Brooks, and Associates, *Career Choice and Development.* San Francisco: Jossey-Bass, 1984.

Super, D. E., and Bowlsbey, J. A. *Guided Career Exploration.* Cleveland, Ohio: The Psychological Corporation, 1979.

Super, D. E., and Carlson, R. "What Adolescent and Adult Stamp Collectors Learn from the Hobby." *Journal of Genetic Psychology,* 1942, *60,* 99–108.

Super, D. E., and Nevill, D. D. *The Salience Inventory.* Palo Alto, Calif.: Consulting Psychologists Press, 1985a.

Super, D. E., and Nevill, D. D. *The Values Scale.* Palo Alto, Calif.: Consulting Psychologists Press, 1985b.

Super, D. E., Thompson, A. S., and Lindeman, R. H. *The Adult Career Concerns Inventory.* Palo Alto, Calif.: Consulting Psychologists Press, 1985.

Terkel, S. *Working.* New York: Random House, 1972.

Watts, A. G. *Education, Unemployment and the Future of Work.* Milton Keynes, England: The Open University Press, 1983.

Yankelovich, D., and Lefkowitz, B. "Work and American Expectations." *National Forum,* 1982, *42* (2), 3-5.

4

꧁꧁꧁꧁꧁꧁꧁꧁꧁

Breaking
Career Routines:
Midcareer Choice
and Identity
Development

Douglas T. Hall

Gaps in Current Career Theory, Research, and Practice

In 1971, the author published a theoretical paper describing career growth as a process of identity development through personal choice (Hall, 1971). At that time, the major gap in the career literature was the lack of attention to the ways careers unfold in organizational settings. Since that time, a considerable body of literature has developed on the topic of organizational career development (see, for example, Hall, 1976; Schein, 1978). At present, the gaps in the literature are more specific. A major deficiency now in the organizational career literature centers on the issue of what happens to a person who has successfully explored and made an

Note: I am grateful for the helpful comments of Chris Argyris, Connie Gersick, Raymond Katzell, Kathy Kram, Janina Latack, and Asya Pazy on earlier drafts of this chapter.

initial occupational choice, gone through a period of entry, trial, and settling down, and become established in his or her career field. Most of the organizational career research to date has dealt with these early stages, as indicated in Table 1.

Similarly, the *adult socialization* literature typically has dealt with the educational or early occupational experiences of individuals making the transition into their work careers—for example, medical or nursing students (Becker, Geer, Hughes, and Strauss, 1961), management trainees (Schein, 1978; Louis, 1980), and air traffic controllers (Crump, Cooper, and Maxwell, 1981). Thus, adult socialization, in fact, has been implicitly defined in the literature to mean *early* adult socialization. The reason for this is that the central assumption of the research on role transitions has been a tilted power relationship, with a low-power individual moving into a high-power work environment, with a resulting one-way influence process: The organization socializes the person, but the person does not innovate or otherwise act on the organization.

Table 1. Current Status of Organizational Career Research
and Practice, in Relation to Career Stages.

Career stage	Amount of research[a]	Representative citations
Exploration	+++++	Holland, 1973
Entry	++++	Wanous, 1980
Trial	+++	Berlew and Hall, 1966
Establishment/ Advancement	+++	Bray, Campbell, and Grant, 1974
Maintenance/Midcareer	+	Slocum, Cron, Hansen, and Rawlings, 1985
Disengagement	++	Latack and Dozier, 1985

[a]Key: +++++ A tremendous amount
++++ A great deal
+++ A moderate amount
++ A small amount
+ Virtually none

As Schein (1978) has pointed out, as the individual advances and becomes more established in his or her career, there is relatively less organizational socialization and more individual innovation. Thus the "adult" socialization studies have tended to systematically exclude later career stages during which the person exerts more influence in the organization.

In the psychological literature, however, work on what is termed *adult development* has covered (indeed stressed) the middle years (see, for example, Levinson and Associates, 1978; Levinson, 1984; Osherson, 1980; Gould, 1978). However, since the focus here has been on the total life structure of the individual, the primary focus has been on midlife, not necessarily mid*career* experiences. Changes in personal identity (especially in relation to aging and mortality), interpersonal and family relationships, and generativity issues have been of primary concern. Of course, critical career experiences are certainly a major influence on personal development in midlife. Osherson (1980) presents an especially sensitive summary of these major midlife issues.

In the last few years, as a result of the volatile external environment, a literature on *organizational life cycles* has developed (see, for example, Kimberly, Miles, and Associates, 1980). The focus here generally has been on business strategy and how that strategy can best be fitted to the organization's life state (birth, growth, maturity, or decline). This notion of a system life cycle fits beautifully with the stages of an individual's career development (where organizational birth is analogous to exploration for the individual, growth to establishment and advancement, maturity to maintenance, and decline to disengagement). (This idea is discussed in greater detail in Hall, 1984; see Figure 1.) However, this very logical topic of how individual career stages relate to organization stages has been largely unexplored, although the work of Gupta (1984; Gupta and Govindarajan, 1984) and Slocum, Cron, Hansen, and Rawlings (1985) is a step in the right direction.

The author (Hall, 1984) has proposed some theoretical ideas in person-organization life cycle matching. The first assertion is that the organization's career management process and the person's career planning tends to place employees in congruent environments: That is, young, growing employees tend to be found in

Figure 1. Individual and Organizational Life Stages.

Individual

Organization	Establishment	Advancement	Maintenance	Disengagement
Birth	X			
Growth		X		
Maturity			X	
Decline				X

Source: Hall, 1984.

young, growing organizations, while mature, stable organizations tend to have more older, midcareer employees. In other words, the X's in the congruent cells (on the diagonal) in Figure 1 represent the most common combinations of people and organizations.

However, maximum development does not necessarily occur when a person is perfectly in tune with his or her environment. Some degree of challenge or "stretch" is required for the person to acquire new skills and abilities (and thus grow). One promising area for strategic human resource development, then, would be the creation of *strategic misfits,* where a person is placed in an off-diagonal environment (that is, one that does not fit his or her career stage). For example, if the young "go-go" manager were placed in a mature organization, this might force him or her to develop more careful planning, budgetary control, and other administrative skills. Similarly, placing a maintenance-stage manager in a birth-

or growth-stage organization might reignite the person's creative energies and spark a midcareer renewal.

Such strategic misfitting also would promote the development of the organization, as well as that of the individual. The go-go manager in the mature organization might restore a degree of organizational growth, for example. The mature manager in the high-growth organization might impose discipline and a more controlled growth, a necessary ingredient in many young organizations (Greiner, 1972).

A subset of the work on organizational life cycles has been the literature on *organizational decline*—studies focusing specifically on retrenchment, plant closings, job elimination and work force reduction ("downsizing"), and organizational restructuring (eliminating layers of management). For example, the Winter 1983 (volume 22, number 4) issue of *Human Resource Management* contains an excellent collection of studies on organizational decline. However, the literature in this area has focused on the exit process alone: Research typically has not taken a career perspective and considered how the process of leaving related to the person's career stage concerns or how the exit aided or hindered development. One reasonable hypothesis would be that the threat or fact of losing one's job would tend to be a trigger that could stimulate a major career reexamination and renewal (Latack and Dozier, 1985). However, most of the research has been limited to the transition of the person out of the organization (and, sometimes, into the new job), with little examination of career consequences (Kaufman, 1982).

This literature, in a major omission, also has ignored the problem of how to facilitate career growth for the individuals who remain in the downsized ("lean and mean") organization. It appears that in managing the slow-growth organization, all the easy steps have been taken (in other words, we have separated people from the organization). Now it is going to be necessary to achieve additional efficiencies with the bare-bones staff that remains and to provide career growth for those people. Retaining established strong performers in a low-opportunity organization is a major challenge of career management in the late 1980s.

In the area of *individual learning*, several critical questions remain unanswered. How do people make major and minor shifts in their career specialties and competencies? The author (Hall, 1980) proposed a methodology for assessing the degree of career change a person makes when he or she moves to a new job. What is needed now is research on *trigger events and influences* that stimulate various types of changes. We know more in a descriptive sense about what types of changes people make and about the consequences of changes (Brett, 1982) than we do about their causes.

Following on the learning theme, what causes some people to be in a *continual learning or exploratory mode*, with small shifts throughout the career (as opposed to long periods of stability, punctuated by one or two massive, crisis changes)? This issue of learning will be addressed in detail later in this chapter.

The Midcareer Experience

What Is Midcareer? The first issue to consider here is the definitional one: What do we mean by "midcareer"? There are several possibilities, each with its own merits. One option would be to work from our definition of *career,* which is the sequence of individually perceived work-related experiences and attitudes that occur over the span of the person's work life (Hall, 1976). Midcareer, then, would be the middle phase, or the beginning of the middle phase of the person's work life. The point where that middle occurs thus would depend upon the person's work life pattern. For a person with a traditional, uninterrupted career, starting work at age twenty-one and retiring at sixty-five, the middle third would roughly cover the years from thirty-six to fifty-one. This is close to some approaches which have used chronological age as a basis and arrive at ages thirty-five to fifty as being midcareer (Hall and Mansfield, 1971).

However, in the case of a person with an interrupted or delayed career, the middle would come at a quite different point. Say a person embarked on a career at age twenty-one, worked for two years, and then left the labor market for twenty years (as might be the case for a woman raising a family and being a full-time homemaker). If she reentered the work force at age forty-three and worked until age seventy, the middle nine years of her twenty-seven-year career would be ages fifty-two to sixty-one.

Or say a person had an uninterrupted career but made two major career switches. Assume that the person was trained as an engineer and worked in that field between the ages of twenty-one and thirty-one, rising to the level of senior project engineer. Then assume that the person went to law school for three years and practiced law from age thirty-five to fifty. And then assume he or she became a professor of business law, rising through the ranks of a tenure-track position between the ages of fifty-one and sixty-five. In this case, there are stages to the person's work in each career field, and in a sense he or she would have three "midcareers." In this approach, midcareer would be defined by the amount of time the person had been in a given career field. An example of this approach would be Stumpf and Rabinowitz's (1981) study of academics, in which career stage was measured in terms of time in the academic ranks: Postentry socialization (up to two years), advancement (two to ten years), and maintenance (over ten years). Rush, Peacock, and Milkovich (1980) refer to this type of measure as a "career clock."

This definition, with its notion of multiple midcareers, is in marked contrast to the adult development approach, which considers life stages rather than career stages. Since the person has only one life (as far as science can prove today), there is only one midlife period. Levinson and Associates (1978) define the transition into midlife as occurring between the ages of forty and forty-five, while the stage of midlife is defined as ages forty-five to sixty.

Another approach is to focus on the passage a person perceives him- or herself making through a particular career role and to define the middle in terms of the person's psychological adjustment to that role. This adjustment could be viewed in terms of the familiar career stages (exploration, trial, establishment, maintenance, disengagement), but here the references would be to stages of perceived transition through the occupational career role. Thus, referring back to the person described earlier who made two major career switches, he or she would, by this definition, have three midcareers, but they would be measured by his or her degree of role adjustment, not by chronological time spent in that role.

The midcareer stage of the perceived intracareer role transition would commence after the person felt established in that role. This would be the time at which the person had mastered the role, was no longer a "newcomer" and had become an "insider" (Wanous, 1980; Louis, 1980), and before the process of disengagement or withdrawal. At this point, the status passage from the previous role (for example, from school or from a previous occupational role) into the new role would have been completed and the person would have acquired the knowledge, values or attitudes, and skills required of incumbents in the new role (Van Maanen and Schein, 1979). At this point, the person feels established in the role, experiences mastery, and has entered a period in which work is more scripted, habitual, routine, and nonconscious (Louis, 1980).

The latter approach (perceived intracareer role adjustment) will be the approach to midcareer taken here. What this approach means is that midcareer must be assessed subjectively, based on the person's experienced career concerns (Hall, 1976). The timing of midcareer may be affected by the passage of time in that role, but it is not defined by time.

This also means that we can make a clear distinction between "midcareer," "midlife," and "midworklife" (that is, a distinction between midcareer and chronological age and time in career role). As we will see later, it will be important for analytical purposes to be able to examine variations in age and midcareer in relation to each other. And for people with traditional, uninterrupted work lives, these various middles would tend to coincide.

Thus, to sum up, we are defining midcareer as the period during one's work in an occupational (career) role after one feels established and has achieved perceived mastery and prior to the commencement of the disengagement process.

Themes in Midcareer Experience. Interviewer: "How does it feel to be in midcareer in this organization?" Midcareer purchasing administrator: "The opportunities are less. The number of opportunities is shrinking. The company is not growing fast. In fact, it's shrinking. No matter how good you are, you're not going anywhere. You're in a declining universe." These comments reflect the feelings of one administrator regarding midcareer. As we identify the major themes of the midcareer experience (summarized in Table 2), his comments capture what is probably the core concern of this career stage: there is a *perceived constriction of career opportunity*. Whereas in early career opportunities seemed wide open and the major issue was *choosing* which opportunity to pursue, in midcareer the task is *finding* viable career options. One cause for this is the narrowing pyramidal structure of the organization: In midcareer, the individual has probably advanced to a level at which competition for promotions becomes more severe. Also, most organizations have an implicit or explicit career timetable such that if a person has not progressed to a certain level within a certain number of years, the probabilities of further promotion are sharply reduced (Lawrence, 1984). This plateauing is the result of a "tournament" process of advancement, under which a person must keep "winning" (gaining promotions) in each round (grade level) to be a candidate for the next round (level). Once a person loses in one round (is passed over for promotion too often),

Table 2. Themes in the Midcareer Experience.

1. Perceived constriction of career opportunity
2. Organizational maturity (slow growth, no growth, or decline)
3. Ambiguity and uncertainty about one's future career role
4. Midcareer change experienced as dysjunctive and individualized
5. Shift from influence of socialization to influence of
   - change within the work role or
   - change in the person or
   - awareness of lack of change
6. Heightened awareness of the longer-term dimensions of career effectiveness:
   - adaptability
   - identity
7. Increased awareness of responsibility for own career
8. Increased salience of separation from old roles
9. Disruption of the psychological success cycle; need to disrupt habitual behavior and trigger exploration
10. Shift in balance from work roles to personal roles
11. Increased connectedness between career transitions and life event changes

he or she is out of the game (is no longer a candidate for further promotions) (Rosenbaum, 1979).

Another reason for declining opportunity at midcareer is the result of the life stage of many contemporary organizations: a period of *organizational maturity marked by slow growth, steady state, or decline.* As one executive in a large international bank said recently, "Unfortunately, the bank has hit 'midcareer' precisely at the same time as a large group of our employees." The organizational response to slower growth is often the elimination of jobs and layers of management, which further reduces the opportunities for established employees (Hall, 1984). This constrained organizational environment is in marked contrast to the rapid-growth environment experienced in the early career stages of many of today's midcareer employees. These changing organizational growth rates have been affected largely, of course, by the slow growth in the national and world economy.

Related to this feeling of constrained opportunity is a sense of *uncertainty and ambiguity about one's future career role.* In interviews with people in midcareer, many comments reflected a feeling that there had been more of a perceived career path in early career but that in midcareer there was no clear future path. Many organizations' training progams move people through a fairly standard program of jobs and promotions for the first few years of service, and often people advance together, as a cohort. Then in later years, future advancement is determined more by individual potential and performance. If the person stops moving for several years, in the absence of career feedback from the organization there is a feeling that the career trajectory has leveled off, and the person is left hanging in an organizational limbo.

This uncertainty about the future career role is different from the earlier stages of trial and establishment, in which the person was entering a clear organizational role (or roles) and was being socialized. Thus, in early career the role is clear and fixed, while the person's subidentity is changing. In midcareer, the career subidentity has been established, and the career role appears to be shifting and unclear. The issue is still one of achieving career role and subidentity fit, but the person is trying to hit a moving and unclear target. And in the process of achieving midcareer fit, the subidentity may change, too, but in the beginnings of the midcareer transition process, the career subidentity is clear and established.

Because of this ambiguity in the future career role, the *midcareer change is likely to be experienced as dysjunctive and individualized*—that is, the change process may be experienced as unique, as though the person were the first to face the particular situation and were going through it alone rather than as part of a group. In contrast, early career in many organizations is often characterized by a serial socialization process (where one is living through a transition experienced by previous newcomers) and a collective one (in which a group of newcomers goes through entry together).

The *source of influence for change* is also different in midcareer. In the early career transition, the major force for change is external: the socialization by members in the career role set. In midcareer, the dawning of the need for change is more subtle. As one manager said, "It just gradually creeps up on you." And there can be several sources of change. First could be a *change within the career role.* Such work role changes can result, for example, from new technology (as in the secretary's role with office automation), new products (as the banker's role has changed with the introduction of new financial services), and new clients or customers (as the professor's role has changed with an older student population). An awareness of an altered career role creates a need to change one's subidentity to restore fit. Or there could be a *change in the person,* perhaps a heightened awareness of one's identity (values, needs, interests, or skills), perhaps a desire for a different balance between work and personal involvements, or perhaps a growing awareness of negative attitudes toward the current career role. And, finally, the influence could be simply an *awareness of a lack of change,* a sense that the person has experienced few new experiences in many years, with a resulting lack of new learning and growth. For example, in a large bank many midcareer employees expressed great satisfaction with their current jobs but greater frustration that they saw few prospects for doing anything new and developmental in the years ahead. And this awareness of no change can trigger a person's desire to seek change at midcareer.

The increasing importance of the career subidentity, attitudes, and need for change at midcareer suggests that there is a *heightened awareness of the longer-term dimensions of career effectiveness at midcareer.* These dimensions, shown in Figure 2, are attitudes, performance, adaptability, and identity. In early career, the short-term outcomes (performance and attitudes) are more salient, as in the exploration and trial stages the person is attentive to how he or she feels (attitudes) about the various career roles and how much talent and potential (performance) he or she has in these roles. In establishment, the person has made a commitment and is probably aware of growing involvement (attitudes) caused by success (Hall, 1976), but his or her attention is most likely focused primarily on performance (getting established by mastering the career role).

Only after the intense performance pressures of the establishment stage are over does the person become aware of the longer-term future and has to confront such identity issues as, "What do I want to do with the rest of my life?" and such adaptability issues as, "How can I make the changes necessary to remain on top in my field or to move into a new field?" It is still important to perform well (although there is less external pressure or sense of being tested) and to experience positive attitudes toward one's work, but the sense of self and the sense that one is responsible

Figure 2. Dimensions of Career Effectiveness.

		Focus on Self	Task
Time Span	Short Term	Attitudes	Performance
	Long Term	Identity	Adaptability

Source: Hall, 1976.

for creating and implementing a self is very new and very strong, as is the need for flexibility and change. Thus, a wider, richer set of career tasks becomes salient in midcareer.

The process of making role transition changes at midlife in other ways, as well. One result of the heightened sense of ambiguity and the perceived lack of clear career paths or progress is a growing feeling of *personal responsibility for one's career.* As one manager said, "I finally realized that they (management) weren't going to do anything for me, so I'd have to make something happen for myself." Ironically, this lack of progress can lead to a strong sense of taking charge, assuming control over one's career. Thus, at midcareer, the career often becomes self-directed or more protean (Hall, 1976). This is in contrast to the early career experience of the organization's being in control of the career.

The phases in the role transition process are also different, as well. The movement from one role to another involves three distinct phases: separation from the old role and environment, initiation into the new role, and incorporation (or integration) of the new subidentity (created by that new role) into the prior identity (Van Gennep, 1960). Separation needs much more attention in research on midcareer changes.

In early career, separation from the old role is not a major problem, since it is often accomplished through institutionalized events (such as graduation from college or graduate school or departure parties and ceremonies when leaving an earlier career role). The main task of the person in early career is to successfully undergo the socialization tasks of the initiation process and to incorporate the new career subidentity into one's total self. In midcareer, however, there are less likely to be institutional influences to force a separation from the old role (unless one is fired or retired involuntarily). As the awareness of a need for change gradually grows, the decision to separate and the act of separating from the old career role are more often the person's responsibility. Thus, at midcareer, the person experiences *two difficult transition tasks: leaving the old role and entering the new role.* In early career, only the entry task seems salient. The midcareer separation process can be especially painful, since much of the person's sense of identity had become based on his or her career role (Hall, 1976).

Osherson (1980) provides a good discussion of the emotional tasks of separation or "letting go," as he calls it. The process of separation from the old role (desocialization, if you will) has been largely ignored in the literature on transitions to date.

There are also differences in the role of habitual and exploratory behavior in early and midcareer. In early career, there is a great deal of conscious, cognitive, exploratory behavior (Hall, 1976; Louis, 1980, 1982). The purpose of this exploratory behavior is to find a good fit, to settle down in one's "niche," where many tasks become habitual and noncognitive. Movement is from exploratory to habitual behaviors. In midcareer, the opposite order occurs: habitual behaviors, because they no longer work as well, become questioned, and cognitive, exploratory behavior is initiated in the search for change. Thus, the task in early career is to reduce exploratory behavior and establish a career routine, while *in midcareer there is a need to disrupt habitual behavior and trigger exploration.*

Part of the way a career routine is established in early career is through the experience of psychological success. The process by which work goals lead to good performance, psychological success, heightened self-esteem, involvement, and higher future goals is shown in Figure 3. This is a self-reinforcing cycle, as success leads to further involvement and even greater future success (Hall, 1976). Howard (1984) has found evidence for this process by which "success breeds success" over a period of twenty years in a longitudinal study of AT&T managers. A key task of early career is to become established by demonstrating strong performance and experiencing psychological success.

In midcareer, this success cycle often becomes disrupted. Often the opportunity to work toward challenging, relevant career goals is reduced (either because of fewer promotional goals to work toward or because mastery of one's job reduces the challenge of task goals). Therefore, even exceptional performance in an unchallenging task will not produce psychological success, and self-esteem, job involvement, and motivation suffer. Also, there is less feedback and recognition at midcareer (Hall, 1985), which further reduces psychological success. Also, if the person experiences a major career

Figure 3. The Psychological Success Model of Career Development.

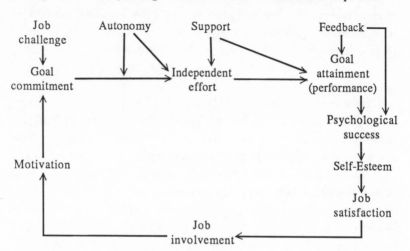

Source: Adapted from Hall, 1971.

Source: Adapted from Hall, 1971.

setback, such as being fired or being passed over for a key promotion, this can also disrupt the success cycle. Thus, *in early career the psychological success cycle is established, and in* midcareer the person experiences greater responsibility for man- then, is to establish new career goals that would initiate new cycles of the psychological success experience.

There are also important differences in midcareer in the relationships between work roles and personal roles: The issue of balance between work roles and personal roles becomes more salient. As the person establishes mastery over the career role, more of his or her time and energy becomes available for investments in personal or home roles. And, after the great effort of becoming established, the person may experience a desire to reap the rewards of that hard work by enjoying his or her personal life more. Thus, *balance shifts from work to personal roles in midcareer.* In early career, work often takes higher priority, and personal life is neglected. Further, in midcareer, just as a result of the passage of time, the person probably has more life roles (as parent, person responsible for aging parents, community leader, and so on) than in early career. These roles create their own demands, which further strengthen the desire for work/personal role balance.

A related issue is the degree of interdependence of personal life roles and the career role (distinct from the balance of energy invested in each). Sokol and Louis (1984) describe the differences between career transitions and life event adaptations. They define a career transition as "a boundary crossing, a role shift or status transformation that is in some way tied to the organization" (p. 83). A life event adaptation, in contrast, is seen as "temporal in nature (that is, of short duration), involving major changes as well as disequilibrium for the individual in transition." Sokol and Louis describe the similarities and differences in the tasks of the two types of transitions, the coping strategies used, resources available, and impacts on nontransitions. The tasks and coping strategies for career transitions and life event adaptations are reproduced in Tables 3 and 4, respectively.

Although he does not wish to go into each task and strategy in detail, the author is struck by the fact that the career transition studies cited in Tables 3 and 4 tend to relate to early career stages, where the main task is organizational entry and establishment. In early career, the organization is responsible for creating change, the career role is clear, the person's identity is malleable, and work changes are not strongly related to other life events. In midcareer, however, a career transition is a critical life event; and life events can trigger career changes. (For example, if one's health or that of a family member suffers, the person may move into a less demanding career role in order to have more energy for family relationships.) The strategies listed in Table 4 suggest that the organization is the active member in career transitions, while the person is the responsible party in coping with life events. This is probably the case in early career. However, for reasons discussed earlier, in midcareer the person experiences greater responsibility for managing the change process. And, from the adult development perspective, in midlife the whole issue is a reexamination of the total life structure, of which career is a major component. The career role is no longer a bounded segment of the total identity.

Table 3. Tasks of Transition.

Career Transition Literature	Life Event Adaptation Literature
Feldman (1976, 1980). Learn attitudes, behavioral norms and skills. Louis (1982). (1) master job basics; (2) build role identity; (3) build relationships; (4) update frame of reference (that is, how and why things are done); (5) map key people and social networks in the organization; (6) locate oneself in networks; (7) learn organizational vernacular; (8) assess unit functioning. Schein (1978). (1) accept reality of the human organization; (2) deal with resistance to change; (3) learn how to work; (4) deal with the boss; decipher the new reward system; (5) develop an identity and a place within the organization. Van Maanen (1977). Normalize the situation. Locate oneself in time and space relative to the organization and one's career, and develop causal meanings to explain why events occur as they do.	Hamburg (1977). (1) contain stress within tolerable limits; (2) maintain self-esteem; (3) preserve interpersonal relations; (4) meet conditions of new environment. Moos and Tsu (1976). (1) respond to requirements of the external situation; (2) respond to one's own feelings about the situation. R. Rapoport (1965). Tasks of newlywed couple—(1) establish couple identity; (2) sexual adjustment for engagement period; (3) agreement on family planning; (4) system of communication between the pair; (5) patterns with regard to relatives and friends; (6) patterns with regard to work; (7) patterns with regard to decision making; (8) plan for wedding, honeymoon, and early months of marriage.

Source: Sokol and Louis, 1984. (Note: Works cited in this table are listed in Sokol and Louis and will not be reported in the references to the present chapter.)

Thus, in midcareer, career transitions and life event changes become increasingly interconnected. This idea is supported by recent data from Latack (1984), who found in a group of experienced managers and professionals (average age thirty-nine) that major career transitions were associated with major personal life transitions. Latack's data suggest that career transitions can act as a major trigger for personal life instability.

In this analysis, our focus has been on general tendencies in the midcareer experience. Of course, there are individual differences

Table 4. Strategies of Transitioners.

Career Transition Literature	*Life Event Adaptation Literature*
Feldman (1976); Wanous (1980). Anticipatory socialization; develop and revise expectations about organization prior to actual transition.	Caplan (1964). (1) explore reality issues and search for information; (2) express feelings and tolerate frustration; (3) invoke help from others; (4) break problems into manageable bits; (5) be aware of fatigue; pace efforts; (6) master feelings and accept inevitable events; (7) trust oneself and others.
Glaser and Strauss (1971). Describe multiple strategies available to transitioner as well as to the "legitimator" of the transition.	
Katz and Kahn (1978). Role sending as implicit strategy of group and newcomer for communicating and shaping role expectations of the newcomer.	Hamburg (1977). (1) regulate timing and dosage of acceptance; (2) handle one crisis at a time; (3) seek information from multiple sources; (4) develop expectations for progress; (5) formulate attainable goals; (6) rehearse and test behavior patterns in safe situations; (7) appraise reaction; (8) try multiple approaches; (9) prepare contingency plans.
Louis (1980a). Sensemaking—cognitive strategy for selecting appropriate behavioral responses, for interpreting surprises, and for revising expectations about the work place and oneself.	
McConkie (1980). Organizational myths used to teach morals and values.	Lieberman (1975). Individual strategies assessed from relevant past behaviors, history of crisis management, and traits.
Sokol and Neumann (1981). Newcomer taking perspective of organizational diagnostician—mapping boundaries and relationships between others.	L. Rapoport (1965). If crisis is viewed as challenge, then it will be met with energy mobilization and purposive problem solving.
Van Maanen and Schein (1981). Several strategies of organizational "people processing."	Schlossberg (1981). May need to cut down or seek more information.
	Weiss (1976). Utilize cognitive materials, find support, find place within a temporary community.
	White (1976). Have appropriate levels of information—too much or too little increases difficulty of choosing adaptive action.

Source: Sokol and Louis, 1984. (Note: Works cited in this table are listed in Sokol and Louis and will not be reported in the references to the present chapter.)

at midcareer such that some people continue to experience psychological success and growth with no career shifts, while others feel secure and/or satisfied with work that has become routine. Later in the chapter, we will examine some individual differences that affect midcareer change. In the next section, we will consider a major characteristic of the person: age.

Experiencing Midcareer at Different Ages. Earlier, in our definition of midcareer, we said that midcareer should not be equated with a particular chronological age. In fact, the experiences of midcareer will vary according to the age at which it occurs. What happens when midcareer occurs at different ages? In a study of engineers in a large manufacturing organization, the author examined the career experiences of people who had become established in middle-level professional or managerial positions. (The organization had a dual-ladder job-grading system, under which engineers could advance to the equivalent of a plant manager's job level on the technical promotion ladder.) All members of the sample were at the same job level (level 36), where there was a serious "bottleneck" problem: 30 percent of the positions in the department were at level 36, while only 2 percent were at level 37. Thus, the probability of promotion above level 36 was quite low, although some promotions did occur occasionally.

Thus, these people were professionally established and had mastered their work and were, by our definition, in midcareer. Their ages ranged from late twenties to sixties, but the majority were in their thirties, forties, and fifties. We were interested in seeing what differences there were in being at midcareer in each of these three age (decade) groups.

People who had hit midcareer in their thirties (these were the fast trackers) were very concerned about their continued advancement as well as angry and frustrated about the organizational bottleneck and the resulting low likelihood of further promotions. They felt that they had risen rapidly and plateaued just as suddenly. Their quick early success had led to high expectations, which the current organizational reality could not satisfy. As a result, these people were either exploring other routes to career advancement (inside and outside the company) or rethinking the balance between their investments in work versus personal life. On the latter issue, their thinking was "Why continue to kill myself and my home life over this job if the rewards won't be there?" But many still saw advancement *somewhere* as a strong likelihood.

In people in their forties, there was more uncertainty about promotion anywhere, a vague uneasiness that they had gone as far as they would go, but still there were just enough examples of people promoted in their forties to provide some hope. However, there was a sense of "hoping against hope" and a growing awareness of career limits. There was also a feeling that it might soon be too late to make a career switch and that if any change were to be made it would have to be soon. But since most people in their forties had become committed to the company and comfortable in their careers, there was much ambivalence about change.

The people in their fifties were quite clear about the fact that their careers had plateaued and had the feeling that if any new career excitement were going to occur for them they would have to take their own action to make it happen for them. They were seeking satisfaction and fulfillment, either by enriching the present job (which many did quite well by seeking a new assignment), through outside work activities (such as starting their own financial investment organizations), or through family and community activities. Many were planning ahead for retirement. There was a high level of protean career activity for midcareer people in their fifties. In fact, the trend seemed to be from a perceived external midcareer orientation in the thirties ("the organization should develop my career") to a protean (self-directed) midcareer orientation ("I'm in charge here") in the fifties.

Routine-Busting: A Model of Midcareer Development

Since the essence of midcareer is the fact that the person has become established and settled into a career routine, a critical issue is what triggers change in the career routine to stimulate new learning (the acquisition and development of new information, skills and attitudes). A model of midcareer development is presented in Figure 4. The career routine is shown in the large block in Figure 4 to illustrate the barrier that this habitual, noncognitive behavior presents to career growth. The career routine is created largely as the

result of earlier workings of the psychological success cycle shown
in Figure 3. The model describes how various triggers (in the
organizational environment, work role, and person) can disrupt a
career routine and lead to new exploration behavior. Under the
proper conditions, this exploration can lead to trial activity in new
areas, subidentity changes, increased adaptability, and a heightened
sense of self as agent (in charge of one's own career.)

   Midcareer Triggers. Several causal factors are hypothesized to
trigger disruptions in the career routine. These factors are grouped
under three general sources: organization (or society), work role,
and person. The first trigger, which comes from *organizational or
societal sources,* would be a major change in the job or organization
that calls for significantly different work skills. As technology
changes within a job, or if a person is assigned to a new job, one's
job is eliminated, or the company is reorganized, the person could
be suddenly placed in a situation in which the old routines no
longer work. This would lead to an awareness that some change
would be necessary, which, in turn, would lead to exploratory
behavior. Latack (1984), using Hall's (1980) measure of magnitude
of career transition, found that the more major the shift in job
responsibilities was, the more stressful and disruptive the change
was (and thus the stronger the trigger value was). Table 5 shows
how Latack operationalized the concept of job change.

   Major external events could create motivation for change in
much the same way as job and organizational changes. Economic
fluctuations affecting one's external labor market, either positively
or negatively, might stimulate thoughts of change, even if one's
own job or organization had not yet been affected. An example here
would be an engineer in a military-oriented contracting firm who
made a career switch to law when he saw military expenditures
reduced in the mid 1970s, even though his firm still had plenty of
work.

   Qualities in the organizational climate and reward structure
(in other words, a growth environment) can enhance midcareer
learning. If the culture stresses growth and learning, if development
is "built into" the human resource policies of the organization
(Hall, 1984), then midcareer learning is more likely to be an
ongoing process, not a major, discontinuous event. If the

Figure 4. A Model of Midcareer Subidentity Development.

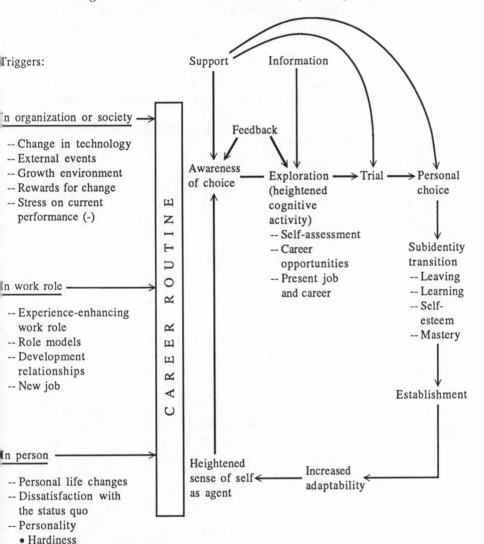

Table 5. A Measure of Degree of Change in a Job Transition.

Change in:	Increasing intensity →	Scale value
Job + level + function + occupation + occupational field		12
Job + function + occupation + occupational field		11
Job + level + occupation + occupational field		10
Job + level + function + occupation		9
Job + occupation + occupational field		8
Job + function + occupation		7
Job + level + occupation		6
Job + level + function		5
Job + occupation		4
Job + function		3
Job + level		2
Job		1
No change		0

Source: Latack, 1984 (based on a model proposed by Hall, 1980).

organization rewards change (by facilitating job rotation and/or by rewarding managers for promoting later cross-functional moves and for developing subordinates), again change is more likely to occur naturally.

An important restraining factor in midcareer change is the extent to which the organization stresses current performance and low-risk behavior. This encourages people to develop, refine, and persist in successful career routines, which works strongly against innovative behavior.

The second kind of trigger in the model involves *work role sources.* If the work role is one that is experience enhancing, such that experience leads to both continual variety and increased mastery, then midcareer development is built into the work role. Hall (1985) found that project managers were in such an experience-enhancing role, so that plateaued project managers experienced *greater* career growth than their less experienced colleagues. Thus, certain job characteristics seem to make one immune to the negative consequences of plateauing.

In a similar vein, if there are positive role models and opportunities for developmental relationships, either as mentor, protege, or peer, then relationships can be a powerful stimulus for change (Kram, 1985). Again, these developmental relationships can be built into the work environment and made available on a voluntary, self-selection basis by the individual. Kram finds that such naturally occurring developmental relationships are more effective than organizationally imposed arrangements, as reported in Chapter Five.

Personal sources of career transition might include a change in one's personal life (Osherson, 1980). As we discussed earlier, major changes in one's family, personal health, age, personal insight, and so on, could cause the person to reexamine career priorities. In a similar vein, the person could simply experience dissatisfaction with the status quo and finally reach the point at which the frustration was great enough to trigger a change. (By the same token, satisfaction with the present state of the career could lead to no change.)

There is also a set of personality characteristics that can disrupt career routines. (Conversely, low levels of those qualities could lead to no change in midcareer.) Kobasa (1982) has identified a construct of personality hardiness that gives a person a more proactive, protean orientation toward managing the life structure and reduces the negative consequences of work stress. Hardiness includes three existential elements: commitment, perceived control, and perceived challenge. This relates to Staw's (1984) notion of a "basic personality predisposition" (a positive or negative orientation toward the work environment) which either empowers or debilitates the individual.

Ann Howard (1984), in a twenty-year longitudinal study of AT&T executives, found a constellation of personality constructs that correlated with midcareer organizational success (grade level attained). Her criterion, then, was not necessarily midcareer change, but one could argue that some degree of adaptability would be necessary to achieve midcareer corporate promotions. In fact, flexibility was a major correlate of advancement, as was the motivation for advancement. Also, in view of our comments about the presence of ambiguity in midcareer, it is not surprising that

tolerance of ambiguity and uncertainty were strong correlates of
midcareer success. Also, dominance and independence were
important factors, again reflecting one's ability to proactively create
impact (or be protean) in one's work environment. Dominance and
independence seem closely related to the concept of hardiness. More
information on how managers can be trained in such areas as
flexibility is found in Chapter One.

  Exploratory Learning Cycle. Once the career routine has
been disrupted, it is hypothesized that an exploratory learning cycle
is stimulated. Because the routine no longer exists or because the
person perceives the opportunity for more satisfactory behaviors,
there is a heightened *awareness of choice.* External support and
feedback from others can enhance the awareness. With awareness of
choice, the person begins *exploration* (cognitive activity). This
could be a self-exploration (self-assessment of values, needs,
interests, skills, satisfactions, relationships, future potential in
current role, and so on), a search for other career opportunities, or
a reassessment of the present job and career. External information,
counseling, and coaching can be useful in the exploration stage.

  As a result of this exploration, the person might try out some
new activities. This could be a very tentative *trial,* such as taking
some university courses in a new field, signing on to a project team
or task force in a new area, or participating in trial job interviews
in a new field. There is no commitment at this point, and
information about the self in these trial activities feeds back into the
exploration process.

  Often enough data are generated in the trial process that the
person becomes confident enough to make a *personal choice.* This
could mean staying in the current role (with a new orientation,
perhaps) or it could mean changing to a new role, whose distance
from the former role could vary greatly (Latack, 1984). This choice
would lead to a *subidentity transition,* a transformation of the
career subidentity in important ways. The transition entails first
leaving the old role and then learning new skills, information, and
attitudes for the new one. This process modifies self-esteem (which,
initially, might drop sharply, as the person feels that he or she has
moved from a state of high mastery and status in the former role to
low status or competence in the new one). The goal is to gain

credibility and mastery in the new role in one's own eyes as well as in others'. London and Stumpf's chapter on career resilience (Chapter One) provides useful practical ideas for helping people make this sort of transition.

At the conclusion of the transition, the person becomes *established* in the new role, incorporating the new subidentity into the total identity and meshing it with the past identity. A new career routine has been established. Paradoxically, however, with each new level of routine established comes a heightened level of *adaptability*, as the person experiences confidence in his or her ability to learn how to learn new career roles. This leads to a heightened awareness of *self as agent* of the career (as opposed to passive object), which can then feed back and increase the probability of future career learning cycles.

Facilitating Midcareer Growth

On the basis of the themes and the model of the midcareer experience just described, it is possible to identify specific needs of the individual at midcareer. With these needs in mind, as well as an examination of research on midcareer interventions, we will conclude with a set of suggested methods of promoting midcareer development. The midcareer needs and interventions discussed here are shown in Table 6.

Midcareer Needs. Probably the single most important need in midcareer is *recognition*. In interview after interview, the author has heard experienced employees talk with great feeling about the many ways the organization devotes attention to new employees in a particular field—they get the choice assignments, they get the best pay raises, they get sent to seminars and conferences, the company has a career development plan for them, and management worries about retaining them. Established employees often feel that no one cares about their careers, since there has been little career movement in recent years. As one engineer put it, "They seem to assume that once you reach a certain level, you're an independent, fully functioning professional who should be helping other people develop and who doesn't need any help yourself."

Table 6. Facilitating Midcareer Growth.

Midcareer needs	*Midcareer interventions*
1. Recognition	1. Stimulation of awareness of choice and exploration

2. Information (ambiguity/uncertainty reduction)
  a. career opportunities
  b. self-assessment
	2. Provide growth environment
	  a. employee development in performance appraisal
	  b. subordinate development as prerequisite for manager's move
	  c. reward mentoring activity
	  d. career exploration workshops

3. Opportunity to use unique skills and abilities	3. New job
	  a. career brokers
	  b. management personnel committees
	  c. lateral movement policy
	  d. loaned employees

4. Job and career movement	4. New organization
5. Job redesign	5. Create surprise
6. Continuing training and development	6. Experience-enhancing work roles (such as project work)
	7. Formal career-planning program

This recognition deficiency fits with the disruption of the psychological success cycle described earlier. If the link between work goal attainment and self-esteem becomes severed in midcareer, this intrinsic loss of self-esteem combines with the extrinsic loss of esteem (through recognition) to produce a "career double whammy," leaving the person with severe questions about his or her self-worth.

Because of the ambiguity and uncertainty of the midcareer, there are strong needs for *information*. One type is information about career opportunities. When midcareer employees were asked what resources they needed for career development, this was the most frequently cited one. Most people, even after many years with a single organization, know very little about career possibilities in other departments, other geographical units, or other business units. And their managers generally lack this information, as well.

The second type of information needed is self-assessment information. The person may lack feedback about his or her strengths and weaknesses (even good performance feedback may be lacking), clarity about his or her values, interests, needs, and work-style/life-style preferences, or a sense of personal priorities about tradeoffs he or she would be willing to make for a better career fit. As Minor shows in Chapter Six, computer-based career programs are now being utilized to help people obtain self-assessment information and information on organizational career opportunities.

The *opportunity to use one's unique skills and abilities* is especially important to a person who has devoted years to honing these components of his or her identity. However, the goal in placing an experienced employee is often to meet a particular corporate need rather than to stretch that person and tax his or her most important skills. This is especially apparent when an organization's business focus changes and attempts are made, in good conscience, to redeploy employees who possess formerly needed skills (but not the new ones). One example here is a marine biologist who was a world expert on undersea habitats, who had been doing pioneering research on undersea communities for a submarine manufacturer (when the focus was on basic research). Then, when military spending was reduced, there was a move to develop specific new products with an immediate profit potential. This scientist was reassigned to a project on the adhesion of barnacles to submarine hulls, much to his frustration.

The experience that seems most difficult for such a person to accept in midcareer is that of feeling "stuck." Therefore, there is a strong need for *job and career movement* of some sort. In various surveys, the author has found that midcareer employees would be willing to accept lateral moves—and even downward moves (Hall and Isabella, 1985)—if they were career enhancing in some way. This movement does not have to be upward. There simply has to be some specific sense that the organization has a plan and a program to assist midcareer employees with the process of career development. (At a minimum, a career program specifically devoted to midcareer employees would communicate a real form of recognition.)

To illustrate this point, one major manufacturing company initiated a career development program for new engineers, using the manager as a mentor to provide career coaching and challenging initial assignments. The program foundered because of the unenthusiastic response of the managers (most of whom were in midcareer). The feedback from the managers was, "Why should we help these young kids when no one's doing anything for us?" As a result, the company designed a midcareer growth program for the managers, helping them do self-assessment and exploration of various company career opportunities. Once the managers' career needs were met, their resistance to assisting their engineers disappeared (and the managers' learning from their own career program made them more effective career coaches, as well).

An alternative to career movement that is sought by some people is in-place career development. What this means is the opportunity to *redesign the present job* to permit work on new, more challenging career goals. Indeed, many professional and managerial positions contain enough discretion to permit the individual to explore such options for change without leaving the present job. In most cases, however, the consent and cooperation of the boss is required, or at least helpful. Specific needs for within-job career change would include: greater participation in decision making, greater autonomy, more variety in assignments, and more feedback on the impact of one's work.

A final, more specific need that is often expressed by the midcareer person is for *continuing training and development.* Again, management's assumption often is that the established person already is fully trained and thus needs no further assistance. However, midcareer is often precisely the point at which one's particular technology changes abruptly, leaving one with an increasingly obsolescent set of skills. This obsolescence often is not detected until it reaches crisis proportions, calling for either retraining, outplacement, or early retirement. If training and development were an ongoing activity associated with any job, career renewal would be built into the job.

Most of these midcareer developmental needs seem to grow out of the deterioration of the psychological success cycle described earlier. The loss of recognition, as we said, seems related to the loss of perceived challenge and self-esteem from the work itself. As a person becomes more senior and established, clear feedback on his or her work and skills becomes less available (as younger people, peers, and supervisors find it harder to confront older colleagues). There is less feeling of support from the environment, relating to the feeling that management does not really care about the careers of established employees. Self-assessment of one's personal career goals is difficult to do alone, and work goals gradually become less motivational. Information about opportunities to pursue new goals in other places is not available in most cases. Training to keep one's knowledge and skills current, so that high effort will continue to lead to good performance, also becomes less available over time. Thus, all of these midcareer needs seem to result from, and then contribute to, the deterioration of the success cycle. As a result, a person might attempt to cling to the midcareer routine even more desperately with the hope of preserving past successes.

Midcareer Interventions. What steps might be taken to reverse this process of declining success in the face of the midcareer routine? Some clues can be found in Figure 4, the cycle of midcareer learning. The critical factor is the *stimulation of awareness of choice and exploration.* The personality factors and some of the trigger events that disrupt the career routine are beyond the scope of organizational intervention and thus will not be discussed in detail here. However, we suggest that the more the proactive personality pattern (positive predisposition, flexibility, advancement motivation, dominance, tolerance of uncertainty and ambiguity, and independence) is sought in the selection process, the more likely it is that the employee will be adaptive in midcareer. As shown at AT&T, the assessment center method permits an organization to select individuals with this personality pattern (Howard, 1984).

The more the work environment stresses growth, the more midcareer change will be facilitated. A growth environment can be manifested in many ways. One method is to hold managers accountable for employee development, as measured on the manager's performance appraisal. A related approach is to establish the norm that a manager will have a difficult time gaining a promotion if he or she has not yet developed possible successors (Laidlaw, 1984). Another method is to develop systems that encourage and reward mentoring and other types of developmental relationships, which help the midcareer manager at least as much as the younger protege (Kram, 1985). See Kram's chapter in this volume for more ideas on how to build growth into the work environment (Chapter Five).

One specific aspect of a growth environment is career exploration workshops, which have grown in popularity in recent years. In many cases, these seminars have been created in response to organizational retrenchment, as a means of helping employees cope with sharply reduced career opportunities. An example here would be Ford Motor Company, which now has roughly half the work force it had in 1979. Because of the interest expressed by employees and the concerns of management that the company might lose its remaining high-potential employees, a series of career workshops was developed for salaried employees. The purpose was to help them do self-assessment of skills, values, and interests, to get information on company career opportunities, to identify their own career goals, and to learn how to implement a career plan in the realities of the corporate environment (in other words, how to "work the system"). A companion seminar was developed for supervisors so that they would be able to provide follow-up assistance to employees after they finished their workshops. (Supervisors could also participate in the employee career-planning workshops if they desired.) Demand for the workshops has been growing sharply, and employees seem to come out of them with a clearer sense of their own goals, a realistic view of the career environment, and some practical ideas on how to work toward their career goals (Horner, 1984).

A similar career-planning program was developed as part of a general career management system at Monsanto (Christiansen, 1983). Surveys conducted before and after the program indicated that, after the workshop, employees were more open to lateral or even downward movement for career growth, were more optimistic about making a move in the next five years, and were more willing to take a job change involving relocation. In terms of their own career possibilities, there was an increase (from around 40 percent to almost 70 percent) in the number who felt that they knew where they stood in the organization, what their prospects were for the future, and whether they could expect to be promoted or not. And, on a positive note, there was little change in their likelihood of leaving the company and an increase in perceived career opportunities at Monsanto. There was also an increase in exploratory activity and in proactive career activities.

Some questions also were included in the follow-up survey about the perceived effectiveness of the career workshops. The most frequently cited benefit was greater understanding of one's own strengths and weaknesses (60 percent). The next most common responses were better career information (41 percent) and help in clarifying career goals and letting one know where he or she stood in the organization (40 percent) (Christiansen, 1983). An earlier study by Miller, Bass, and Mihal (1973) also found an increase in self-development activity following a career-planning intervention. This combination of providing career assessment and planning workshops for employees, coupled with career-coaching training seminars for managers, seems to be a growing method for building growth into the work environment.

Changes in the job or organization can be a potent means of stimulating midcareer exploration. Bailyn and Lynch (1983) found, in a study of experienced engineers, that those who had made a move in recent years were more satisfied than those who had stayed in the same job. This does not mean that just any move would provide development—the new job should stretch the person in important new directions. But job movement is more likely to promote growth than is nonmovement. Movement to a new function, a new product, or a new project is more likely to yield growth than is a move within one of their entities.

There are various ways to facilitate job moves. One is to create a human resource position (such as internal placement manager) with "career broker" responsibilities. Another, often growing out of a succession-planning process, is management personnel committees: interdepartmental groups of managers who make staffing decisions for jobs at the level just below them, with the aim of encouraging interdepartmental moves. A top-management policy statement endorsing such cross-functional moves is extremely helpful here. Job switches are another form of job move. Ford is experimenting with letting employees trade jobs as a way of exploring careers in a different part of the company (Horner, 1984). In a gas pipeline company, the vice-president of engineering was faced with a surplus of professional employees. Rather than lay people off, he offered to loan them to other departments. They were promptly snapped up by such departments as finance and marketing research, which could utilize their quantitative skills but which could not hire from the outside, owing to a freeze on new hiring. It was agreed that the loaned employees would remain the "property" of engineering but that permanent career switches could be arranged at the employee's request. And for employees who returned to engineering, professional horizons and skills had been broadened considerably.

What these organizations and job changes do is reactivate the sense-making process (Louis, 1980, 1982). Whereas in early career socialization the goal was to reduce the sense of surprise caused by change, in midcareer development the object is to *create surprise,* which in turn will stimulate growth through renewed sense making. The more the organization can replicate the feeling of being a newcomer for the established employee, the more likely it is that midcareer growth will occur. Mihal, Sorce, and Comte (1984) present a general process model showing how such a career role discrepancy can lead to the creation of new roles.

As part of an effort to create new job experiences, a focus on *experience-enhancing work roles* is an unexplored, yet high-potential area. In a study of established engineers, the author examined three paths in an organization's triple career ladder (Hall, 1985). The first two paths were the traditional technical specialist and management advancement paths. The third was a cross between the two, a technical generalist or project management career path. On this path, one's work is a series of responsibilities for projects of varying size, scope, purpose, and corporate significance. Moving from one project to another resembles what Driver (1980) calls a spiral career path, as each new project requires some sort of important new learning but also builds on previous learnings. When plateaued employees were compared with their nonplateaued counterparts in the author's study, expected differences were found among the managers and technical specialists: Plateaued people reported less favorable career experiences and attitudes than did those who were not plateaued.

However, for technical generalists the opposite was true: Plateaued project managers reported more positive career attitudes and experience than did their nonplateaued colleagues. Further examination of the data revealed that in this type of work, past experience adds to one's "portfolio" of varied skills, which makes one ever more competent and effective in managing future projects. And future projects always demand the development of some new skills. Thus, experience enhances career growth in this particular work role.

Thus, the more the organization can build experience enhancement into work roles, the more natural midcareer growth will occur. This can be done through the creation of more "project-management-type" jobs, such as temporary task forces, product teams, project teams, and so on. IBM's use of autonomous project teams to develop such new products as the personal computer is a good example here. Kidder (1981) provides a fascinating examination of the career growth and excitement experienced by members of a project team to develop a thirty-two-bit computer at Data General. Team members explained their excitement and growth as the "pinball model of motivation"—your reward for success is that you get to play the game again, with more challenge and resources (see Figure 3).

Trouble-shooting and internal consulting assignments are another way to provide temporary project-type experiences. One large manufacturing company needed some consulting assistance in the design and construction of a proposed new industrial furnace, and the initial plan was to hire an outside firm at the cost of several million dollars. As it turned out, someone realized that the company had a world expert on the subject on its own corporate engineering staff. (In fact, he often did outside work for the consulting firm about to be hired!) Thus, the company sent this man to the plant for a six-month internal consulting assignment, and it was a tremendous psychological success experience for him—as well as a financial boon to the company. This experience has led to a concerted corporate effort to save money on external consultants by identifying and utilizing internal experts whenever possible.

Rotation of technical specialists is another way to provide more of the career breadth of the technical generalist function without going quite that far. Research and development professionals, for example, tend to be more career adaptive if they switch specialties every five to ten years (Pelz and Andrews, 1976). The military uses the dual-specialty model, in which a person initially masters a primary specialty (such as infantry) and then learns a second specialty after seven or eight years (such as human resource management). Subsequent assignments then could alternately be in either of these two specialties.

An emerging model for continual career renewal is skill-based (not position-based) career paths. Here advancement takes place in terms of tasks and skills mastered rather than positions and levels attained. For example, employees in banking could rotate through the different areas of consumer banking, progressing to mastery of all basic functions. Then they could rotate and start over, learning the basics of commercial lending or investment banking. Many of these moves would be lateral and some even downward, but they would all build new career skills. This would require a skill-based or experience-based compensation system, as well.

All of these career interventions should be done with an eye toward facilitating the midcareer learning cycle shown in Figure 4 so that the employee is an active participant in the career growth process. The employee should have an opportunity to have someone to talk to for information, support, feedback, or coaching and to help him or her move through the stages in the cycle. The more involvement and control the person has in this career exploration process, the more career self-direction he or she will have as a result of the career change. But if the change is simply organizationally induced with little opportunity for personal inquiry and choice, the effects may be minimal.

To illustrate, in one high-tech organization, several midcareer professionals had just been transfered to jobs requiring more general skills (the kind of job change we have just advocated). However, the change was never discussed with these employees: They were given no choice, and they had no understanding of the developmental purpose behind the move. They experienced it as something that was done *to* them, and they were upset and stressed. The result: no learning.

One way to facilitate the participation of the employee is through the creation of a *formal career-planning program,* which would provide opportunities for self-inquiry through computer-based career-planning seminars, developmental working relation-ships, and career counseling. (See Chapters Two and Six for more detail on these programs.) All of this, of course, should be on a voluntary basis. And such a program does not have to be specifically for midcareer employees. In fact, if it is labeled as such, it may be promptly dismissed as a "retread program." Instead, if it is available to employees at all career stages, it will reinforce the idea that midcareer growth is simply one part of a lifelong process of career development.

Conclusion

This has been an initial step in the formulation of some theoretical notions about growth in the middle of a career. As we have attempted to show, the basic process of growth through psychological success is the same at all stages in a career, but it does tend to get interrupted in midcareer. Development at this point is a process of triggering new career exploration and mastery of new skills. The concerns and tasks at midcareer, however, are different from those of early career, and the interventions discussed represent possible ways of meeting the needs of this career stage.

References

Bailyn, L., and Lynch, J. T. "Engineering as a Life-Long Career: Its Meaning, Its Satisfactions, Its Difficulties." *Journal of Occupational Behavior,* 1983, *4,* 263–283.

Becker, H., Geer, B., Hughes, E., and Strauss, A. *Boys in White.* Chicago: University of Chicago Press, 1961.

Berlew, D. E., and Hall, D. T. "The Socialization of Managers: Effects of Expectations on Experience." *Administrative Science Quarterly,* 1966, *11,* 207-223.

Bray, D. W., Campbell, R. J., and Grant, D. E. *Formative Years in Business.* New York: Wiley, 1974.

Brett, J. M. "Job Transfer and Well-Being." *Journal of Applied Psychology,* 1982, *67,* 450-463.

Christiansen, K. C. "Case Study of a Career Management System." Workshop presented for Division 14, American Psychological Association, Anaheim, Calif., Aug. 1983.

Crump, J. H., Cooper, C. L., and Maxwell, V. B. "Stress Among Air Traffic Controllers: Occupational Sources of Coronary Heart Disease." *Journal of Occupational Behavior,* 1981, *2,* 293-303.

Driver, M. "Career Concepts and Organizational Change." In C. B. Derr (ed.), *Work, Family, and the Career.* New York: Praeger, 1980.

Gould, R. *Transformations: Growth and Change in Adult Life.* New York: Simon & Schuster, 1978.

Greiner, L. "Evolution and Revolution as Organizations Grow." *Harvard Business Review,* 1972, *50,* 37-46.

Gupta, A. K. "Contingency Linkages Between Strategy and General Manager Characteristics: A Conceptual Examination." *Academy of Management Review,* 1984, *9,* 399-412.

Gupta, A. K., and Govindarajan, V. "Business Unit Strategy, Managerial Characteristics and Business Unit Effectiveness at Strategy Implementation." *Academy of Management Journal,* 1984, *27,* 25-41.

Hall, D. T. "A Theoretical Model of Career Subidentity Development in Organizational Settings." *Organizational Behavior and Human Performances,* 1971, *6,* 50-76.

Hall, D. T. *Careers in Organizations.* Glenview, Ill.: Scott, Foresman, 1976.

Hall, D. T. "Socialization Processes in Later Career Years: Can There Be Growth at the Terminal Level?" In C. B. Derr (ed.), *Work, Family, and the Career.* New York: Praeger, 1980.

Hall, D. T. "Human Resource Development and Organizational Effectiveness." In C. Fombrun, N. M. Tichy, and M. A. Devanna (eds.), *Strategic Human Resource Management.* New York: Wiley, 1984.

Hall, D. T. "Project Work as an Antidote to Career Plateauing in a Declining Engineering Organization." *Human Resource Management,* 1985, *24,* 271–292.

Hall, D. T., and Isabella, L. "Downward Moves and Career Development." *Organizational Dynamics,* 1985, *14,* 5–23.

Hall, D. T., and Mansfield, R. "Organizational and Individual Responses to External Stress." *Administrative Science Quarterly,* 1971, *15,* 271–281.

Holland, J. L. *Making Vocational Choices: A Theory of Careers.* Englewood Cliffs, N. J.: Prentice-Hall, 1973.

Horner, P. "Career Planning at Ford Motor Company." Presentation at annual meeting of the American Society for Personnel Administration, Chicago, Apr. 27, 1984.

Howard, A. "Cool at the Top: Personality Characteristics of Successful Executives." Presentation as part of symposium, "Industrial Assessment and Personality Psychology," annual convention of the American Psychological Association, Toronto, Ontario, Aug. 1984.

Kaufman, H. G. *Professionals in Search of Work.* New York: Wiley, 1982.

Kidder, T. *The Soul of a New Machine.* Boston: Little, Brown, 1981.

Kimberly, J. R., Miles, R. H., and Associates. *The Organizational Life Cycle: Issues in the Creation, Transformation, and Decline of Organizations.* San Francisco: Jossey-Bass, 1980.

Kobasa, S. "The Hardy Personality: Toward a Social Psychology of Stress and Health." In G. S. Sanders and J. Suls (eds.), *Social Psychology of Health and Illness.* Hillsdale, N. J.: Erlbaum, 1982.

Kram, K. E. *Mentoring at Work.* Glenview, Ill.: Scott, Foresman, 1985.

Laidlaw, D. "Succession Planning at IBM." Presentation at annual meeting of the American Society for Personnel Administration, Chicago, Apr. 27, 1984.

Latack, J. C. "Career Transitions Within Organizations: An Exploratory Study of Work, Nonwork, and Coping Strategies." *Organizational Behavior and Human Performance*, 1984, *34*, 296–322.

Latack, J. C., and Dozier, J. B. "Job Loss as a Career Transition." Presentation as part of symposium, "Down or Out: Strategies for Managing Involuntary Career Movement," annual meeting of the Academy of Management, San Diego, Calif., Aug. 13, 1985.

Lawrence, B. S. "Age Grading: The Implicit Organizational Timetable." *The Career Center Bulletin*, 1984, *4*, 6.

Levinson, D. J. "The Career Is in the Life Structure, the Life Structure Is in the Career: An Adult Development Perspective." In M. B. Arthur, L. Bailyn, D. J. Levinson, and H. A. Shepard, *Working with Careers.* New York: Center for Research in Career Development, Columbia University, 1984.

Levinson, D. J., and Associates. *The Seasons of a Man's Life.* New York: Knopf, 1978.

Louis, M. R. "Surprise and Sense Making: What Newcomers Experience in Entering Unfamiliar Organizational Settings." *Administrative Science Quarterly*, 1980, *25*, 226–251.

Louis, M. R. "Managing Career Transitions: A Missing Link in Career Development." *Organizational Dynamics*, 1982, *8*, 68–77.

Mihal, W. L., Sorce, P. A., and Comte, T. E. "A Process Model of Individual Career Decision Making." *Academy of Management Review*, 1984, *9*, 95–103.

Miller, J., Bass, B. M., and Mihal, W. L. "An Experiment to Test Methods of Increasing Self-Development Activities Among Research and Development Personnel." Publication T-43. Rochester, N.Y.: Management Research of Rochester, 1973.

Osherson, S. D. *Holding On or Letting Go.* New York: Free Press, 1980.

Pelz, D. C., and Andrews, F. M. *Scientists in Organizations.* (Rev. ed.) Ann Arbor: Institute for Social Research, University of Michigan, 1976.

Rosenbaum, J. E. "Tournament Mobility: Career Patterns in a Corporation." *Administrative Science Quarterly*, 1979, *24*, 220–241.

Rush, J. C., Peacock, A. C., and Milkovich, G. T. "Career Stages: A Partial Test of Levinson's Model of Life/Career Stages." *Journal of Vocational Behavior,* 1980, *16,* 347–359.

Schein, E. H. *Career Dynamics: Matching Individual and Organizational Needs.* Reading, Mass.: Addison-Wesley, 1978.

Slocum, J., Cron, W. L., Hansen, R. W., and Rawlings, S. "Business Strategy and the Management of the Plateaued Performer." *Academy of Management Journal,* 1985, *28,* 133–154.

Sokol, M., and Louis, M. R. "Career Transitions and Life Event Adaptation: Integrating Alternative Perspectives in Role Transition." In V. L. Allen and E. Van de Vliert (eds.), *Role Transitions: Explorations and Explanations.* New York: Plenum, 1984.

Staw, B. M. "Organizational Behavior: A Review and Reformulation of the Field's Outcome Variables." *Annual Review of Psychology,* 1984, *35,* 627–666.

Stumpf, S. A., and Rabinowitz, S. "Career Stage as a Moderator of Performance Relationships with Facets of Job Satisfaction and Role Perceptions." *Journal of Vocational Behavior,* 1981, *18,* 202–218.

Van Gennep, A. *The Rites of Passage.* Chicago: University of Chicago Press, 1960.

Van Maanen, J., and Schein, E. H. "Toward a Theory of Organizational Socialization." In B. M. Staw (ed.), *Research in Organization Behavior.* Greenwich, Conn.: J.A.I. Press, 1979.

Wanous, J. P. *Organizational Entry.* Reading, Mass.: Addison-Wesley, 1980.

5

ЯЯЯЯЯЯЯЯ

Mentoring in the Workplace

Kathy E. Kram

Like other behavioral science concepts, mentoring has captured the attention of human resource specialists, practicing managers, and scholars in a variety of disciplines. Some have claimed that finding a mentor is essential for career advancement in almost any organization (Roche, 1979; Collins and Scott, 1978; Missirian, 1982; Phillips-Jones, 1982). Others have stated that mentoring can be an effective management development tool that can benefit both individuals and organizations by enabling experienced managers to develop younger talent in their work settings (Dalton, Thompson, and Price, 1977; Clawson, 1980; Digman, 1978; Hall and Kram, 1981). Finally, scholars have attended to the central role that relationships between younger and older adults play in psychosocial and career development at every stage of adulthood (Levinson and others, 1978; Gould, 1978; Erikson, 1980).

Some of these claims have compelled employees, managers, and human resource professionals to attend systematically to the quality of relationships at work; others, however, have been quite misleading, suggesting that mentoring is a panacea without limitations. The purpose of this chapter is to present a realistic view of mentoring, including its potential benefits and its potential destructive characteristics, the various forms of developmental relationships that can exist in work settings, and the ways in which organizations enhance or create obstacles to an effective mentoring process.

Mentoring can best be understood using a systems framework that considers individual, interpersonal, and organizational levels of analysis. Therefore, drawing on recent research, I will examine how individuals' career histories and current developmental tasks shape the need for mentoring alliances, or alternatively, interfere with establishing them. Then, to ensure a comprehensive perspective that dispels the myth that the classical mentor relationship first described by Levinson and others (1978) is the only mentoring alternative, I will delineate the various forms that these developmental relationships can take. Finally, I will illuminate how organizational practices shape relationships at work and account for differences in the mentoring process that have been observed.

Mentoring can be defined generally as relationships between junior and senior colleagues, or between peers, that provide a variety of developmental functions (Kram, 1985). Since the concept has been used to connote a number of different types of relationships, it is useful to first specify a working definition that outlines critical developmental functions and the variations in relationships that have been described.

Defining Mentoring

Relationships between junior and senior colleagues that contribute to career development have been alternatively referred to as mentor relationships (Levinson and others, 1978; Phillips-Jones, 1982; Dalton, Thompson, and Price, 1977; Kram, 1983a), sponsor relationships (Kanter, 1977), patron relationships (Shapiro, Haseltine, and Rowe, 1978), godfather relationships (Kanter, 1977), or as a relationship between good friends. Each of these suggests a slightly different view; while there is agreement about the potential value of developmental alliances, there are differences in perceptions about the range of developmental functions provided, the intensity of the relationship, and the exclusivity of the relationship (Phillips-Jones, 1982; Clawson, 1979; Shapiro, Haseltine, and Rowe, 1978).

Among completed studies, a set of functions converges that can be summarized in two broad categories (Kram, 1985). Career functions are those aspects of a relationship that enhance learning the ropes and preparing for advancement in an organization. Psychosocial functions are those aspects of a relationship that enhance a sense of competence, clarity of identity, and effectiveness in a professional role (see Table 1). While career functions serve primarily to aid advancement up the hierarchy of an organization, psychosocial functions affect each individual on a personal level by contributing to self-worth both inside and outside the organization. Together these functions enable individuals to address the challenges of each career stage.

Career functions are possible because of the senior person's experience, organizational rank, and influence in the organiza-

Table 1. Mentoring Functions.

Career functions	Psychosocial functions
Sponsorship Opening doors. Having connections that will support the junior's career advancement.	*Role modeling* Demonstrating valued behavior, attitudes and/or skills that aid the junior in achieving competence, confidence, and a clear professional identity.
Coaching Teaching "the ropes." Giving relevant positive and negative feedback to improve the junior's performance and potential.	
Protection Providing support in different situations. Taking responsibility for mistakes that were outside the junior's control. Acting as a buffer when necessary.	*Counseling* Providing a helpful and confidential forum for exploring personal and professional dilemmas. Excellent listening, trust, and rapport that enable both individuals to address central developmental concerns.
Exposure Creating opportunities for the junior to demonstrate competence where it counts. Taking the junior to important meetings that will enhance his or her visibility.	*Acceptance and confirmation* Providing ongoing support, respect, and admiration, which strengthens self-confidence and self-image. Regularly reinforcing both are highly valued people and contributors to the organization.
Challenging work Delegating assignments that stretch the junior's knowledge and skills in order to stimulate growth and preparation to move ahead.	*Friendship* Mutual caring and intimacy that extends beyond the requirements of daily work tasks. Sharing of experience outside the immediate work setting.

tional context. It is this structural role relationship that enables him
or her to provide critical support that helps a junior colleague learn
to navigate effectively in the organizational world and to
simultaneously gain respect among peers and superiors for
developing talent for the organization.

In contrast, psychosocial functions are possible because of an
interpersonal bond that fosters mutual trust and increasing
intimacy. These relationship qualities enable the junior to identify
with his or her senior colleague and the senior to offer counsel on
crucial dilemmas that surface as the novice launches a career. Each
individual experiences acceptance and confirmation of self-worth
through interaction with the other.

The range of career functions and psychosocial functions
observed in developmental relationships varies. When a hierarchical relationship provides all of the possible functions outlined
above, it best approximates the classical mentor relationship that
Levinson and others (1978) describe. Relationships that provide
both kinds of functions are characterized by greater intimacy and
commitment and are viewed as more indispensable, more critical to
development, and more exclusive than other relationships at work.
Relationships that only provide career functions are characterized
by less intimacy and are valued primarily for the instrumental ends
that they serve in an organizational context. More often than not,
relationships provide a subset of the possible mentoring functions,
and, in general, career functions are more prevalent (Kram, 1985).

For example, in her study of female managers, Phillips-Jones
(1982) made a distinction between primary mentors and secondary
mentors. Primary mentors are individuals who are labeled as
mentors and who are viewed as unselfish, altruistic, and caring. In
contrast, secondary mentors are individuals who are part of a more
businesslike relationship in which exchanges benefit both
individuals' career advancement. Phillips-Jones noted that primary
mentors are more scarce and are described with greater indebtedness,
while secondary mentors are easier to come by; a manager might
have several during a particular period of a career. Primary mentors
provide both career and psychosocial functions, whereas secondary
mentors provide only career functions.

Shapiro, Haseltine, and Rowe (1978) describe a continuum of advisory/support relationships that range from mentor to sponsor to guide to peer pal. This continuum suggests, on the mentor end, that relationships are highly exclusive, characterized by a hierarchical or parental role relationship, and high in emotional intensity. As one moves toward the other end of the continuum, relationships become more available and less exclusive, less parental, and less emotionally involving. These dimensions parallel the variations noted in other studies. Again using Phillips-Jones's (1982) terms, primary mentors are those who provide both career and psychosocial functions; they are relatively scarce, exclusive, parental, and intense. Secondary mentors are those who provide only career functions and on the continuum would be sponsors or guides.

Finally, Clawson (1979) offers two dimensions for distinguishing developmental relationships that parallel the continuum, the primary and secondary classification, and the career and psychosocial function categorizations. In his study of effective boss-subordinate relationships, he delineated (1) comprehensiveness of influence—that is, how many different aspects of an individual's life a relationship affects; and (2) mutuality of individual commitment to the relationship, where high commitment on the part of both individuals characterizes the primary mentor relationship.

Thus, mentoring is embodied in a variety of relationships that fulfill a number of developmental purposes. While most of the research to date has focused on the nature of hierarchical mentoring, a recent study indicates that peer relationships offer critical developmental functions as well (Kram and Isabella, 1985). The systems perspective illustrates that variations in mentoring experiences, within and across work settings, are due to differences in individuals' needs, attitudes, and interpersonal skills, as well as differences in organizations' cultures and practices.

The Role of Mentoring in Development

Both adult development and career development perspectives have established that individuals face predictable developmental tasks at successive life and career stages (Levinson and others, 1978; Schein, 1978; Hall, 1976; Gould, 1978; Erikson, 1968; Baird and Kram, 1983). Several studies of how these developmental tasks manifest themselves in work settings have suggested that relationships with senior colleagues and peers might facilitate work on these tasks. Attention in these studies was first given to how young adults benefited from the guidance and support of more senior colleagues as they entered the world of work and attempted to establish a professional identity while learning the ropes of organizational life (Dalton, Thompson, and Price, 1977; Schein, 1978; Hall, 1976). More recent studies of mentoring have indicated that, indeed, individuals at every career stage can benefit from such developmental alliances (Clawson, 1980; Hall and Kram, 1981; Kram, 1985).

Relationships in the Early Career Years. The early career years can be characterized as a period of initiation and new beginnings. In this period, individuals are generally exploring a possible career path, developing knowledge and skills that will prepare them for advancement, and establishing competence and confidence in the adult world and, more specifically, in a work context (Hall, 1976; Levinson and others, 1978; Dalton, Thompson, and Price, 1977). Each of these tasks is facilitated by the interest, guidance, and support of more experienced colleagues.

Relationships with more senior colleagues can provide a variety of developmental functions. Career functions, including sponsorship, coaching, exposure, challenging work, and protection, all aid an individual in preparing for career advancement. Psychosocial functions, including role modeling, counseling, acceptance and confirmation and friendship, all aid an individual in developing competence, confidence, and a clear sense of professional identity (Kram, 1985). Both kinds of functions are important, yet in most instances particular relationships provide only some of these developmental functions.

Since relationships are limited in terms of the range of developmental functions they offer and in terms of how long they endure through organizational changes and individual transitions, it appears necessary for individuals in the early career period to build several developmental alliances rather than just one. The search for one mentor who will guide and coach a young adult through the entire duration of the early career period is almost always a futile one. Instead, with awareness of personal and professional concerns and of how relationships can support work on these developmental tasks, individuals can consciously attempt to initiate contacts that support their growth and well-being in a work context.

Interestingly, relationships with senior colleagues are not the only ones that can support development in the early career years. A study of peer relationships indicated that peers can provide a variety of career functions and psychosocial functions similar to those provided in a hierarchical mentoring alliance (Kram and Isabella, 1985). However, individuals in this career stage generally look for guidance more from their bosses and other senior colleagues than from their organizational and age peers. Not only do young adults need the parental guidance and sponsorship of older mentors, but organizational circumstances frequently discourage collaboration among peers.

Sometimes, individuals' career stage and chronological age are "out of sync." For example, a person who begins a new career at midlife is a novice at work while having considerable experience and expertise in other spheres. In this instance, developmental needs are somewhat different from those of a younger entering employee, and the relative ages of novice and potential mentors may be the reverse of what is usually encountered. These differences may result in unique dilemmas, since individuals' needs may not be as complementary as they might be in the more traditional hierarchical mentoring relationship; also, competition as well as authority issues may be exacerbated, since it is quite likely that the career novice may be more expert in certain domains than are his or her senior colleagues at work. It seems important to investigate these complexities, since these midlife career changes are becoming increasingly prevalent.

Relationships in the Midcareer Years. The midcareer years are generally characterized by a period of reassessment and reappraisal as individuals look back over what they have accomplished, how their careers and lives have unfolded, and whether earlier life dreams have been realized. In contrast to those in early career, individuals in midcareer have a substantial history of jobs and relationships behind them; their primary task is to assess and, if necessary, modify the present in order to reconcile past aspirations with current circumstances (Osherson, 1980; Jacques, 1965; Dalton, 1959; Levinson and others, 1978).

Relationships with junior colleagues can enable individuals in midcareer to enhance self-esteem, to strengthen further advancement prospects, and to pass on personal values and experiences to the next generation. In providing a range of mentoring functions, individuals in midcareer gain technical and psychological support, recognition from peers and superiors for effectively developing younger talent for their organizations, and personal satisfaction in seeing how efforts at coaching and counseling enable junior colleagues to develop competence and succeed in their professional worlds. Overall, the opportunity to mentor provides a vehicle for reliving earlier experiences and decisions and thus facilitates the primary task of reappraisal. As active participants in junior colleagues' growth and development, individuals in the middle career years benefit from such developmental alliances.

Not all individuals in midcareer embrace the role of mentor. It appears that the capacity to assume such a stance is related to self-esteem and prospects for further growth and development (Hall and Kram, 1981). If, for example, a manager is facing blocked opportunity and is frustrated at seeing no further advancement, he or she is unlikely to be psychologically available to help junior colleagues who still face seemingly limitless opportunities in their own careers. Alternatively, if a manager is content with his or her current status and accomplishments to date and he or she experiences positive self-esteem, it is more likely that providing mentoring functions will be seen as an attractive and creative endeavor. Finally, if the individual in the middle career period is beginning to anticipate retirement, the opportunity to pass on wisdom to junior colleagues is likely to offer a vehicle for making a final mark before leaving one's work identity behind. Whether individuals are evolving toward further growth, maintenance, or stagnation will, to a large extent, determine the extent to which they will benefit from alliances with junior colleagues.

Other factors influence whether individuals in midcareer will seize the opportunity to mentor their junior colleagues. First, organizations' cultures and practices either encourage or impede individuals' efforts to develop their subordinates (Peters and Waterman, 1982; Deal and Kennedy, 1982). Those organizations that reward mentoring behavior and offer opportunities for juniors and seniors to collaborate will have more individuals at midcareer embracing the mentoring role than will those that minimize the importance of people development and relationship-building efforts.

Interviews with managers in the middle career years indicate that individuals who have had positive mentoring alliances in the early career years are more inclined to seek out opportunities to coach and counsel their junior colleagues than are those who have not (Kram, 1985). It appears that individuals learn to mentor from the models of their significant others in previous years and recognize the value of developmental relationships from their own early career experiences.

Finally, mentoring relationships can become destructive if during the middle career period the senior colleague enters a midlife transition in which self-esteem and identity are called into question. Frequently, such a significant period of reappraisal and redirection can disrupt the complementarity of an alliance; the senior becomes too self-absorbed to continue to provide mentoring functions and/ or the junior becomes a threat rather than an asset during a period of personal upheaval. However, in rare instances it is precisely the continued support and admiration of a junior colleague that enables a midcareer individual to manage a major transition without loss of self-esteem.

As in the early career years, individuals in the middle career years can benefit from developmental alliances with peers. It appears, however, that at this career stage relationships with subordinates and other junior colleagues offer a unique opportunity to achieve a new self-image as an expert with knowledge and wisdom to share. Furthermore, while relationships with peers become increasingly important in accomplishing organizational tasks and in facing the personal and professional dilemmas of midcareer, competition may interfere with establishing intimate alliances with peers in the same organizational hierarchy.

Relationships in the Late Career Years. The late career years are generally characterized by the anticipation of retirement as well as increased awareness of substantially greater life and organizational experiences than the majority of one's work colleagues (Kram and Jusela, 1978). Whereas individuals in midcareer are in a process of reappraisal and reassessment, individuals in the late career years face impending retirement and must begin to consider what life will be like without a work identity.

At this career stage, relationships with junior colleagues provide a vehicle for passing on wisdom and experience and thus for creating a legacy that will be left behind after leaving the organization. Through mentoring junior colleagues, individuals in the late career years are able to maintain a sense of being contributing and valued members of their organizations. In addition, relationships with subordinates allow late career individuals to get reacquainted with their youthful selves. In identifying with those that they mentor, these individuals can relive some of their earlier experiences as the process of moving into retirement begins. The gratification and psychological support found in mentoring younger colleagues are significant.

Individuals who fail to develop a sense of "ego integrity" (Erikson, 1968) as their careers come to an end are not likely to engage in supportive relationships with junior colleagues. They may resent their younger colleagues' youthfulness and continuing growth, and negative self-esteem as well as anger or depression can interfere with providing mentoring to others. Paradoxically, close relationships with subordinates are an important source of support during the late career years; yet those who could most benefit from mentoring alliances are least available to participate in them.

Relationships with peers become increasingly important during the late career years (Kram and Isabella, 1985). Individuals can reflect on the past and also share concerns about the future with those of the same age and similar career histories. Peers can empathize with fears and anxieties about retirement, and they also remember the many organizational changes over the years that had influence on their careers. Talking about how it was different in earlier years with those who have been part of that history serves an important developmental function: It unites the past with the present. Finally, peers can provide information and psychological support for managing the transition into retirement.

Competition with peers is not as great during this career stage as in earlier years. Individuals no longer aim for the next promotion; they are more likely than those in midcareer to be coaching younger organizational members and advising on strategic or policy issues. Those who find movement into a less central (or more consultative) role difficult might resent peers who do remain more integrally involved in the organization. In general, however, relationships with peers seem to complement relationships with junior colleagues well. Both kinds of developmental alliances enable late career individuals to accomplish the tasks of this period.

The Relationship Constellation

The first studies of mentoring clarified its role in career development and delineated a range of functions that relationships between younger and older adults in the workplace can serve (Clawson, 1979; Missirian, 1982; Phillips-Jones, 1982; Kram, 1983b). With this increased understanding, the subtle yet important variations in such developmental alliances became apparent. First, since mentoring relationships are limited in duration and availability, some individuals do not find such alliances at critical points in their development. Second, men and women describe significantly different experiences with their male mentors. Finally, some individuals actively seek relationships with senior colleagues, while others are content to operate without the guidance of more experienced coaches; in many instances, relationships with peers and/or subordinates provide equally important developmental functions.

These variations are important to note so that the nature of mentoring in organizations is not oversimplified or glorified. The concept of the relationship constellation is introduced to account for the range of relationships with seniors, juniors, and peers that can provide mentoring functions (Kram, 1985). The complexities of cross-gender alliances are delineated in order to illustrate how mentoring is shaped by demographic characteristics of the parties involved. And, while systematic research is still needed to test certain premises, interviews with managers suggest that fundamental attitudes toward competition, competence, authority, intimacy, and learning significantly influence the relationships that evolve.

In response to the finding that many individuals do not form significant relationships with senior colleagues and, in addition, that some mentoring alliances become destructive over time with changes in individuals' needs and/or organizational circumstances, an inquiry into mentoring alternatives was begun. This resulted in the delineation of a continuum of peer relationships that provide a variety of mentoring functions (Kram and Isabella, 1985). This study indicated that not only do relationships with peers provide a variety of mentoring functions but also the dominant themes characterizing them as well as their relative importance in individuals' development vary with career stage.

The relationship constellation is the range of relationships with superiors, peers, subordinates, and (outside work) family and friends that support an individual's development at any particular time (see Figure 1). It reflects the fact that mentoring functions frequently are embodied in several relationships rather than just one. While a hierarchical mentor relationship may stand out as providing the widest range of career and psychosocial functions, it is also possible that relationships with peers offer several functions as well as the opportunity to engage in a relationship characterized by greater mutuality of exchange. In peer relationships, individuals can share wisdom and feel like experts while also learning and deriving support from a colleague. It is precisely this circumstance that enables one to move from the apprentice stage to the independent contributor stage of a career (Dalton, Thompson, and Price, 1977).

Relationships with bosses, subordinates, and friends and family members also can provide a range of developmental functions. Bosses often provide coaching, challenging work, role modeling, and visibility (Baird and Kram, 1983; Berlew and Hall, 1966). However, it appears that their mentoring activities are

Figure 1. The Relationship Constellation.

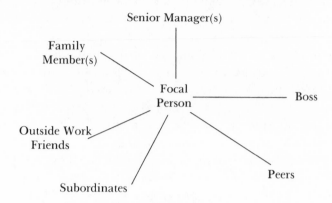

Each relationship constellation includes those relationships that provide mentoring functions for this focal person. The particular individuals noted vary over time as individuals' needs and/or organizational circumstances change.

Source: Adapted from Kram, 1985.

frequently limited by their position and/or career stage; for example, because they evaluate subordinates' performance, it may be difficult to also serve in the role of confidante. Alternatively, they may be reluctant to sponsor a subordinate because his or her movement would be a significant loss and/or a threat to his or her advancement or self-confidence (Baird and Kram, 1983).

Outside work family members and friends are unencumbered by the formal role relationships of organizational life. It is precisely this structural detachment that enables them to provide counseling, coaching, role modeling, confirmation, and support at critical times. Peers from outside work often can provide critical functions because they are not competing within the same profession or organizational hierarchy. Family members often have a broader understanding of the total person and his or her life (rather than just career) concerns. While it is possible that family ties could interfere with effective mentoring, these sources of support have not been sufficiently highlighted to date.

Finally, relationships with subordinates appear to offer a variety of developmental functions (Thompson, 1982). For individuals at midcareer or beyond, subordinates offer the opportunity to meet generative needs and to achieve the self-image of one who has wisdom and experience to share. At the same time, subordinates most obviously provide technical and psychological support to individuals, regardless of their career stage. Indeed, in some industries, subordinates have become coaches and mentors in technical areas because they have more expertise than their more senior colleagues; understanding that learning from subordinates is not only legitimate but essential is key to ongoing performance and development.

The character of a relationship constellation is not static and, indeed, evolves as individuals' needs and organizational circumstances change. For example, as individuals get older and become more experienced, the desire to teach others and to assume a mentoring role undoubtedly will result in subordinates becoming part of a relationship constellation. Similarly, as individuals are promoted to new organizational levels, a new set of peers and subordinates becomes essential not only for getting work done but also for learning the new ropes and developing supportive alliances. Finally, organizational changes can result in significant others no longer being available to provide critical developmental functions.

Just as developmental tasks have been delineated for each adult life and career stage, so it seems essential to delineate the patterns of relationship constellations that evolve over the course of careers. This understanding would enable individuals to consciously identify the kinds of developmental alliances that are critical at a given time, and it would enable organizations to create avenues for employees to build such relationships through job design and various human resource management practices. Then, as individuals feel unsupported or exposed to considerable stress, they could consider how their relationship constellations could be modified to provide critical developmental functions. Similarly, as organizations note unusually high turnover among novices or considerably low morale and disengagement among plateaued individuals at midcareer, they could consider how creating conditions that encourage mentoring alliances between juniors and seniors or among peers would alleviate these human resource problems.

The concept of a relationship constellation eliminates the misconception that mentoring is embodied in one hierarchical relationship. In addition, it implies that the character and qualities of mentoring alliances vary with age and career stage, with organizational context, and with the unique complexion of individuals' characteristics. Finally, this complex view suggests that in order to understand the role of mentoring in individuals' careers or in the performance and development of an organization's human resources, it is necessary to periodically assess the various factors that shape these developmental alliances.

Cross-Gender Mentoring

Additional complexities are found in mentoring alliances that involve both men and women. In contrast to mentoring among men, there is considerable confusion and anxiety about how to work closely with individuals of the opposite gender (Sargent, 1977; Crary, 1985; Jamison, 1983; Josefowitz, 1982). In addition, sex role socialization creates (albeit unconsciously) relationship dynamics that can reduce individual performance, competence, and well-being (Kanter, 1977; Martin, Harrison, and DiNitto, 1983). Finally, in an organizational context cross-gender mentoring alliances attract notice and scrutiny, which adds negative pressures to an already complex situation (Clawson and Kram, 1984; Missirian, 1982; Bowen, 1985). It is not surprising, then, that cross-gender mentoring relationships sometimes are avoided because of these complexities; and if not avoided, they often are limited in the range of developmental functions they provide.

The most salient issue for managers is the concern about increasing intimacy and sexual attraction that frequently characterizes cross-gender mentoring alliances (Kram, 1985; Jamison, 1983; Quinn, 1977; Bowen, 1985). Anxiety about the boundaries of the relationship can lead either or both individuals to withdraw or at least to avoid frequent contact that might otherwise provide a forum for coaching and counseling discussions. This concern appears not only to affect ongoing alliances but also to discourage initiation of relationships that could provide meaningful developmental functions if they were nurtured. Finding the appropriate level of intimacy and distance is difficult; and rather than tackle this obstacle, relationships remain, instead, superficial (Crary, 1985; Clawson and Kram, 1984).

Second, both men and women have a strong inclination to rely on traditional sex-role stereotypes in cross-gender relationships (Kanter, 1977; Sargent, 1977; Epstein, 1970; Hennig and Jardim, 1977). In the face of the unknown, they will collude in keeping the woman in traditional roles that reduce her overall contributions and competence in the organization. Thus, for example, a male mentor is protective of his female protege who is attempting to fight the barriers to women's advancement in the organization. At the same time, she becomes so comfortable with his support that she does not risk venturing out from his turf in order to establish her own reputation as an independent contributor. What appears to be mentoring at work is, in fact, the subtle undermining of a young woman's performance and potential.

Third, in cross-gender mentoring relationships the role-modeling function is frequently unsatisfactory to the junior person and sometimes to the mentor as well. While women in the early career years face developmental dilemmas similar to those of male counterparts, they face some that are unique to being female in male-dominated settings (Kanter, 1977; Missirian, 1982; Baker-Miller, 1976). Concerns about the appropriateness of particular behavior may appear unwarranted to the male mentor who does not understand that what works for a man may not work for a woman. Concerns about balancing work and family commitments are exacerbated for women in their thirties who are simultaneously advancing their careers and assuming roles of wife and/or mother. These unique gender-related concerns make it difficult for male mentors to empathize, to provide role modeling and counseling, and to identify with their female proteges.

Fourth, cross-gender relationships are subject to public scrutiny; others study these relationships with interest and, more likely, with some suspicion (Clawson and Kram, 1984; Kram, 1985). If the external relationship is not carefully managed, rumors develop that can be destructive to one or both individuals' careers.

The possibilities of sexual involvement and favoritism rather than competence as the criteria for sponsorship can threaten the reputations of both individuals. This puts considerable stress on the relationship as the public image becomes the priority, increasing the likelihood that certain developmental functions are forfeited.

Finally, cross-gender relationships are subject to peer resentment (Kram, 1985). Because of the competition that occurs among peers aspiring to advance, the solo woman stands out as one who receives special attention if she is regularly coached by a male superior. Although this relationship may be important to her, she may be reluctant to maintain it for fear of becoming isolated from or ridiculed by her male peers. In this situation, the junior individual usually feels trapped into choosing between relationships with peers and a relationship with a mentor; while such a choice should not be necessary, the stress created by peer resentment is compelling.

Similar dynamics are likely to occur in mentoring relationships in which the mentors are women and the proteges are men. To date, however, these situations have not been systematically studied, since until recently they were not readily encountered in most work settings. Concerns about sexuality and intimacy, the limitations of role modeling, public scrutiny, and peer resentment are likely to be similar. However, given what is known about sex-role socialization, one can predict that there are likely to be some unique dynamics in situations in which the woman is more senior and more powerful. When the power relationship is opposite to traditional relations between the sexes in this culture, it is likely that some unpredictable dynamics occur to manage these discrepencies.

These added complexities make forming and maintaining cross-gender mentoring alliances relatively difficult. It would not be surprising to survey organizations and discover that women find less access to mentoring than their male colleagues or that the mentoring they do experience is more limited in the range of functions that are provided. In addition, it is likely that the particular challenges encountered in managing cross-gender mentoring alliances vary across organizations with differences in task design, norms, and organizational practices (Spelman, Crary,

Kram, and Clawson, 1986). Finally, a parallel study of interracial mentoring is necessary in order to identify the dynamics that interfere with the quality and availability of mentoring for minority group members. It appears that some of the difficult dynamics encountered in cross-gender relationships would be similar, and, undoubtedly, unique aspects would be discovered as well.

It appears that in the face of limited role modeling, avoidance behavior due to sexual tensions or public scrutiny, or dissatisfaction that occurs when stereotypes govern behavior, women find mentoring opportunities in relationships with their female peers. While this alternative is very beneficial in making relationship constellations more supportive and developmentally responsive, it does not eliminate the problems of unequal access, sponsorship, and coaching that result from the complexities of cross-gender alliances.

Demographic characteristics, including gender, race, ethnicity, education, socioeconomic class, and age, all shape the complexion of mentoring alliances. First, most individuals find it easier to establish mentoring alliances with others who are similar rather than different with regard to key demographic characteristics. (It appears, however, that in some instances women find it difficult to mentor other women when competition is severe, and it is all too common to be labeled as the one who only mentors other women.) Second, when the age differential between potential mentor and protege is small or the reverse of what generally occurs, competition, resentment, self-doubt, or awkwardness can interfere with establishing productive alliances. Finally, it appears that the culture of an organization significantly affects the extent to which differences in demographics will interfere with establishing development alliances; in some contexts avoidance behavior will predominate, while in others attempts to transcend differences and build supportive alliances across demographic boundaries are encouraged and rewarded.

Fundamental Attitudes, Postures, and Skills

Variations in mentoring alliances appear to be explained in part by differences in fundamental attitudes and postures that are brought to relationships at work. While further research is needed to delineate how particular attitudes shape relationship constellations, managers' personal accounts, as well as the psychoanalytic and psychiatric literature, provide sufficient data and theory to speculate about several (Kram, 1985; Levinson, 1976; Zalesnick, Dalton, and Burns, 1970; Sullivan, 1954).

Individuals' attitudes toward authority are likely to affect whether they seek out mentor relationships with senior colleagues or peers. In addition, this stance will affect the extent to which mutuality in relationships is possible. For example, the individual with a generally rebellious stance toward authority is less likely to seek out supportive relationships that involve coaching and guidance from senior colleagues. In contrast, the individual who seeks approval from those in authority is more likely to gravitate toward senior colleagues for guidance and support and thus also to form significant mentor relationships. The former may seek developmental functions from peers, while the latter may focus only on senior colleagues and overlook the potential value of peer relationships.

Another important factor here is individuals' attitudes toward intimacy, which are likely to influence the extent to which they develop open and enhancing relationships with mentors, peers, and subordinates. If sharing personal and professional concerns with individuals in the workplace is perceived as legitimate and one has the skills to self-disclose, listen, build rapport, and so on, then he or she is likely to build strong mentor and peer alliances. The individual who has a radically different view of what is appropriate may have few or distant connections at work; in this instance, a relationship constellation might consist of a boss, limited sponsorship from senior colleagues, and primarily instrumental relationships with peers.

Individuals' views of their competence affects the extent to which they are able to develop peer relationships characterized by mutuality and two-way helping (Kram and Isabella, 1985). In addition, self-concept affects the extent to which individuals in midcareer are available and willing to become mentors for junior colleagues (Levinson and others, 1978; Hall and Kram, 1981). For example, in early career years, individuals form peer relationships of increasing developmental importance only if they feel that they have expertise to offer. Similarly, in the middle and later career years, individuals are likely to embrace the mentoring role only if they have accepted their accomplishments to date and can enjoy helping junior colleagues succeed and perhaps even surpass them.

A further major influence is individuals' attitudes toward competition and conflict: While competition and conflict are inevitable, how they are managed determines whether supportive relationships can evolve. For example, the individual who has strong competitive feelings may not be willing to collaborate with peers; as a consequence, a two-way helping relationship cannot emerge. In contrast, the individual who can put aside the competitive dimensions of organizational life when support and collaboration are beneficial will build mutually enhancing relationships with peers. Similarly, if conflict is managed effectively, it will not interfere with relationships at work. If conflict is avoided at all costs, intimate relationships with potential mentors and peers probably will be curtailed.

Individuals' attitudes about the importance of work and personal domains are likely to shape the evolution of relationships at work. When work is considered to be relatively unimportant, developmental functions are likely to be provided primarily by relationships outside the work context. In contrast, when work represents a primary commitment of time and personal involvement, relationship constellations are likely to contain relationships with peers, mentors, bosses, and subordinates.

Finally, attitudes toward learning appear to affect the extent to which an individual looks to relationships for developmental functions. If individuals assume that learning must be accomplished alone, then they probably will not seek out coaching, counseling, or other developmental functions. But if they perceive learning as an ongoing collaborative process, they are more likely to initiate relationships and build relationship constellations that provide a wide range of developmental functions.

These postulates are derived from interviews with managers in which they described how and why certain developmental relationships evolved as they did. Their personal accounts reflected fundamental attitudes and assumptions that significantly shaped how relationships at work were approached and managed. We can also assume that most of these fundamental stances were established early in life in relationships with parents, teachers, and siblings (Levinson, 1976; Storr, 1960). Indeed, mentoring alliances are frequently potent because of the transference from earlier life relationships and the projection of desired attributes and competencies onto these significant others. As a consequence, the patterns found in a current relationship constellation can be understood in part by examining individuals' life histories and previous relationships.

Whether such fundamental attitudes and postures change significantly during life in an organization remains open to investigation. Certainly, major life changes and experiences in therapy can enable an individual to alter stances that have interfered with developing satisfying relationships at work and at home. What remains to be tested is whether human relations training and management development programs offered on-site and in public forums can provide the stimulus and support to change attitudes that interfere with building relationship constellations that support development.

It is also clear that interpersonal skills are necessary in order to initiate and build mentoring alliances with juniors, seniors, and peers. Even with the desire to form intimate connections with and learn from colleagues, the lack of effective skills in listening, self-disclosure, conflict management, giving and receiving feedback, and building rapport will thwart the best intentions. Organizations are beginning to investigate whether skill building of this kind can be accomplished in an educational context.

How Organizations Shape the Mentoring Process

Organizations influence the nature of relationships between juniors and seniors and among peers in a variety of ways. More often than not, these practices are not intentionally designed to encourage an effective mentoring process. If the potential of mentoring is to be realized, organizations will have to examine whether they are creating conditions that support or interfere with forming developmental alliances at every career stage. Certain conditions must exist in order for an effective mentoring process to evolve (Kram, 1983a). First, there must be opportunities for frequent and open communication between individuals at different career stages and hierarchical levels so that the relationships that respond to current developmental needs can be established. Second, organizational members must have the interpersonal skills to build supportive relationships as well as the willingness and interest to do so. Third, the organization's reward system, culture, job design, and management practices must value and encourage relationship-building activities.

Frequently, significant obstacles to achieving these conditions are observed. For example, if the reward system is such that only short-term bottom-line results are valued in promotion and pay decisions, then individuals will be discouraged from investing in people development and relationship-building activities. In addition, if the design of work is such that jobs are highly individualized and there are few job-related reasons to interact with others who might provide mentoring functions, then it is less likely that individuals will find the vehicles for building supportive alliances with peers, seniors, or juniors. Similarly, if the culture of the organization is characterized by low trust, little valid communication across hierarchical and departmental boundaries, and little attention to the quality of relationships at work, then it will be difficult for developmental alliances of high trust and intimacy to evolve. Finally, while such performance management systems as performance appraisal, succession planning, and career development can provide a forum for counseling and coaching, these systems frequently are poorly utilized either because they are perceived as irrelevant or because individuals lack the skills to make them effective.

Three different strategies have been attempted for overcoming these obstacles and for building conditions that support an effective mentoring process. First, several oganizations have set up formal mentoring programs that match juniors and seniors for the purpose of supporting the junior's career development (Phillips, 1978; Klauss, 1979). Second, educational programs for managers and employees at different career stages have been designed to enable individuals to build supportive alliances at work. Third, an organizational change approach that combines diagnosis, education, and changes in structure, norms, and processes has been implemented to build individuals' knowledge and interpersonal skills while simultaneously attending to the ways in which the context facilitates or interferes with the mentoring process. Each of these has its benefits and limitations, and further research is needed to assess their long-term impact on relationships and on development in general.

Formal Mentoring Programs

A number of formal mentoring programs have been implemented in both the private sector and the federal government. These programs vary in terms of the target population served, the degree of structure and formal requirements, how mentors and proteges are assigned to each other, and the extent to which education is offered to help individuals learn their mentoring responsibilities. For instance, the Internal Revenue Service, the Federal Executive Development Program, the Presidential Management Intern Program, and the U.S. Department of Agriculture have formal systems in which the training and development staffs assign coaches or mentors to junior-level employees (Klauss, 1979). In the private sector, the Jewel Companies assign each new MBA to a senior manager for coaching and mentoring when he or she joins the organization (Collins and Scott, 1978). AT&T Bell Laboratories have junior and senior engineers share the same office for several months, Glendale (California) Federal Savings and Loan has volunteer leaders in each unit counsel employees, and Merrill Lynch, Pierce, Fenner and Smith has bosses nominate junior managers to be assigned to seniors, who act as mentors (Phillips-Jones, 1982). Finally, Federal Express has a structured mentoring system that includes education and involvement of immediate supervisors as well as an advisory board that monitors the system's effectiveness and any problems that might occur (Lean, 1983).

While systematic evaluation of these programs has yet to be conducted, a partial assessment of their impact raises questions about their actual value in creating conditions that encourage an effective mentoring process (see Table 2). First, while the primary objective is to incorporate and develop newcomers (and, in some instances, particular groups of newcomers, such as women, minorities, and/or high-potential candidates), assigned mentors and proteges frequently fail to accomplish this goal and sometimes these relationships even have destructive consequences. For example, a senior who is uncomfortable with his or her own growth potential may be prone to express resentment and to undermine the

Table 2. A Formal Mentoring Program.

Sample implementation

1. Define a population for whom relationships should be established. Invite potential mentors and proteges to help define the criteria for matching pairs and the process for doing so.
2. Collect data on potential participants that are needed to maximize an effective matching process (such as career goals, performance records, developmental needs).
3. Assign juniors and seniors to each other *or* foster a voluntary selection process. Provide guidelines on goals of the program, role expectations, and staff support services, and encourage participation in relevant educational offerings.
4. Set up monitoring procedures for providing feedback to the organization concerning how the program affects employee development over time.

advantages	*disadvantages*
• Ensures that juniors and seniors find each other	• Individuals may feel coerced and confused about responsibilities
• Increases the likelihood that matches will be good ones	• Those who are not matched feel deprived and pessimistic about their futures
• Provides ongoing support to the pairs	• Assumes that volunteers can learn the requisite skills; some may be ill suited
• Makes mentoring relationships legitimate and more accessible	• Destructive dynamics may evolve within formal pairs or with immediate supervisors

junior's career. Or if the two individuals involved are not compatible in interpersonal and learning styles, either may come to resent the association and seek to disrupt it. Second, even if the program is made voluntary in order to limit potential destructiveness, there is often negative reaction from those who have not been included or from those who are indirectly affected by the arranged relationships. Finally, individuals frequently lack the interpersonal skills and self-awareness needed to carry out the responsibilities of the program; without adequate training, they experience frustration and lowered self-esteem.

It appears that formal mentoring programs are most likely to fail when mentors and proteges are *assigned* to each other. Both juniors and seniors may feel mismatched in or coerced into a relationship that they do not particularly want to cultivate; yet the organization pressures them to continue their interaction. In these instances, seniors may resent their responsibilities as mentors, and juniors are likely to grow pessimistic about the value of relationships with senior colleagues. Negative mentoring experiences, in which either colleague feels undermined, smothered, or abandoned, can be minimized by making participation voluntary. Screening procedures can help individuals think through a decision to participate, and data can be collected to facilitate a good match between potential mentors and proteges (Phillips-Jones, 1982).

Even if the match is voluntary and a good one, both individuals may become anxious and confused about their new responsibilities as mentor or protege. Seniors, when asked to mentor or coach, frequently have an idealized image of what this may entail, and this can cause considerable self-doubt about their ability to succeed. Or individuals at midcareer who are concerned about their own advancement potential may be ambivalent about supporting the growth of their junior colleagues. Finally, individuals who have not experienced developmental relationships earlier in their careers are unlikely to have the intuitive and interpersonal skills needed to cultivate supportive alliances. Education can alleviate some of these anxieties and concerns by defining mentoring functions and by providing interpersonal skills training.

Voluntary participation and relevant education and training can reduce the risks of failure in a formal program, but they cannot eliminate all negative reactions. For example, in a system designed for high-potential candidates, juniors who are not labeled as such may feel deprived, resentful, and increasingly pessimistic about their own opportunities for development. Similarly, in a mentoring program designed to facilitate affirmative action goals, majority group members may become resentful of the guidance and support offered special-interest group members. These side effects affect relationships among peers as well as individuals' long-term commitment to the organization. Finally, immediate supervisors of the juniors who participate in a formal mentoring program may become uncomfortable and feel threatened by these new alliances. The risk of losing influence over the performance and career decisions of a subordinate increases as the bond between mentor and protege strengthens.

The risks of a formal mentoring program are high, and the potential benefits have not been clearly demonstrated. It appears, as I have said, that the risk can be minimized if participation is voluntary and relevant education is provided; it is also helpful if immediate supervisors are informed and included in some advisory capacity, there is flexibility in the program so that relationships can be gracefully ended when they no longer fulfill individuals' needs, and the organization's culture supports open developmental alliances through its norms and practices and, in particular, through the behavior and values of senior management.

These conditions are feasible, but they are not easily achieved. Aside from the practical difficulties inherent in creating a formal mentoring program, the premises on which this kind of intervention is based are of questionable validity. First, research to date indicates that mentoring relationships cannot be engineered but must emerge from the spontaneous and mutual involvement of two individuals who see potential value in relating to each other (Levinson and others, 1978; Kram, 1985). Second, we now know that individuals are likely to develop a variety of relationships that provide some mentoring functions rather than trying to get all their developmental needs met in just one relationship (Shapiro, Haseltine, and Rowe, 1978; Rowe, 1980; Kram and Isabella, 1985).

Still, the formalization of a program does encourage and reinforce the importance of mentoring activities. It is critical that these programs be systematically evaluated over time to determine whether, in fact, the advantages actually outweigh the disadvantages that have been identified.

Education

Educational programs can increase understanding of mentoring and its role in career development and create a learning context in which relationship skills and positive attitudes toward mentoring can be developed. In addition to enhancing knowledge, skills, and attitudes, effective education can change the culture of an organization by reinforcing new values that give priority to relationship-building activities. It is possible, then, that in an organization with practices that encourage mentoring alliances, education will have far more impact than a formal mentoring program.

Many educational offerings are possible, and the appropriate mix depends on the particular setting and objectives that have been defined. For example, when career development systems are functioning well, education related to mentoring can be incorporated into training that supports this performance and development system (Lewis, 1983). Alternatively, when the management education or training department of an organization is expected to offer innovative programs to employees at all career stages, a specific program on mentoring and careers, for example, can be tailored to training populations in early, middle, and late career stages. Finally, when higher quality and greater availability of mentoring for women and minority groups are desired, specialized training events for these groups and their potential mentors can be designed (Lean, 1983; Kram, 1985).

In one organization, managers, engineers, and technicians all participated in a workshop on career planning in which they learned the elements of a new system and the interpersonal skills to make it work for them. Within this workshop, mentoring was introduced as a critical career development tool: Individuals had the opportunity to assess their readiness to provide mentoring or to initiate mentoring alliances with senior colleagues. They were also given the opportunity to role play situations in which developmental relationships could be initiated. Since the workshop was first offered to the most senior managers, by the time those in most need of mentoring participated, they were assured that their senior colleagues were behind the concept and willing to respond to their developmental needs for coaching and guidance. While the actual changes in mentoring behavior have not been monitored systematically, it appears that more opportunities for developmental alliances have been created for those who wish to pursue them.

In one division of a large high-tech firm, senior management was concerned about the lack of mentoring available to their female engineers. Evidence of high turnover among high-potential female engineers led them to inquire about this problem. A series of diagnostic interviews indicated that women had not formed developmental alliances with senior colleagues and that senior male mentors were wary of coaching and counseling young female engineers for a variety of reasons related to sex-role stereotypes, fears of intimacy and sexual tensions, and the traditional values of the surrounding social context. Subsequently, education was designed for two target populations: The young female engineers attended a workshop on mentoring and its role in their career development, where they practiced skills in initiating and cultivating relationships with potential mentors. Then, managers were invited to attend a parallel workshop in which they learned more about the role of mentoring in career development and attended to the particular complexities of managing cross-gender alliances. Since the culture of the organization is generally open and supportive of people development and relationship-building efforts, this education is likely to eliminate the personal and interpersonal obstacle to providing an effective mentoring process for female engineers.

The appropriate objectives, design, and target populations for education of this kind depend on which programs already exist, the role of training activities, and the needs of organizational members. Regardless of the particular objectives and target populations, however, certain principles of laboratory education are important for building knowledge, reorienting attitudes, and developing new behavioral skills (Bass and Vaughn, 1966; Beer, 1980; Hall, 1970): Participants should have the opportunity to explore their own career histories and current attitudes toward mentoring, to learn the range of mentoring functions that are possible and discover how developmental alliances can be initiated, managed, and terminated, and to practice the interpersonal skills needed to build supportive relationships with colleagues (see Table 3). Role plays, self-assessment activities, and case studies offer vehicles to experiment with new behavior, to see models of effective coaching and counseling, to obtain constructive feedback from other participants and instructors, and to plan for back-at-home application of new skills to current and future relationships.

Education has a number of limitations. First, not all potential participants are interested in mentoring; prior experiences in relationships as well as current organizational status and prospects shape the extent to which individuals will embrace opportunities to develop relationship-building skills in an educational context. Second, unless the education is introduced with a clear rationale about how it fits with participants' job situations and broader organizational objectives, it may be viewed as interesting but superfluous. Finally, if organizational practices do not support the attitudes, knowledge, and skills developed in the educational context, new learnings will fade rapidly (Argyris, 1970).

These limitations suggest that participation should be voluntary and that within the context of an educational program, individuals' reluctance and anxieties about building mentoring alliances should be addressed. In addition, third-party consultation with participants as they attempt to build supportive relationships and implement new skills will facilitate transfer of learning in the immediate work situation. A good alternative to this staff resource is structuring peer-counseling agreements among program participants so that they can serve as sounding boards for each other as they venture into new relationship behavior.

Having the support of senior management is critical to ensuring that mentoring education is viewed as legitimate and important. These managers should actively articulate how mentoring efforts contribute to organizational objectives; they should model effective mentoring behavior in their relationships

**Table 3. Mentoring and Career Development: General Outline
for a Two-Day Workshop.**

Objectives:
- To clarify the role of mentoring in career development
- To develop a realistic understanding of the range of mentoring functions and the benefits and limitations of various developmental relationships
- To assess personal career issues, attitudes toward mentoring, interpersonal skills, and current relationship constellations
- To develop requisite interpersonal skills for effective mentoring alliances
- To develop a specific plan for improving the mentoring process on the job

	Day one	*Day two*
Morning	Introduction and overview Definitions of Mentoring; potential benefits and costs; organizational priorities and practices Review of personal experiences with mentoring	Interpersonal skills assessment Role plays • Initiating a mentor alliance • Cultivating an ongoing relationship • Terminating a relationship
After-noon	How career stage affects relationships at work (self-assessment and conceptual input) How the organization's culture and practices shape mentoring opportunities (organizational assessment and conceptual input)	Planning for back-at-home application of mentoring knowledge and skills
Evening	Complexities of demographic diversity in the mentoring process	

with subordinates; and they should provide strong role models as well as positive reinforcement so that participants will find the skills and attitudes acquired during training to be consistent with organizational norms and practices.

In order to ensure that education has impact, organizational structures, norms, and practices must support the skills and attitudes developed during participation in such a program. Without this support, individuals will quickly revert to former attitudes and behavior. If organizational conditions contradict new attitudes and, more specifically, if the reward system only values short-term, bottom-line results and task design does not allow for frequent interaction among colleagues who might have complementary relationship needs, then those who have participated in an educational program on mentoring are likely to become frustrated or angry and ultimately fail to use their newly acquired skills.

An Organizational Change Approach

While formal mentoring programs create opportunities for juniors and seniors to interact on a frequent basis, they do not necessarily produce effective mentoring behavior and, indeed, they may result in a number of destructive consequences for both participants and nonparticipants. Similarly, while education has the potential to increase self-awareness, build knowledge of the range of mentoring functions and their possibilities, develop requisite interpersonal skills, and enhance attitudes toward mentoring alliances, if the job context does not encourage back-at-home application of these learnings, the positive impact will be minimal. The limitations of formal mentoring programs and education indicate the need to attend to characteristics of the organizational context that are either encouraging or obstructing an effective mentoring process.

An organizational change approach to improving the mentoring process is a system-wide process of data collection, diagnosis, action planning, intervention, and evaluation (Beer, 1980). Organizational members are asked about their experiences in relationships, their career concerns, and their perceptions of the organization so that researchers can develop an understanding of where mentoring is lacking, what the obstacles are, and what features of the organization may be contributing to these obstacles. This diagnostic process usually involves a collaboration among the target population of individuals for whom mentoring is desirable, the management group that must commit resources and support, and the internal and/or external change agents who have the behavioral science knowledge and skill to orchestrate this process.

The result of a systematic diagnosis may be a decision to implement educational offerings and possibly to set up some kind of formal mentoring program as well. What makes this process unique is that it ensures that the requisite organizational conditions for an effective mentoring process are simultaneously developed so that programs are not undermined by inconsistencies in the reward system, the culture, the task design, or ongoing human resource management practices. The implementation plan of such organizational change is not formulated until sufficient diagnosis of individuals' attitudes and skills and organizational practices has been completed. After implementation of education or structural changes, ongoing monitoring of their impact on the mentoring process ensures continual learning and further intervention as needed (see Table 4).

Let us now turn to an example of the organizational change approach. In a large public utility, there was growing interest in increasing the quality and availability of mentoring for junior managers in order to ensure effective development of managerial talent for the organization. In addition, there was considerable concern that mentoring for women and minority group members was severely lacking. The first inclination was to offer education and training to managers at every career stage in order to ensure that all had the knowledge and skills necessary to cultivate effective mentoring alliances. A task force consisting of about five line managers, two internal organizational development (OD) consultants, and me as an external consultant was formed to determine whether education would be appropriate and sufficient. Interviews with managers at several career stages indicated that education was desirable (that is, managers wanted to learn more about mentoring, their own career development needs, and the interpersonal skills necessary to build effective alliances) but that problems existed in

Table 4. Improving the Mentoring Process: Guidelines
for Establishing a Change Strategy.

1. Establish the objectives and scope for the project
    • What is the population in need of mentoring?
    • What population can provide mentoring?
    • Are resources available for a system-wide change or for a smaller-scale departmental change?
2. Complete a diagnosis of the factors that create obstacles to mentoring and identify alternative methods for alleviating these
    • What factors are discouraging relationship-building efforts? The reward system? The design of work? The culture? The absence of performance management systems? The lack of requisite interpersonal knowledge and skills?
    • What educational and structural change strategies are feasible and desirable? Are other change efforts or established programs underway in which a strategy to encourage mentoring could be incorporated?
    • Who needs to be involved in choosing the appropriate strategy so that requisite management support is provided and resistance is minimized?
3. Implement the strategy
    • Which should happen first, education or structural change(s)?
    • Who should be consulted and involved in implementation?
    • What depth of intervention is required in order to accomplish the objectives?
4. Evaluate the impact of the intervention and define appropriate next steps
    • How did individuals respond?
    • What other steps are needed to support the desired changes in attitudes and behavior?
    • Who needs to be informed of the impact in order to ensure long-term support for the change?

Source: Adapted from Kram, 1985.

the environment that, if not attended to, would sabotage the educational experience.

The organization was in a period of major transition due to recent changes in government regulation, technology, and market structure. This transition created substantial anxiety, lack of trust, and uncertainty about the future, which made it difficult for managers to attend to developing their subordinates. In addition, a short-term, bottom-line results orientation encouraged increasingly competitive and self-protective behavior that undermined an effective mentoring process. On the positive side, project teams and quality circles were becoming a necessity; if individuals developed adequate interpersonal skills, these structures would provide a forum for building supportive developmental alliances.

The diagnosis suggested that education would be helpful but not sufficient. Indeed, the task force predicted that education alone would leave participants feeling frustrated and disillusioned because they would not be rewarded for attending to relationships. In addition, the turmoil and low trust in the environment would discourage them from implementing new mentoring behavior back on the job. A decision was made to start with a workshop and a survey feedback process aimed at identifying the organizational obstacles that would have to be addressed. The survey was designed with the help of another external consultant, and it was conducted before, during, and after the workshop. During the workshop, initial data about the reward system, the culture, task design, and human resource management practices were examined, and participants were asked to develop strategies for overcoming the obstacles to mentoring that existed. After the workshop, participants, original task force members, senior managers, and the consultants met to review additional data generated at the workshop and to identify further actions needed to create an environment that would support an effective mentoring process.

The actions to date have been consistent with an organizational change approach. Several more workshops are anticipated in the future, and, more importantly, the line organization is now working with the internal consultants to identify steps that can be taken to build greater trust, to genuinely incorporate mentoring into the overall mission and objectives, to modify the reward system so that development is considered as important as financial results, and to maximize the benefit of the already emergent task team structure. A considerable amount of work remains to be done, and there is some doubt as to whether there is sufficient commitment among senior managers to ensure that significant obstacles are identified and alleviated. Systematic diagnosis, action planning, and monitoring of interventions through the survey feedback process increase the likelihood that substantial actions will be taken to enhance the mentoring process.

An organizational change approach to building an effective mentoring process ensures that efforts to alleviate obstacles to relationship-building activities are relevant and acceptable and have their intended impact (Beer, 1980). This implies that strategies that are effective in one setting may be inappropriate in another and that an organization must consider its objectives and resources carefully when choosing among educational and structural change possibilities. Frequently, organizations choose the intervention that appears to be most efficient in order to conserve resources; yet this same alternative may be inadequate in altering the practices that create the most significant obstacles.

As a vivid example of an inappropriate strategy, one organization decided to set up a formal mentoring system for women and minority professionals in an attempt to support affirmative action objectives. While setting up formal relationship pairs appeared to address the fact that these special-interest group members did not have access to senior colleagues, it failed to facilitate relationships that provided mentoring functions. First, seniors resented the new responsibility and felt inadequate to the task. Second, the reward system did not recognize and reward efforts to actively develop subordinates. Finally, those who had not been matched with mentors—the white males in particular—became resentful and angry. What appeared to be a good answer to the obstacles to cross-gender and interracial mentoring created a number of negative consequences. Without skills training, adequate sharing of information with nonparticipants, and a reward system that encouraged developmental alliances, frustration mounted in the wake of the initial enthusiasm about the program.

An organizational change approach ensures that the necessary sequence of education and changes in structures, systems, and practices is identified. For example, if opportunities for interaction among those who might build developmental relationships are lacking, then changes in task design or the organization's culture may be needed. If organizational members do not understand the role of mentoring or if they do not have the requisite self-awareness and interpersonal skills, then education is warranted. Finally, if people development and relationship-building activities are unimportant in promotion and pay decisions, then changes in the reward system will have to be made.

An organizational change approach points out the need to involve individuals at all levels and career stages in the diagnosis, action-planning, and evaluation phases. Each phase in the process is enhanced by having representatives of major interest groups involved. A temporary project team, with the primary objective of creating conditions that encourage an effective mentoring process should be designated (Beckhard and Harris, 1977; Beer, 1980; Alderfer, 1976).

Conclusion

Considerable progress has been made in developing a comprehensive understanding of the mentoring process. Research has dispelled a number of myths and replaced them with a more complex view of developmental relationships. We now know that mentoring is embodied in a variety of relationships between juniors and seniors and between peers that comprise individuals' relationship constellations. In addition, it has become clear that the potential value of these developmental alliances is rarely realized in most organizational settings. Finally, with the identification of the complexities of mentoring—including the dynamics of cross-gender relationships, the factors that contribute to destructive relationships, and the ways in which organizations inhibit effective mentoring—further inquiry seems essential.

Sufficient understanding has been achieved to guide individuals in managing their own careers. Clearly, individuals benefit from relationships that support both psychosocial development and career advancement. However, it is generally unwise to search for one mentor who will provide the full range of developmental functions that are desired. Rather, individuals should proactively assess what kinds of relationships will be responsive at each successive career stage and who might be available to provide important developmental functions both inside and outside the organization. With the requisite interpersonal skills and knowledge about the role of relationships in careers, individuals at every career stage can initiate relationships that will support their development.

Studies of managers in corporate settings have established that mentoring alliances can facilitate socialization into an organization (Clawson, 1980; Berlew and Hall, 1966), reduce turnover among valued young professionals (Dalton, Thompson, and Price, 1977; Kram, 1985), minimize the potentially difficult adjustments at midcareer (Hall and Kram, 1981; Levinson and others, 1978; Kram, 1985), facilitate the transfer of knowledge and values that support an organization's mission (Peters and Waterman, 1982; Kram 1983a), and ease the transition into retirement (Schein, 1978; Hall, 1976). These contributions to productivity and the quality of work life are significant, and in high-performing organizations mentoring is considered a basic part of a manager's job. Indeed, developing subordinates is viewed as mainstream activity in these contexts. More often than not, however, most organizations do not reap the benefits that mentoring has to offer. Recent research indicates that organizations can become more self-conscious about how their practices (the reward system, the task design, the culture, performance management systems) encourage or impede an effective mentoring process and then make changes to create conditions that facilitate relationship-building efforts.

A number of situations might lead organizations to become concerned about the quality and availability of mentoring. Whether the initiative comes from senior managers concerned with the development of young talent and the transmission of key organizational values, various constituencies concerned with affirmative action, or junior members concerned with their own development, it is likely that human resource specialists will be active participants in any effort to improve the mentoring process. In some instances, the impetus to examine the quality of developmental relationships and their role in career development may even come from the human resource specialists within an organization. Those interested in responding to a concern about the quality of mentoring now have three strategies from which to choose.

Initial review of formal mentoring programs, educational interventions, and organizational change efforts to improve the mentoring process suggests that the latter is likely to be most effective (and may in some instances incorporate the first two as well). While mentoring programs are the most tangible and apparently direct way to facilitate mentoring alliances between juniors and seniors, the potential negative consequences limit its appeal. Similarly, while education has been demonstrated to increase knowledge about mentoring and the interpersonal skills and attitudes needed to build supportive relationships, unless the environment in an organization encourages back-at-home application of learnings, new skills will fade rapidly and frustration or resentment will develop. The organizational change approach—collaboration among relevant staff and line groups in diagnosing and planning appropriate education and structural changes that will remove obstacles to mentoring—appears to minimize the risk that efforts will have no impact or negative consequences and increase the likelihood that significant opportunities for mentoring will be created.

Recent efforts to understand the mentoring process have produced a new agenda for scholars working in the areas of adult development, career development, and the quality of work life. Now that it has been established that individuals at every career stage can benefit from developmental relationships, it seems essential to investigate what relationship constellations look like at successive career stages as well as the individual and organizational forces that shape their various forms. In addition, the complexities of cross-gender alliances demonstrate the need to also investigate the complexities of interracial alliances and to create strategies for overcoming obstacles created by demographic diversity. Finally, while a number of educational and organizational change strategies designed to improve the quality and availability of mentoring in organizations have been identified, their relative value and real impact remain to be assessed. There is still considerable uncertainty as to whether education can indeed increase interpersonal skills and modify fundamental attitudes or assumptions that shape behavior in relationships at work. And, while organizational interventions appear to have great potential in creating conditions that encourage an effective mentoring process, they have yet to be systematically monitored over time.

As a realistic view of mentoring has evolved, its appeal also has been strengthened. While it no longer can be seen as a panacea, it certainly offers a potentially significant developmental tool for individuals at every career stage and for organizations concerned with employee productivity and the quality of work life. It is now up to practicing managers, human resource specialists, and organizational researchers to continue the inquiry that promises to further enhance the quality of mentoring in the workplace.

References

Alderfer, C. P. "Change Processes in Organizations." In M. D. Dunnette (ed.), *Handbook of Industrial and Organizational Psychology*. Skokie, Ill.: Rand McNally, 1976.

Argyris, C. *Intervention Theory and Method: A Behavioral Science View*. Reading, Mass.: Addison-Wesley, 1970.

Baird, L., and Kram, K. E. "Career Dynamics: Managing the Superior-Subordinate Relationship." *Organizational Dynamics*, Summer 1983, pp. 46-64.

Baker-Miller, J. *Toward A New Psychology of Women*. Boston: Beacon Press, 1976.

Bass, B. M., and Vaughn, J. A. *Training in Industry: The Management of Learning*. Belmont, Calif.: Wadsworth, 1966.

Beckhard, R., and Harris, R. *Organizational Transitions*. Reading, Mass.: Addison-Wesley, 1977.

Beer, M. *Organizational Change and Development: A System View*. Santa Monica, Calif.: Goodyear, 1980.

Berlew, D. E., and Hall, D. T. "The Socialization of Managers: Effects of Expectations on Performance." *Administrative Science Quarterly*, 1966, *11*, 207-223.

Bowen, D. "Were Men Meant to Mentor Women?" *Training and Development Journal*, 1985, *39* (2), 31-34.

Clawson, J. G. *Superior-Subordinate Relationships for Managerial Development*. Unpublished doctoral dissertation, School of Business, Harvard University, 1979.

Clawson, J. G. "Mentoring in Managerial Careers." In C. B. Deer (ed.), *Work, Family, and the Career.* New York: Praeger, 1980.

Clawson, J. G., and Kram, K. E. "Managing Cross-Gender Mentoring." *Business Horizons,* May–June 1984, pp. 22–32.

Collins, E., and Scott, P. "Everyone Who Makes It Has A Mentor." *Harvard Business Review,* 1978, *56* (4), 89–101.

Crary, L. M. "The Intrapersonal Issues in Attraction at Work: Looking from Inside Out." Working paper, Department of Management, Bentley College, Waltham, Mass., 1985.

Dalton, G. W., Thompson, P. H., and Price, R. L. "The Four Stages of Professional Careers—A New Look at Performance by Professionals." *Organizational Dynamics,* 1977, *6,* 19–42.

Dalton, M. *Men Who Manage.* New York: Wiley, 1959.

Deal, T. E., and Kennedy, A. A. *Comparable Cultures: The Rites and Rituals of Corporate Life.* Reading, Mass: Addison-Wesley, 1982.

Digman, L. A. "How Well Managed Organizations Develop Through Executives." *Organizational Dynamics,* Autumn 1978, pp. 63–80.

Epstein, C. *Woman's Place: Options and Limits in Professional Careers.* Berkeley: University of California Press, 1970.

Erikson, E. H. *Identity, Youth, and Crisis.* New York: Norton, 1968.

Erikson, E. H. (ed.) *Adulthood.* New York: Norton, 1980.

Gould, R. *Transformations: Growth and Change in Adult Life.* New York: Simon & Schuster, 1978.

Hall, D. T. *Careers in Organization.* Santa Monica, Calif.: Goodyear, 1976.

Hall, D. T., and Kram, K. E. "Development in Midcareer." In D. H. Montross and C. J. Skinkman (eds.), *Career Development in the 80's.* Springfield, Ill.: Thomas, 1981.

Hall, J. "The Use of Instruments in Laboratory Training." *Training and Development Journal,* 1970, *24* (5), 48–55.

Hennig, M., and Jardim, A. *The Managerial Woman.* New York: Doubleday/Anchor Books, 1977.

Jacques, E. "Death and the Mid-Life Crisis." *International Journal of Psychoanalysis,* 1965, *46,* 502–514.

Jamison, K. "Managing Sexual Attraction in the Workplace." *Personnel Administrator,* 1983, *28* (8), 45–51.

Josefowitz, N. "Sexual Relationships at Work: Attraction, Transference, Coercion, or Strategy." *Personnel Administrator,* 1982, *27* (3), 91–96.

Kanter, R. M. *Men and Women of the Corporation.* New York: Basic Books, 1977.

Klauss, R. "Formalized Mentor Relationships for Management and Development Programs in the Federal Government." *Public Administration Review,* Mar. 1979, pp. 489–496.

Kram, K. E. "Creating Conditions that Encourage Mentoring in Organizations." *Enhancing Engineers' Careers,* Institute for Electrical and Electronic Engineers Catalog No. VH0158-6, Palo Alto, Calif.: 1983a.

Kram, K. E. "Phases of the Mentor Relationship." *Academy of Management Journal,* 1983b, *26* (4), 608–625.

Kram, K. E. *Mentoring at Work.* Glenview, Ill.: Scott, Foresman, 1985.

Kram, K. E., and Isabella, L. "Mentoring Alternatives: The Role of Peer Relationships in Career Development." *Academy of Management Journal,* 1985, *28* (1), 110–132.

Kram, K. E., and Jusela, G. "Anticipation and Realization: A Study of Retirement." Unpublished research report, Department of Administrative Sciences, Yale University, 1978.

Lean, E. "Cross-Gender Mentoring—Downright Upright and Good for Productivity." *Training and Development Journal,* 1983, *37* (5), 60–65.

Levinson, D. J., and others. *Seasons of a Man's Life.* New York: Knopf, 1978.

Levinson, H. *Psychological Man.* Cambridge, Mass.: Levinson Institute, 1976.

Lewis, A. D. "Developing Technical Careers in Large Corporations: Where Do the Responsibilities Rest?" Paper presented at Institute for Electrical and Electronic Engineers conference, Palo Alto, Calif., Oct. 1983.

Martin, P. Y., Harrison, D., and DiNitto, D. "Advancement for Women in Hierarchical Organizations: A Multilevel Analysis of Problems and Prospects." *Journal of Applied Behavioral Science,* 1983, *19* (1), 19–33.

Missirian, A. K. *The Corporate Connection: Why Executive Women Need Mentors to Reach the Top.* Englewood Cliffs, N.J.: Prentice-Hall, 1982.

Osherson, S. D. *Holding On or Letting Go.* New York: Free Press, 1980.

Peters, J., and Waterman, R., Jr. *In Search of Excellence.* New York: Harper & Row, 1982.

Phillips, L. L. "Women Finally Get Mentors of Their Own." *Business Week,* Oct. 23, 1978.

Phillips-Jones, L. *Mentors and Protégés.* New York: Arbor House, 1982.

Quinn, R. E. "Coping with Cupid: The Formation, Impact, and Management of Romantic Relationships in Organizations." *Administrative Science Quarterly,* 1977, *22,* 30–45.

Roche, G. R. "Much Ado About Mentors." *Harvard Business Review,* 1979, *57* (1).

Rowe, M. W. "Building Mentoring Frameworks for Women (and Men) as Part of an Effective Equal Opportunity Ecology." Working paper, M.I.T., Oct. 1980.

Sargent, A. (ed.) *Beyond Sex Roles.* St. Paul, Minn.: West, 1977.

Schein, E. H. *Career Dynamics: Matching Individual and Organizational Needs.* Reading, Mass.: Addison-Wesley, 1978.

Shapiro, E., Haseltine, F., and Rowe, M. "Moving Up: Role Models, Mentors, and the 'Patron System'." *Sloan Management Review,* Spring 1978, pp. 51–58.

Spelman, D., Crary, L. M., Kram, K. E., and Clawson, J. G. "Managing Male-Female Attraction at Work." In L. Moore (ed.), *Women in the Workplace.* Lexington, Mass.: Lexington Books, 1986.

Storr, A. *The Integrity of Personality.* New York: Atheneum, 1960.

Sullivan, H. S. *The Psychiatric Interview.* New York: Norton, 1954.

Thompson, P. "Learning from Subordinates." Working paper presented at meeting of the National Academy of Management, New York City, Aug. 1982.

Zalesnick, A., Dalton, G. W., and Burns, L. B. *Orientation and Conflict in Careers.* Cambridge, Mass.: Division of Research, Harvard University, 1970.

6

꧁꧁꧁꧁꧁꧁꧁꧁

Computer Applications in Career Development Planning

Frank J. Minor

Today's business environment, driven by changing technology, operating methods, and social forces, has created a need for organizations to enhance their career development programs. Changing technology and new business methods cause ongoing shifts in job duties, skill demands, and numbers of employees needed in different types of jobs within an organization. This information must be communicated to both employees and managers via the organization's career development programs to assure that employee career-planning, skills development, and job placement activities are responsive to and consistent with the organization's changing environment.

Note: I would like to acknowledge the contributions made to this chapter by organizations using or implementing computer-based systems to support their career development programs. Descriptions of their systems were contributed by Richard Bastian of the Cleveland Clinic Foundation, Barbara H. Feldman of Corning Glass Works, Sheila A. Pidgeon of Digital Equipment Corporation, Lila Norris of Educational Testing Service, and Dale N. Parisi of Merck & Company. I would also like to acknowledge the constructive suggestions of Professor Roger A. Myers of Teachers College, Columbia University, and JoAnn Bowlsbey of The Discover Center, American College Testing Program.

Social forces also have motivated organizations to improve their career development programs. For instance, in order to achieve equal employment opportunity and affirmative action goals, organizations are seeking ways to assist women and minority group members in identifying and examining career paths and requirements for their growth and development within the organization (Lancaster and Berne, 1981; Duval and Courtney, 1978). Another social force is the growing desire on the part of employees for information about the organization's job skill demands and career paths so that they can manage their career planning more effectively. This employee interest stems from a desire to plan for growth, reduce ambiguity, and satisfy their work values. The payoff to the individual is an opportunity for more satisfying work, increased dedication to a field of specialization, and greater involvement in one's career decision making. Formalizing an organization's career development program can do much to increase employee commitment, involvement, and satisfaction in the organization (Morgan, Hall, and Martier, 1979).

An internal organizational pressure has been created by the increasing number of midcareer employees competing for a fixed or shrinking number of management positions (Hall and Richter, 1984). This increase in the number of slow-growth or potentially plateaued employees is the result of the post-World War II baby boom, which, according to U.S. Bureau of Labor Statistics, will increase the population between the ages of thirty-five and forty-four by 42 percent between 1980 and 1990. Further curtailing the career mobility of this group are organizational trends to reduce the number of middle managers. In response to this problem, organizations are encouraging their midcareer employees to manage their own careers and providing them with career-planning information for exploring job options and skills development opportunities that can open new avenues and reduce the likelihood of plateauing and obsolescence (Hall and Richter, 1984; Bardwick, 1984).

Career development programs in organizations can be grouped into a variety of specific categories that reflect the nature of the service performed (Lancaster and Berne, 1981). Some of the more prevalent services are:

- Career planning in group workshops or seminars and individualized career counseling conducted by personnel staff, managers, and/or specialized counselors
- Career information services that provide employees with information about career paths in the organization, equal employment opportunity and affirmative action policies, educational assistance programs, training and development opportunities within and outside the organization, and the posting of job openings
- Personnel planning programs designed for employee placement planning, redeployment planning, identification of skills training needs, and management succession planning
- Special population programs and practices developed to support the unique career-planning needs of such groups as minorities, women, management trainees, preretirees, midcareer employees, and handicapped employees
- Assessment centers for the evaluation of employees' management potential and the identification of their career interests and their skill and experience development needs
- Training and development programs that assist both nonmanagers and managers in the acquisition of job-relevant core skills needed for growth and development within the organization (such as interpersonal communication skills, technical skills related to the company's business, and business-planning skills)

In a study of career development programs in organizations (Gutteridge and Otte, 1983), the techniques reportedly used by the majority of the organizations were career-planning seminars or workshops and individualized career counseling by staff counselors.

The career development services categorized in the preceding list can be grouped into two general types of career development programs: career-planning programs and career management programs (Leibowitz and Schlossberg, 1981; Storey, 1981). Career-planning programs are designed to help individual employees explore career development areas and make decisions about personal objectives and development plans. Career management programs are designed to help managers make more informed decisions about employees in regard to the organization's human resource needs. The areas of concern in career management programs include such activities as employee placement, identification of skills training needs, employee development, redeployment of employees to accommodate business demands, and management succession planning (see Chapter Two of this volume; see also Cloonan and Squires, 1981; Gutteridge and Otte, 1983; Sonnenfeld, 1984). Tables 1 and 2 summarize career-planning and career management activities and explore a typical allocation of these activities among employees, managers, and the organization.

These programs, although described separately, are interrelated and complementary. Ideally, the organization should strive to achieve a balance that accommodates both the needs of the individual and those of the organization (Leibowitz and Schlossberg, 1981). In attempting to satisfy the objectives of these two types of career development programs, organizations are finding it

Table 1. Summary of Career-Planning Activities.

Employee's responsibilities:
- Self-assess abilities, interests, and values
- Analyze career options
- Decide on development objectives and needs
- Communicate development preferences to manager
- Map out mutually agreeable action plans with manager
- Pursue agreed-upon action plan

Manager's responsibilities:
- Act as catalyst; sensitize employee to the development planning process
- Assess realism of employee's expressed objectives and perceived development needs
- Counsel employee and develop a mutually agreeable plan
- Follow up and update employee's plans as appropriate

Organization's responsibilities:
- Provide career-planning model, resources, counseling, and information needed for individualized career planning
- Provide training in career development planning to managers and employees and career counseling to managers
- Provide skills training programs and on-the-job development experience opportunities

Table 2. Career Management Activities.

Employees' responsibilities:

• Provide accurate information to management as needed regarding their skills, work experiences, interests, and career aspirations

Manager's responsibilities:

• Validate information provided by employees
• Provide information about vacant job positions for which the manager is responsible
• Use all information provided by the process to: (1) identify all viable candidates for a vacant position and make a selection and (2) identify career development opportunities (job openings, training programs, rotation assignments) for employees and place them accordingly

Organization's responsibilities:

• Provide information system and process to accommodate management's decision-making needs
• Organize and update all information
• Ensure effective usage of information by: (1) designing convenient methods for collecting, analyzing, interpreting, and using the information and (2) monitoring and evaluating the effectiveness of the process

---

helpful to use technological aids. The computer, in particular, is used to help manage the increasingly complex information-handling problems associated with the career development process: classifying, searching, comparing, integrating, summarizing, and updating facts about jobs, careers, training programs, and employees' personal attributes. This chapter describes two types of computer-based systems in which organizations are placing increasing reliance to support their career development programs. They are career-planning information systems (to support career-planning activities) and human resource information (HRI) systems (to support career management activities).

Career-planning information systems, designed to assist employees in the self-management of their careers, represent the most recent computer application to be implemented. This type of system is expected to become increasingly popular because a conversational information system is an excellent tool for supporting personalized career development planning. Also, access to computers by employees is becoming more common as a result of the use of microcomputers. HRI systems used by managers are much more commonplace in organizations than are career-planning information systems. They had their origin in personnel data base systems or skills inventory systems developed during the 1960s.

Career-Planning Information Systems

Computer-based systems to support career planning had their origins in high school and college settings and were designed for use by students. The first few systems to demonstrate usability and acceptance of the concept were: The Computerized Occupational Information System (Impellitteri, 1967), The Computerized Vocational Information System (CVIS) (Harris, 1969), the IBM Education and Career Exploration System (ECES) (Minor, Myers, and Super, 1969; Minor, 1970), and the Information System for Vocational Decisions (ISVD) (Tiedeman and others, 1967). These early systems were designed primarily to retrieve and summarize occupational and educational information based on comparisons of students' profiles with occupational and educational profiles. Super (1970) surveyed these systems and their implications for career counseling, and Myers and Cairo (1983) assembled an overview of computer-assisted counseling as experienced in schools, colleges, and universities. Shortly after their acceptance by educational institutions, extensions of these system concepts were proposed for use in business organizations and military settings (Harris-Bowlsbey, 1983; Minor, 1978, 1984; Myers, 1978). Currently, a number of organizations are using or implementing career-planning information systems for use by their employees. Several examples are described later in this chapter.

Purpose of Computer-Based Career-Planning Information Systems in Organizations

The overall purpose of an organization's career-planning information system is to support ongoing personal growth and development of its employees. The systems communicate job and career information in a form that readily enables employees to make comparisons between their personal attributes and jobs and to compare different jobs within the organization. Because of the types of information services provided in this application, these systems are designed to provide a personalized interactive conversation with the employee similar to that found in computer-aided instruction programs. The computer serves as an information management tool because of its ability to compare and summarize the numerous complex categories of information involved in the process. An information management tool is necessary because neither managers nor their subordinates are able to effectively search, link, and integrate all the subsets of information required for exploration and analysis of the detailed facts describing employees' attributes, jobs, and avenues of development. Organizations, in some cases, have developed their own computer software programs to provide career-planning services to their employees or have acquired commercially available software programs that can be customized or localized to meet their requirements.

A career-planning information system provides benefits to employees, managers of employees who use the system, and the organization. It gives employees greater control over the management of their careers and helps them identify realistic goals and plans and become aware of the variety of developmental avenues within the organization. The system gives managers a model for counseling their subordinates and relieves them of the responsibility of gathering and disseminating career information. Also, managers can communicate more effectively with employees about their objectives and plans because the employees are more prepared to deal with specific issues. For the organization, the system provides a standardized media for communicating to employees and managers information about the organization's skills demands, job content, and career paths.

Examples of Systems in Organizations

The experiences of several organizations currently using or implementing career-planning information systems are described next:

IBM Corporation. The National Service Division of the IBM Corporation has developed for use by its employees a computer-based system to support the organization's existing employee development process. The system was designed by Minor (1984) of IBM as an information aid or tool to help employees plan and manage their careers and personal growth within IBM. It is called the Employee Development Planning System (EDPS) and was developed for use by employees at all levels: nonexempt employees, exempt professionals, and managers. It supports IBM's existing employee development program and practices. EDPS does not replace or change any of the IBM employee development procedures or roles of employees and managers. The employees' role in career planning is to formulate and communicate their career objectives and perceived development needs to their managers. The managers' role is to assess and counsel their employees with respect to their goals and plans. Action plans are jointly formulated and implemented.

The functional objective of EDPS is to help employees define career development objectives and goals that are consistent with their personal attributes and IBM's career paths. It helps them recognize their potential and the wide range of development avenues by which they can realize their potential. Finally, it assists them in defining self-improvement needs and action plans for achieving desired objectives.

EDPS is organized into five general sections: *Section 1, orientation and planning readiness assessment:* In this section, employees receive an explanation of the system objectives and operating procedures and an inventory of items with which they assess their readiness for career decision making. Implications of their inventoried readiness are reviewed by means of an individualized interactive dialogue. *Section 2, employee self-assessment:* The employees create a self-description profile based on their work-related interests, abilities, skills, and desired in-depth work experiences. *Section 3, system job search:* The system permits searches through a file of generic job types that exist within the organization in order to identify those with profiles compatible with the employees' self-described profiles. A list of these job types is displayed to the employee. *Section 4, employee analyzes jobs of interest:* The employees select from a list of displayed job types those about which they would like to learn. While analyzing a job type, employees can express their likes and dislikes about various job features. Based on the employees' reactions in combination with their planning readiness scores, personalized messages are displayed to the employees. The messages describe potential planning problems, consistencies and inconsistencies in the employees' response patterns to the job types analyzed. The employees are not limited to analyzing jobs in their list but can analyze any job type contained in the system. *Section 5, summarizing personal development needs:* After the employees have analyzed all job types of potential interest to them, the system helps them summarize their development needs. The summary reflects the employees' perceptions of how well their current skills and work experiences support the potential objectives they identified while using the system. The system organizes this information into a table useful for planning self-improvement activities.

The system enables employees to skip or return to selected modules. At critical checkpoints, the system automatically prints summary reports for the employees, which can be used for review with their managers and as a personal record of their activities with the system. The employees review with their managers their views, ideas, and preferences about goals, plans, and needs based on their experience with the system.

Before making EDPS available to all employees in the IBM National Service Division, it was decided that a pilot test would be conducted and that the system design and user procedures would be reviewed on the basis of the test results. The system thus was made available to employees in a variety of occupations at selected sites across the country. Workshops were conducted at each site to introduce managers and employees to the system. The system was introduced as an information tool and an adjunct to IBM's present employee development planning program, practices, and materials. Employees were advised that the system was to be used on a voluntary basis during normal work hours. A one-year pilot test was concluded late in 1985.

A test plan was designed to evaluate EDPS in terms of its usefulness and impact on employees and their managers. The criteria for assessing EDPS for use by employees included opinions regarding the system's usefulness, changes in the employees' choice of career development objectives, changes in their level of expectation of achieving objectives, and satisfaction with their personal career development plans. Criteria for managerial assessment of the system included evaluation of the system's usefulness to employees, opinions regarding change in the realism of employees' expressed career development objectives, and the managers' desire to keep the system for continued use by their employees.

Additional data collected included measures of the amount of time invested by employees in system use and human factor problems experienced. While these data were collected on-line after each use period, overall measures of system usefulness and its impact on career planning allowed sufficient time for career-planning discussions between the employee and his or her manager, as well as time for initiating the implementation of plans. Follow-up studies of system users are planned.

Several hundred employees representing a cross-section of exempt professionals and nonexempt employees responded to both a presystem and a postsystem use questionnaire. Almost all of the employees rated the system as being highly useful to their career development planning on several criteria. Table 3 presents a list of the criteria referenced. Shortly after using the system, a majority of the employees reported that the system influenced decisions about their development action plans. Most of the remaining employees reported that the system had helped them confirm or validate previously established plans. Comparisons between employees' responses before and after using the system showed no increase in the percentage of employees selecting promotion as their next career objective or in employees' expectations of being promoted. This finding suggests that the system does not act as a catalyst for raising employees' desires or expectations for promotion. It is important that a career planning aid not raise employees' expectation for advancement that cannot be achieved within the organization, since this would be a source of frustration to employees.

Additional comparisons show that after using the system employees demonstrated statistically significant increases in their:

Table 3. Employees' Opinions of System Usefulness.

Criteria of usefulness

1. Provides useful information about different job types
2. Introduces employees to new job types
3. Identifies types of work experiences and training development needed to meet specific objectives
4. Prepares employees for planning discussions with managers
5. Improves self-assessment of skills, abilities, and interests
6. Helps employees become more specific about development plans
7. Helps employees plan further ahead
8. Provides more systematic approach to career development planning
9. Helps employees assume more self-control of career development
10. Provides flexibility in development plans

- satisfaction with their ability to manage their own career development
- satisfaction with their current development goals and plans
- satisfaction with their perceptions about opportunities for a "better" job
- ability to plan for the future with more certainty
- satisfaction with the information needed for personalized career development planning
- perception of management's commitment to employees' career development
- satisfaction with the helpfulness of the organization's career development process

Correlations based on employees' opinions after using the system show that the more favorably the employees perceive the organization's career development program, their managers' commitment to their career development, their ability to manage their own careers, and their satisfaction with their career goals and plans, the greater is their commitment to the organization and their satisfaction with their present job and the more strongly they focus their career development plans within the organization. These correlations were all highly significant.

These pilot test results demonstrate that EDPS, as perceived by employees, makes a positive contribution to the organization's employee development planning program and that effective employee development improves employee attitudes and commitment to the organization.

Managers of employees who used EDPS were surveyed to ascertain their reactions to the system. The managers were asked to rate the usefulness of the system for their employees. (The managers' opinions are important because they are their employees' career counselors and participants in the formulation and implementation of their development plans.) As was the case with employees, almost all of the managers rated EDPS as being highly useful to their employees on the career development planning criteria listed in Table 3.

When asked about the realism of their employees' development objectives and plans after using the system, a majority of the managers reported their employees as being more realistic, and the remainder indicated that their employees' original plans had been realistic and the system had sustained that realism. The managers participating in the pilot test expressed the desire to keep the EDPS system on an ongoing basis for use by their employees, and most of them wanted to have the system available for their own management development planning. Following the pilot test phase, EDPS was implemented for use by employees.

A number of other organizations are implementing, testing, or operating career planning information systems. Descriptions of plans, activities, and experiences with such systems were written and provided to the author for publication in this chapter by the Cleveland Clinic Foundation, Corning Glass Works, Digital Equipment Corporation, and the Educational Testing Service. The descriptions are presented below as authored and submitted by these organizations. A comparison of their activities shows variations in their implementation approaches that are based on the needs of each organization.

The Cleveland Clinic Foundation. The Cleveland Clinic Foundation (CCF) is a physician-managed group practice that provides medical care supported by innovative research and graduate medical education. The CCF reported that it is implementing a computer-based career-planning information system (Richard Bastian, personal communication, April 1985).

The foundation employs approximately 7,500 individuals. It has doubled in size over the past ten years and is currently engaged in an ambitious expansion program promising new employment opportunities. This demands that the organization carefully manage the design of its career development program so that it is responsive to both the organization's needs and the unique interests of its individual members.

The foundation reported that its rationale for implementing a computer-based career development and planning system was fourfold. First, the software package selected, which is a commercially available program, matches recently defined foundation career development philosophy and values emphasizing personal responsibility for managing one's own career decisions. Second, it provides a structure for integrating and optimizing numerous other career development resources available to employees via existing human resource systems. Third, such a program represents an innovation consistent with CCF's reputation for state-of-the-art advancements in medical care. And, finally, the system is capable of being customized or "localized" specifically to accommodate CCF's career path environment.

The sequence of events, described by CCF, leading to a computer-based career-planning information system followed an evolutionary process. Prior to 1981, employees relied on an internal job-posting system, education assistance funds, career advice from their managers, personal mentors, and human resource professionals for information on jobs and how to get them. In 1982, the CCF made its first review of computer-based career planning. The foundation next conducted a needs analysis to identify CCF values with regard to career development. The conclusion of the analysis was that pursuit of career is best managed by individual employees with the foundation providing information and educational resources to assist them in making their own well-informed decisions.

As a result of this needs analysis, a career development advisory committee was created. The mission of this group was to build, coordinate, and monitor organization support for career development efforts at CCF. This group served as a focal point for piloting a computer-based career-planning system for the organization. Over seventy managers, employees, and human resource professionals were invited to pilot a prototype version of the system and asked to provide feedback as to its utility for CCF. This group provided feedback and recommendations on every aspect of the program from graphics to structure and philosophy.

The system emphasizes the individual, who is primarily responsible for making choices relative to his or her career. It includes training in career dynamics and provides a continuum of self-assessment, information-gathering, action-planning, and goal-setting logic to assist users in making their own career decisions. The system provides a comprehensive set of management reports, which promises to yield data on a variety of scales useful for planning human resource development support activities.

CCF reported that it acquired the generic system in early 1984 and spent eighteen months resolving system design issues and piloting the system. (At present, employees are required to use the system on their own time as a way of reinforcing the principle that one should take personal responsibility for one's career.) The remainder of 1985 was used to implement the system and announce its availability to employees at CCF, generate employee usage and verify plans to localize the system's information files to meet specific CCF needs. A localization plan is based on feedback provided from the earlier pilot participants. This localization includes CCF job descriptions, organization charts, equal employment opportunity categories, career-related policies, skills-training resources, and so on.

CCF reported several key observations based on implementation experiences to date and on conversations with other organizations that are also implementing computer-assisted career-planning systems. For example, active involvement of managers and employees in system design and implementation is critical to system validity and acceptance. Extensive pilot testing helped managers learn that the system would reinforce realistic employee career planning and support managers in their supervisory roles as career counselors and mentors. Employees have learned that career development involves more than the pursuit of the next job; it requires a studied approach to self-assessment and actively identifying opportunities. Some of the most satisfied users are those who find relief from peer-imposed guilt about lacking ambition to be upwardly mobile. They learn that their satisfaction with their current job is legitimate, yet they can apply the goal-setting/action-planning model to other spheres of interest to them.

However, some of the more dissatisfied users are disappointed to find that the system merely confirms their former or self-derived current aspirations. The system does not provide clear, no-risk alternative career directions to those that might be seeking them. But it does provide a structure useful to employees who wish to identify and develop new opportunities of their own choosing.

CCF also concluded that a computer-assisted system in the CCF cannot function effectively as an independent service. Though one of CCF's objectives is to reduce the amount of time spent by human resource professionals in responding to individual career issues, it seems that employees will still require mentors or sponsors to provide individual support. The CCF system is best at helping create a framework for employees to direct their information needs to the right source at the right time and to educate and support managers by providing a structure for responding to expressed employee career needs. With increasing experience and customizing of the system, CCF reports, its use will become linked with other human resource development practices within the organization.

Corning Glass Works. Corning Glass Works (CGW) reports that it is in the process of implementing a Career Planning and Information System in support of a career development program for approximately 1,400 nonexempt employees at the company's corporate headquarters in Corning, New York (Barbara H. Feldman, personal communication, April 1985). The overall system consists of a computer-based career-planning software package, information videotapes, resource materials, and supervisory training. The decision to initiate a career development program was based on the results of a company-wide climate survey conducted in 1984-1985. The results indicated that a major concern of nonexempt and exempt employees was a lack of information with which to plan their careers. To respond to this need, the corporate human resource department developed the Career Planning and Information System. The nonexempt employees at the corporate headquarters were targeted as the Phase I users of the implemented system. The objective of the initial system is to provide nonexempt employees and their supervisors with information, tools, and skills to facilitate the identification of career goals and development plans congruent with CGW opportunities and needs. CGW established three criteria in designing the system: The system should highlight the employee's and supervisor's role in the career-planning process, promote the development of realistic career goals, and be integrated with the existing employee appraisal and development process.

Prior to selecting a computer-based solution, CGW considered a variety of alternative methods to support its career development program. The primary consideration in choosing a method was that it be independent and available to employees at their convenience. CGW initially proposed developing a set of videotapes with a workbook for employees to complete independently at their own discretion. This proposal was rejected because of management's concern that the potential ambiguity and lack of closure for employees could cause frustration and would place an undue burden for assistance and support on CGW human resource representatives. In addition, it would not reinforce the supervisor's role in the career-planning process.

In lieu of a videotape and workbook solution, the CGW human resource department selected a commercially available generic career-planning software system that could be customized by adding CGW job and career path descriptions. The system provided the structure and disciplined approach to career planning sought by CGW, yet it provided the flexibility for employees to meet their unique needs. Through interactive sessions, the system can help employees assess their skills, values, and interests, identify compatible opportunities with the CGW corporate framework, set multiple career goals, and develop career action plans at their own pace. A steering committee consisting of company-wide human resource representatives along with a group of managers and nonexempt employees determined what changes should be made in the existing software and what additional information or support was needed for an effective career development program. Customizing was accomplished by adding CGW job titles, job descriptions, and employee development policies and procedures. Based on recommendations from the committee, other components were developed by CGW and added to the overall process as follows:

1. Three videotapes were developed to provide more data specific
    to CGW. The first videotape explains the career-planning
    process at CGW and the tools available to help. The second
    videotape identifies the different functional work areas and
    how a selected number of employees have moved within and
    between these areas during their careers. The third videotape
    explains how the employees can use their career-planning
    system information in conjunction with their performance
    appraisal in the development process and how it links to
    CGW's placement process.
2. Career information books containing CGW data on positions,
    salary grades, skills requirements, and sample career paths and
    statistics on career movement were developed.
3. A one-day supervisory training course was developed that helps
    managers link the career development process to the CGW
    performance appraisal and the career-planning system. This
    training enhances managers' skills needed for effective
    appraisal of subordinates' performance and career development
    counseling.

After the software customization and development of the
materials and training was completed, a pilot project was initiated
to further evaluate and test the entire process and its components.
A cross section of managers and nonexempt employees was chosen
to participate in the use of the Career Planning and Information
System. The pilot evaluation resulted in minor changes to both the
software and written materials. Although the system was developed
at the corporate level, it will be implemented and managed on a
decentralized basis. The use of the system by employees is voluntary
and confidential. CGW's philosophy is to link the Career Planning
and Information System to its current performance appraisal and
development system to assure its integration into existing human
resource processes.

The benefits that CGW anticipates from employee use of the
Career Planning and Information System when fully implemented
include:

- Better understanding by employees and supervisors of their roles and responsibilities in the career-planning process
- Greater awareness of employees and supervisors of CGW nonexempt career opportunities and the process for preparing for candidacy for those opportunities
- More realistic career plans developed by nonexempt employees
- More consistent dissemination of career information within CGW's decentralized environment
- Improved quality of job information channeled into the placement process
- Improved satisfaction with career development planning and growth by nonexempt employees
- Improved skill development and utilization of the nonexempt work force

When the system is implemented, CGW plans an evaluation phase. Available within the system is an on-line administrative management report that provides data on employees' use and opinions of system usefulness. Additional data will be collected by CGW via questionnaires and feedback meetings with employees and supervisors to assess benefits and changes needed. CGW reported that a more conclusive assessment of the system's impact on the organization's career development program, however, will be conducted when the CGW company-wide climate survey is readministered in two to three years. After the initial experience with the system, CGW states that it will investigate the feasibility of expanding and modifying the Career Planning and Information System to accommodate all salaried employees.

Digital Equipment Corporation. Digital Equipment Corporation (DEC) is piloting a computerized career-planning system. It is one approach to meeting the challenge of improved work force utilization while at the same time maintaining Digital's "bottoms-up" organizational culture, which it values highly (Sheila A. Pidgeon, personal communication, April 1985). Digital's decentralized structure often makes it difficult for employees to "know the territory": the range of work opportunities outside their own function; the knowledge, experience, and education requirements of different jobs; the transferability of employee skills to other jobs; future work force skill/knowledge requirements.

To increase cross-functional mobility, DEC is introducing, on a pilot basis, a computer-based career-planning system developed by customizing a commercially available generic software system, which DEC has named System-Wide Career Awareness Network (DECscan). Customization is being accomplished through modifications in the system software functions and the addition of descriptions of Digital's jobs, educational resources, and policies and a corporate orientation module.

The goal of DECscan is to provide the information necessary to optimize the match between individual employee needs for career growth and Digital's need for a work force with the skills necessary to meet its changing business requirements. The emphasis is on providing the kind of information that supports career self-management and enhances the employee-manager career-development planning discussions.

DECscan, when completed, will ideally be linked to the organization's existing human resource information systems in order to address the following objectives:

1. Matching the self-assessment profiles of employees who use DECscan with DEC's employment data base containing qualification profiles for vacant positions. (This matching process would produce a list of potential positions for these employees.)
2. Advising the employees of DEC's available training and development resources and opportunities that are compatible with their development objectives.
3. Enabling the employees to browse through DEC's existing open job-posting system—that is, a listing of job vacancies.
4. Creating an employee talent file for management use. The file would include employees' self-descriptions of skills, experience, and job interests. The talent file could be used by management to search for applicants with specified profiles of ability or accomplishment.

DEC initially plans to make the system available to employees through career centers that provide professional career-counseling services. Employees' career development plans, however, would be jointly worked out by the employees with their managers.

The task of collecting current, valid position descriptions and translating them into the competency-based language that best supports self-assessment, development planning, and mobility is proving to be the greatest challenge in implementing DECscan. DEC reported that a valuable by-product of the effort, however, has been the increased integration among the organization's personnel disciplines of employment, compensation, benefits, and employee development. The integration of these disciplines is the result of their sharing the same conceptual model and a common language to describe jobs and job skill demands.

The Educational Testing Service. The Educational Testing Service (ETS) has developed a new computerized career-planning information system called System for Interactive Guidance and Information Plus (SIGI PLUS) (Lila Norris, personal communication, April 1985). Building on the strengths of SIGI, a career-planning information system for college students (Katz, 1974), SIGI PLUS extends its audience from college level to the general population of adults. SIGI PLUS helps users evalute their values, interests, skills, and education and apply these self-assessed personal attributes to their career planning. It addresses users' concerns about preparing to enter a new job or occupation, as well as concerns about advancing in their presently held job.

ETS reported that it is now pilot testing a customized version for use by its employees. This version contains information about jobs at ETS. An evaluation of the usefulness of SIGI PLUS at ETS will cover four major areas: (1) Summary data will be collected describing system usage. (2) Reactions of employees will be collected through a questionnaire and interviews with employee users. (3) The ETS personnel function will track job and career action steps undertaken by employees as a result of using the system. (4) The impact of the system on employee counseling services at ETS will be assessed.

Implementation Issues that Influence System Success

Organizations that already have or are in the process of implementing a career-planning information system have had to resolve questions or problems associated with a variety of issues. Some of these issues are described as follows:

Accuracy of the Job and Career Description Data. The validity of a career-planning information system is dependent upon the accuracy of the job and career path information stored in the system. Managers of the jobs to be described can serve as accurate and economical sources for the system's job descriptions. While an organization's wage and salary position descriptions are an alternative information source, the information content is sometimes lacking in facts needed for individualized career development planning.

Design of Employee Self-Description Inventories. Inventories must be designed by which employees can create their self-description profiles. The profiles are used by the system to identify job types that are compatible with the employees' profiles and provide them with personalized feedback. The inventories used in the earlier described systems draw upon a variety of concepts dealing with work related interests as described by Holland (1973) and Prediger (1976, 1981, 1982), work values as described by Super (1982) and Katz (1969), skills and satisfaction with one's present job as described by Harris-Bowlsbey (1985).

Human Factor Testing of Early Versions of the System. To increase the likelihood that a career-planning information system will provide line managers and their employees with a tool that both will find useful, members of both groups should participate in user trials with prototype versions of the system. Their mission should be to judge system usefulness, identify potential problems in the design of information content and user procedures, and anticipate the system's impact on development planning activities. Managers should advise how best to introduce the system to their employees to assure compatibility with existing management practices. System modifications should be made based on the feedback provided by both managers and nonmanagers during these prototype user trials.

Linking Systems to Established Personnel Programs. A career-planning information system can only be effective if it is linked to the organization's existing human resource planning and development activities currently in place. The linkage methods varied among the organizational career-planning systems described earlier in this chapter. Examples of activities and programs to which career-planning information systems are linked include: the organization's career-planning workshops, workbooks, and career-counseling services, the development planning sessions between employees and their managers, the management development training modules that train managers to be career counselors for their subordinates, employee performance appraisal programs, human resource planning activities, job-posting systems, and employee skills or talent inventory systems for the identification of candidates for vacant positions.

Management Training. Managers must be prepared to counsel and answer questions from employees who use a career-planning information system. Practical experience has demonstrated that managers are more receptive to and proficient in performing such responsibilities following participation in a workshop in which they actually use the system.

Information Entry and Updating. Of critical importance is the method of entering and updating the system information describing the organization's jobs and career paths. System-updating software is needed to allow for selective editing of a job or career description and the addition and deletion of entire descriptions.

Awareness of Potential Problem Areas. A common concern of management is that a career-planning information system can create unrealistic expectations and raise frustrations when these expectations are not satisfied. Research has shown that persons who develop new skills and aspirations expect to be rewarded with growth opportunities (Hall, 1976). Employees, however, often define a growth opportunity or development objective not as consisting of a promotion, a salary increase, a status or responsibility increase, but as a job that offers an opportunity to learn new skills, acquire new experiences and challenges, and develop new career options (Hall, 1983). Such opportunities are common in many organizations today because of frequently changing technology and the introduction of new business methods that lead to new jobs and new career paths. In addition, organizations can create more opportunities for promotion, growth, and reward by adding new job levels within a career path structure, as proposed by Hall and Richter (1984). To avoid unrealistic expectations, a system should be designed to communicate to the employee the interim job steps and work experiences needed to qualify as a candidate for a desired type of job or career path. The employees' immediate managers should also assume the responsibility for testing the reality of their employees' aspirations and counseling them accordingly.

An additional concern is that an improperly designed career-planning program or system can cause employees to perceive a disparity between their personal goals and the goals proposed or designed for them by the organization. Such perceived mismatches can lead to employee dissatisfaction and reduced commitment to the organization (Granrose and Portwood, 1984). This finding suggests that a system should be designed to introduce employees to a wide range of job and career options, thereby increasing the likelihood of discovering new potential matches. An employee furthermore should be encouraged to identify development objectives compatible with a self-description profile based on expected self-improvement ("What if I had these skills or work experiences?").

System Pilot Test and Start-Up: To increase the likelihood of long-range success, career-planning information systems are best introduced for use in the organization using a pilot test phase to identify design features, user procedures, and support materials needing improvement. The introduction must include top-down management support and acceptance. Employee use of the system should be voluntary, and the system should be introduced as an adjunct information tool to support existing employee career development programs and philosophies.

Human Resource Information Systems

Another type of computer-based aid to support career development in organizations is the human resource information

(HRI) system. The HRI systems are designed to help managers make more informed decisions about the development and utilization of their work force for the purpose of satisfying organizational needs (as contrasted with the career planning information systems, which focus on the individual's needs) (Leibowitz and Schlossberg, 1981). The basic component of an HRI system is an employee data file describing each employee in terms of his or her position type, job level, past work experiences, skills, performance appraisals, potential for higher-level positions, educational background, career objectives, and skills development needs. In some applications, an HRI system may include another data file that describes jobs in the organization in terms of level, prerequisite entry jobs, follow-on jobs, preferred employee qualifications, job locations, and positions currently vacant. HRI systems and career-planning systems can and should complement each other. For example, the employees' goals and personal development activities that result from their use of a career-planning system should be used as data input to the employee profiles stored in the HRI systems (Gutteridge and Otte, 1983). The objectives of some of the major types of applications, which draw upon HRI system data files to support career development programs in organizations, are described as follows:

Staffing or Placement

The most common application for HRI systems is the search for and identification of candidates in the organization who possess a profile of personal attributes needed to fill a vacant position. In the past, such applications generally have been referred to as skills inventories (Gutteridge and Otte, 1983; Sonnenfeld, 1984; Walker, 1982). The skills inventory application is becoming increasingly important to organizations as new types of knowledge workers are demanded as a result of changing technology. Ideally designed and used, the HRI system should help managers identify employee candidates who have the greatest likelihood of performing effectively in the positions to be filled and the potential to handle future jobs to which they might later be promoted.

If a vacant position is to be filled, the manager responsible for the position would enter preferred employee qualifications into the HRI system, and the system would respond by producing a candidate list for the manager to consider. The manager then would contact the managers of the most attractive candidates for additional information needed to screen the candidates. An alternative situation is one in which a manager of an employee is interested in placing the employee in a new job in accordance with the employee's career development plan. In this case, the manager would search a job file to identify positions that offer the developmental experiences prescribed in the employee's development plan.

Systems of this type first were adopted in the 1960s, but they fell into a period of disuse because the system vocabularies designed to describe employees' profiles were unreliable—that is, different managers would have different interpretations for the skill words used in the system (Walker, 1981). In addition, the interactive procedures and conversational dialogue required to use the systems, sometimes referred to as "userware," were inconvenient, caused user errors that were difficult to correct, and in general were not user friendly (LaPointe, 1982). In other words, the earlier systems did not consider human factor engineering criteria. To be user acceptable, HRI systems must enable managers to enter search terms conveniently and to receive output messages in a vocabulary that is compatible with their own terminology as well as the system's software. On an ad hoc basis, a manager should be able to reshape the system's output candidate list or job list by asking "what if" questions of the system (for example: "How would the candidate list be reduced if I choose to eliminate candidates who experienced a job transfer during the last eighteen months?") (LaPointe, 1982).

Several organizations have published descriptions of their HRI systems used for staffing or placement applications. For example, Citibank implemented a candidate-job matching system called Jobmatch for use with its nonprofessional employees (Sheibar, 1979). The advantages of the system as cited by Citibank were that it: (1) provided mobility for current employees, (2) provided a discipline for data records to describe job requirements and candidate work experiences, and (3) identified potentially available candidates to fill current job requisitions. There were two types of files in Jobmatch, one containing employee profiles and the other containing job requisition profiles.

Citibank made several assumptions regarding the most valid sources for the information to be stored in the HRI system: First, the supervisor submitting a requisition for a vacant job is the best source of information about the job tasks and employee qualifications needed. Second, the objectivity of the job requisition descriptions prepared by supervisors is superior if based on a vocabulary using employee task activity demands rather than experience and education needs. Citibank also assumed that the employee candidates were the best source of information regarding the tasks they were qualified to perform; consequently, the employees should prepare their own task proficiency profiles to be stored in the Jobmatch system. Validation of the system input data and output results was performed by the Citibank personnel department. Citibank reported that its experiences with Jobmatch supported its validity and usefulness.

Dunn & Bradstreet described its Computerized Management Inventory System (CMIS) as a successful skills inventory system (Dunn, 1982). As in the Citibank system, the employees' profiles stored in the system are based not on skills but on discernible employee tasks. The CMIS was designed to facilitate the transfer of managers among Dunn & Bradstreet's various operating units.

The RCA Corporation reported the implementation and evaluation of an extensive HRI system to support human resource decision making by managers (Edelman, 1982). An evaluation that extended over a period of several years indicated not only acceptance and improved quality of personnel operations but also a labor cost reduction in accomplishing the information-handling process.

Employee Development

Some organizations store employee skills profiles and career-planning data in their HRI systems in order to link employee skills development needs data to available training and development activity opportunities. For example, Merck & Company uses its system to provide developmental feedback, counseling, and training to its exempt employees to ensure that all employees sustain their growth in work-related skills areas (D. N. Parisi, personal communication, April 1985). Disneyland has computerized its employee data files describing employees' work experience, equal employment opportunity category, current job and experiences, desired career interests, and relocation preferences (see Chapter Two). When a job opening occurs, Disneyland draws upon its employee data files to identify candidates who can ideally benefit from the development experiences provided by the job.

Succession Planning

Top and middle management represent the human resource talent and expertise on which the company's future success depends. It is critical that the company identify, develop, train, utilize, and appraise this resource on a continuing basis to ensure the availability of the correct number and quality of managers to meet future organizational goals. HRI systems are being used to support this process by assisting in the identification and placement of managerial talent into positions providing appropriate career development experiences. The basic objective is to ensure that the organization always has the right number of managers in each type of skill position in its management progression networks. In organizations with a large number of management positions, this can only be practically managed with an HRI system that can also identify the appropriate number of managers needed in each area of specialty at each grade level. For the organization, a systematic tracking of management needs should result in an economy in training, development assignments, and identification of manage-rial or executive candidates. For the individual manager, the HRI succession planning system provides personalized career develop-ment planning information: Using such a system, managers can more clearly visualize how to achieve their career goals and the technical or business experience they need (Cory, Medland, and Uhlaner, 1977).

Several organizations that have implemented management succession planning systems have reported their experiences. For example, the Tenneco Company reports several immediate benefits of its computerized succession-planning system (Norton, 1985b). The system fills in information gaps and allows the organization to perform proactive rather than reactive planning, and it can identify the next planned position and date of movement for each executive. According to Norton's report, information maintenance using a refined system for input of all data codes and titles is a major factor in operating a successful system. Northern Telecom reports that its succession-planning system has changed the logic of its planning (Norton, 1985a). Previously, the organization evaluated managers' readiness for progression, but without the benefit of readiness and replacement dates. Its present computer-based progression system provides this information and enables management to detect potential blockages and gaps in management succession, quickly determine who is a candidate for what position, and note the occurrence of duplicate candidates.

Conclusion

This chapter shows several trends taking place in career development programs in organizations. One trend is the introduction of computer-based career-planning information systems for use by employees. These systems provide employees with increased responsibility for the management of their own development and growth within the organization.

The trend is explained by several factors. First, organization management recognizes that a career development philosophy emphasizing employee participation coupled with a powerful information management tool, such as the computer, increases the likelihood that both the organization's changing human resource needs and the individual employee's needs and aspirations will be satisfied. To some extent, this is due to ongoing changes in the job and career environment in many industries resulting from technological change and the introduction of new business methods. In such a dynamic environment, managers are finding it increasingly difficult to perform the personalized information-handling tasks associated with individualized development planning for their employees. A computer-based career-planning information system is a very viable solution. Of greater importance

is management's growing awareness that there is a positive
relationship between the extent to which employees are empowered
to manage their career development and their satisfaction with and
commitment to both their jobs and the organization. Of interest is
the reported enthusiastic cooperation between an organization's
personnel functions and managers and employees participating in
the implementation of an organization's career-planning information system.

A second trend is a movement toward the integration of the
organization's human resource information system—with their
career-planning information system. Integration will help ensure
data reliability and consistency of career development program
services.

A review of the current state-of-the-technological-art of
computer-assisted career development planning indicates a
potential for significant improvements. Microprocessor technology
has already made the concept of individualized career exploration
and planning viable in terms of cost and accessibility to computers. Microcomputers do, however, lack the information-up-
dating capabilities available in a mainframe system with remote
terminals.

A second area of technology that can improve the quality of
the information presented to the system user in the future is the
videodisc. The videodisc not only offers the ability to provide
pictorial information as a vehicle to describe jobs but, in
conjunction with the computer, it can provide the employee with
illustrative problem-solving situations or work samples that can
more accurately communicate the nature of the work. In a work
sample, the employee plays the role of a person in the job of interest
and is confronted with simulated on-the-job problems which
he or she must attempt to resolve. Since the employees are
not expected to be able to solve the problems, the system prompts
them through the problem solution much as in computer-aided
instruction. The work sample therefore is a learning experience
about the job rather than a knowledge test (Krumboltz and
Bergland, 1969; Minor, 1970). Still another area in which the
designers of career-planning and HRI systems seek more flexibility
is their choice of the software that drives the interactive dialogue

between the user and the system. Tiedeman (1983) proposed a set of system functions to make computer information files more flexible for the user during the career-planning and decision-making process. They include the user's ability to create and insert new items, establish hierarchies, cross-reference, transform meaning of terms, and discard unwanted information. According to Tiedeman, the objective is to have the information "you want when you want it and in the forms in which it is needed" for effective career development planning.

Organizations will continue to improve their career development programs in order to satisfy the needs of the organizations and their employees. This will be accomplished by the introduction of more disciplined and structured programs, the communication of career planning information and the empowering of employees with the means for actively managing their careers. The computer has proved a useful tool to support these activities.

References

Bardwick, J. M. "When Ambition Is No Asset." *New Management*, 1984, *1* (4), 22–28.

Cloonan, J. J., and Squires, H. F. "Job Analysis: Key to Integrated Human Resource System." In D. H. Montross and C. J. Shinkman (eds.), *Career Development in the 1980s*. Springfield, Ill.: Thomas, 1981.

Cory, B. H., Medland, F. F., and Uhlaner, J. E. "Developing a Research-Based System for Manpower Management and Career Progression in the U.S. Army Officer Corps." Paper presented at conference on manpower planning and organizational design of NATO Special Programs Panel on Human Factors and on System Sciences, Stesa, Italy, June 1977.

Dunn, B. D. "The Skills Inventory: A Second Generation." *Personnel*, 1982, *59* (5), 40–44.

Duval, B. A., and Courtney, R. S. "Upward Mobility: The GF Way of Opening Advancement Opportunities." *Personnel*, 1978, *55*, 43–53.

Edelman, F. "Managers, Computer Systems and Productivity." *Interfaces*, 1982, *12*, 36–46.

Ference, T. P., Stoner, J. A. F., and Warren, E. K. "Managing the Career Plateau." *Academy of Management Review*, 1977, *2*, 602–612.

Granrose, C. S., and Portwood, J. D. *A Model of Individual Career Strategies—Understanding the Organization's Impact*. Paper presented at the Careers Division of the 44th annual meeting of the Academy of Management, Boston, Aug. 1984.

Gutteridge, T. G., and Otte, F. L. *Organizational Career Development: State of the Practice*. Washington, D.C.: American Society for Training and Development, 1983.

Hall, D. T. *Careers in Organizations*. Glenview, Ill.: Scott, Foresman, 1976.

Hall, D. T. "Career Development Workshop: The 31st Annual Industrial and Organizational Psychology Workshops, Division 14." Paper presented at the 91st meeting of the American Psychological Association, Anaheim, Calif., Aug. 1983.

Hall, D. T., and Richter, J. "The Baby Boom in Midcareer." *The Career Center Bulletin*, 1984, *4* (3), 15–16.

Harris, J. A. "The Computerization of Vocational Information." *Vocational Guidance Quarterly*, 1969, *17*, 12–20.

Harris-Bowlsbey, J. "Discover: A Computer-Based Career Development System for Organizations." A system demonstration at the annual meeting of the Association for Computer-Based Systems for Career Information, Anaheim, Calif., Nov. 1983.

Harris-Bowlsbey, J. *Discover for Organizations: Human Resource Development Manual*. Hunt Valley, Md.: American College Testing Program, 1985.

Holland, J. L. *Making Vocational Choices: A Theory for Careers*. Englewood Cliffs, N.J.: Prentice-Hall, 1973.

Impellitteri, J. T. "A Computerized Occupational Information System." *Vocational Guidance Quarterly*, 1967, *15*, 262–264.

Katz, M. R. "Interests and Values." *Journal of Counseling Psychology*, 1969, *16* (5), 460–462.

Katz, M. R. "Career Decision-Making: A Computer-Based System of Interactive Guidance and Information (SIGI)." In *Measurement for Self-Understanding and Personal Development: Proceedings of the 1973 Invitational Conference.* Princeton, N.J.: Educational Testing Service, 1974.

Krumboltz, J. D., and Bergland, B. "Experiencing Work Almost like It Is." *Educational Technology,* 1969, *9,* 47–49.

Lancaster, A. S., and Berne, R. B. *Employer-Sponsored Career Development Programs.* Columbus: National Center for Research in Vocational Guidance, Ohio State University, 1981.

LaPointe, J. R. "Userware: The Merging of Systems Design and Human Needs." *Data Management,* Feb. 1982, pp. 29–33.

Leibowitz, Z., and Schlossberg, N. "Designing Career Development Programs in Organizations: A Systems Approach." In D. H. Montross and C. J. Shinkman (eds.), *Career Development in the 1980s.* Springfield, Ill.: Thomas, 1981.

Louis, M. R. "Career Transitions: Varieties and Commonalities." *Academy of Management Review,* 1980, *5* (3), 329–340.

Minor, F. J. "An Experimental Computer-Based Educational and Career Exploration System." In D. E. Super (ed.), *Computer-Assisted Counseling.* New York: Teachers College Press, 1970.

Minor, F. J. "Computer Applications to Support Employee Career Planning." Paper presented at 19th International Congress of Applied Psychology, Munich, Federal Republic of Germany, Aug. 1978.

Minor, F. J. "A Computer-Based Employee Development Planning System." Paper presented at the Careers Division of the 44th annual meeting of the Academy of Management, Boston, Aug. 1984.

Minor, F. J. *Evaluation of the Employee Development Planning System.* Internal Report. Franklin Lakes, N.J.: IBM National Service Division Personnel Research, 1985.

Minor, F. J., Myers, R. A., and Super, D. E. "An Experimental Computer-Based Educational and Occupational Orientation System for Counseling." *Personnel and Guidance Journal,* 1969, *47,* 564–569.

Morgan, M. A., Hall, D. T., and Martier, A. "Career Development Strategies in Industry: Where Are We and Where Should We Be?" *Personnel,* 1979, *56* (2), 13–31.

Myers, R. A. "Career Development of Army Officers with Computer Support." Paper presented at 19th International Congress of Applied Psychology, Munich, Federal Republic of Germany, Aug. 1978.

Myers, R. A., and Cairo, P. C. (eds.). "Computer-Assisted Counseling." *The Counseling Psychologist,* 1983, *11,* 7-63.

Norris, L. "SIGI Plus: New System, New Look for SIGI." *ETS Developments,* Winter 1984-85, pp. 1-3.

Norton, L. A. "The Northern Telecom Story." *Executive Resources* (a publication of Corporate Education Resources, Fairfield, Iowa), Apr. 1985a.

Norton, L. A. "The Tenneco Story." *Executive Resources* (a publication of Corporate Education Resources, Fairfield, Iowa), Feb. 1985b.

Prediger, D. J. "A World-of-Work Map for Career Exploration." *Vocational Guidance Quarterly,* 1976, *24,* 198-208.

Prediger, D. J. "Mapping Occupations and Interests: A Graphic Aid for Vocational Guidance and Research." *Vocational Guidance Quarterly,* 1981, *30,* 21-36.

Prediger, D. J. "Dimensions Underlying Holland's Hexagon: Missing Link Between Interests and Occupations?" *Journal of Vocational Behavior,* 1982, *21,* 259-287.

Schein, E. H. "The Individual, the Organization, and the Career: A Conceptual Scheme." *Journal of Applied Behavioral Science,* 1971, *4,* 401-426.

Schein, E. H. *Career Dynamics: Matching Individual and Organizational Needs.* Reading, Mass.: Addison-Wesley, 1978.

Sheibar, P. "A Simple Selection System Called Jobmatch." *Personnel Journal,* 1979, *53,* 26-29.

Sonnenfeld, J. A. *Managing Career Systems: Channeling the Flow of Executive Careers.* Homewood, Ill.: Irwin, 1984.

Storey, W. D. "Strategic Personal Career Management." In D. H. Montross and C. J. Shinkman (eds.), *Career Development in the 1980s.* Springfield, Ill.: Thomas, 1981.

Super, D. E. *Computer-Assisted Counseling.* New York: Teachers College Press, 1970.

Super, D. E. "The Relative Importance of Work." *The Counseling Psychologist,* 1982, *10,* 95-103.

Taylor, J. "Designing a Computerized Personnel Information System." *Personnel Management*, 1983, 33–39.

Tiedeman, D. V. "Flexible Filing, Computers, and Growing." In R. A. Myers and P. C. Cairo (eds.), "Computer-Assisted Counseling." *The Counseling Psychologist*, 1983, *11*, 33–47.

Tiedeman, D. V., and others. *Information System for Vocational Decision Making*. Annual Report. Cambridge, Mass.: Graduate School of Education, Harvard University, 1967.

Walker, A. J. "Management Selection Systems that Meet the Challenges of the '80s." *Personnel Journal*, Oct. 1981, 775–780.

Walker, A. J. *HRIS Development*. New York: Van Nostrand Reinhold, 1982.

Walker, J. W., and Gutteridge, J. G. *Career Planning Practices*. An American Management Association Survey Report. New York: AMACOM, 1979.

7

ᏒᏒᏒᏒᏒᏒᏒᏒ

Career Building: Learning from Cumulative Work Experience

Robert F. Morrison

Roger R. Hock

The members of every organization, from the "mom and pop" store to such giants as American Telephone and Telegraph and the federal government, have had to concern themselves with learning how to perform their jobs. This chapter will focus on the enhancement of the continuous, integrated learning that occurs at work throughout a person's career. The issue is improving the effectiveness of career development to meet both organizational and individual requirements. The organization needs to have specific competencies available within its work force. These competencies may take many years to develop. Individuals need to be able to determine what those competencies are and what they must do to acquire them.

Note: The opinions expressed in this chapter are those of the authors and do not reflect the views of the U.S. Navy. We wish to acknowledge the helpful comments of John Bruni, Jeanette Cleveland, Douglas T. Hall, Raymond Katzell, Kevin Murphy, and Edgar Schein.

The central assumption of this chapter is that experience at work or in a work-related environment is *the* primary source of career learning for each individual. Our focus is on changes in knowledge, skill, behavior, and personal characteristics that occur by building on previous experiences during moves from task to task, job to job, and context to context over long periods of time. The perspective on the change is developmental if one is a psychologist, or occupational socialization if one is a sociologist. Although nearly as many people participate in corporate training and education programs each year as are enrolled in four-year colleges in the United States (Bowen, 1985), the results are not as effective as they should be. If training and education were designed to augment experience-based learning, their effectiveness would be enhanced materially.

Our approach to the learning process will be to propose an experience-based career development model that can be used to research and analyze, design, and manage a series or combination of job assignments and work contexts over a career. The elements and propositions within the model are not new but are based on research from many disciplines, such as sociology, human resource management, psychology, organization behavior, career theory, and so on. Thus, the focus of the model on career development via continuous work experience and the integration of the many sources of ideas and research is unique.

Another unique facet of the model is its ability to provide a bridge between the organization and the individual. When the organization defines its long-term requirements in the form of target role competencies and formulates work role sequences that provide the opportunity for individuals to develop those competencies, the results can be communicated to its members. Individuals then can use the information to make career decisions and plan their own development and career moves.

The key element to define in this chapter is a *career:* "By emphasizing a continuous growth process centered around experiential learning, it can be defined as a sequence of work roles that are related to each other in a rational way so that some of the knowledge and experience acquired in one role is used in the next. This definition is not constrained by such factors as geography,

organizational boundaries, or promotional opportunities"
(Morrison and Holzbach, 1980, pp. 75–76).

Adapting the generic description of Baltes, Reese, and
Nesselroade (1977), we will define individual and organizational
career development as "a system of behavior change related to
learning" at work or in work-related contexts. The focus is on
intraindividual change as a learning process and on the type of
interindividual differences in learning histories that produce
different developmental outcomes (pp. 208–209). This is similar to
the definition of *occupational socialization* put forth by Volpert
(cited in Frese, 1982, pp. 209–210): "changes in the person which
take place in and because of the work situation."

The two major processes contributing to career development
are career management and career planning. *Career management*
represents the organizational perspective as the "process whereby
organizations endeavor to match individual interests and
capabilities with organizational opportunities through a planned
program encompassing such activities as the design of effective
internal career systems, employee career counseling, job rotation
opportunities, and a blend of positional experiences with on- and
off-the-job training assignments" (Gutteridge, 1976, p. 39). The
alternate, individual perspective is *career planning* or self-
management, in which individuals exert personal control over their
careers (Hall and Hall, 1976). This personal process involves
seeking information, establishing career goals, and planning the
routes one will follow to such goals through occupational,
geographical, and organizational choices, job assignments, work
activities, self-development programs, and making and acting upon
career decisions.

An Experience-Based Career Development Model

In this section, we will present a model of individual career
development based on the learning that occurs via continuous work
experience. We are no longer assuming that adult development is
primarily influenced by age; we are shifting toward an emphasis on
situational factors, such as cohort effects (Schaie, 1983), atypical life
events, and atypical daily events, in our framework for career

development. Cohort effects occur when nearly everyone present in a historical time period, occupation, or organization has similar experiences (for example, the advent of the computer). Atypical life events (Frese, 1982) are life events that are differentially distributed within a cohort, such as job changes, new supervisors and colleagues, and so on. Atypical daily events (Frese, 1982) consist of the daily use or nonuse of skills, intellectuality of work tasks, and so forth. All three of these classes of situational factors set the stage for a systematic approach to individual experience-centered development via the design of appropriate career patterns.

The work of two researchers, Feldman (1981) and Brett (1984), has markedly influenced the design of our experience-based career development model. Feldman proposes that appropriate role behaviors are learned, work skills and abilities are developed, and group norms and values are acquired via work experience. He postulates that this leads to outcomes that can be split into organizational (dependable role performance, retention, innovation, and cooperation) and personal (satisfaction, intrinsic motivation, and job involvement) outcomes. Brett (1984) applied some of the same constructs to the developmental process occurring during career transitions. (See Louis, 1980, for a classification of various career transitions. She presents both interrole transitions, such as initial entry and changing professions, and intrarole transitions, including adjustment to changes occurring in a work role and moving across career stages.) Brett splits development into two types, personal and role. We have used these classifications in our model of experience-based career development. Role development is defined as changes in job behaviors in terms of both what is done and how it is done. While role development as a part of work has received some consideration in the past, Brett presents a markedly heavier emphasis on social processes by referring to roles rather than jobs. She defines personal development as changes in the values, attitudes, and abilities of the individual.

Another dimension, the interaction effect, is also key to the analysis of career development eminating from experience. The developmental process is not unidirectional with only the situation affecting the individual's development. Individuals actively influence their situations by selecting the content and contexts in which they perform and by influencing the character of their situations (James, Hater, Gent, and Bruni, 1978; Mortimer and Lorence, 1979; Schein, 1971).

The constructs of personal and role development have been supplemented by interaction effects and projected across sequential career roles to form the model depicted in Figure 1. The model portrays that individuals enter their first job/job context in a series of related positions (central row in the model) with a previously acquired, limited array of knowledges and skills (upper row in the model) and personal characteristics (lower row in the model). As the individuals move through the sequence of job/job contexts, they acquire new knowledges, skills, and behaviors (role development) and adapt some of their personal characteristics to be consistent with the requirements of the roles (personal development). The effect of the job/job context on both the role and the personal development of individuals starts out at a very high level. Although the effect continues throughout the career sequence, the magnitude of the job/job context influence on individuals does not drop as much for role development as it does for personal development by the time the target position in Figure 1 is reached. While role and personal development occur as a result of the job/job context influences on individuals, the job/job contexts are being modified by the people as depicted by the arrows from the two developmental rows to the row of job/job contexts. The magnitude of that reciprocal effect on the job/job contexts changes during the career, as portrayed by the width of the arrows.

The processes that distinguish adult development from child learning (Knowles, 1973) take place not only upon entry into each position shown in our model but also during all the time individuals are in those positions. The learning that occurs is geared toward the acquisition of the skills and knowledge necessary to perform in the present job. If the position sequence is carefully designed, the knowledge, skills, behaviors, and personal character-istics required to learn and perform effectively in a career goal position (see job no. 4 in Figure 1) that is reached five, ten, twenty or even more years after entry (see job no. 1 in Figure 1) will have been initiated, built upon, and developed throughout the career.

Figure 1. An Experience-Based Career Development Model:
How Person-Work Interaction Leads to Development.

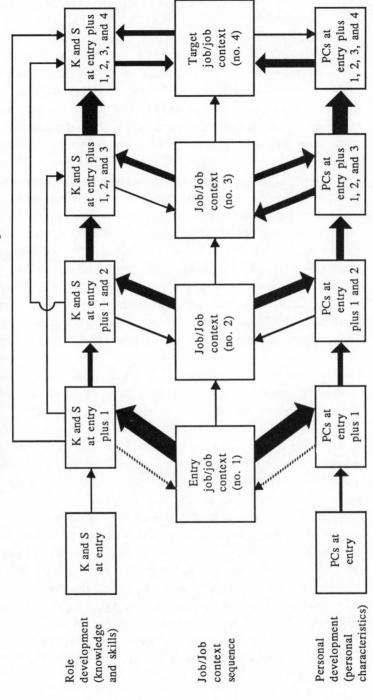

Individual-Level Factors

For many years, individuals and organizations have behaved as though the primary source of learning is the classroom. At work, this belief has resulted in huge sums being poured into education, training, and management development programs. Research results that question this belief and its accompanying policies are slowly starting to accumulate. Work by Morrison (1981), Livingston (1971), and Harold G. Kaufman (1974, and personal communication, September 24, 1980) points out how ineffective organizational training and continuing education programs are and how effective carefully choreographed project work is in the development of scientists and engineers in many settings. Arnold Kanarick (personal communication, April 3, 1984) and Sam Campbell (personal communication, January 4, 1985) have described research in which supervisors and managers from Honeywell reported 80 percent of their learning eminating from their work experience, 50 percent from job experiences, and 30 percent from relationships. According to Vineberg and Taylor (1972), the primary contributor to the effectiveness of navy enlisted personnel is their work experience, not their training. Others have documented research and experiences consistent with those just discussed (Brousseau, 1984; Hall and Fukami, 1979; Morgan, Hall, and Martier, 1979).

Training and education can provide the knowledge necessary for many specific formal job tasks and the elementary level of skill needed for many motor and simple cognitive tasks. The knowledge, skills, and behaviors required for informal and interpersonal roles and complex managerial functions, such as those of "power broker" or "priority setter," cannot be learned via formal training programs. Although these latter knowledges, skills, and behaviors are not even reflected in job descriptions, they are essential to effective performance and reflect the need for a great deal of learning—learning that occurs as a result of job experience. The initial proposition incorporated in the experience-based career development model is: The major source of individual career development is the learning that occurs through experience in work activities, roles, and contexts.

In our model, the fields of developmental psychology and learning theory start to merge in spite of their past philosophical separation stemming from different time perspectives. Developmental psychology has been concerned with changes in behavior over years, while learning theory addresses periods of minutes or days (Zigler, cited in Goulet and Baltes, 1970). Several components of learning theory appear to be robust enough to survive extrapolation from the microcontext in which they were produced to the macrocontext of career development. One of these is vicarious learning.

Vicarious Learning. A great deal of experience-based learning is derived indirectly by imitating, observing, hearing about, and reading about the experiences of others in similar shared conditions—that is, via vicarious learning. In this way, information is obtained regarding the opportunities and restrictions of the environment and the probable consequences of certain behaviors.

For example, division officers (job no. 1 in Figure 1) in a navy ship's department know that a career advancement for them would be movement into the next position, department head (job no. 2 in Figure 1). As subordinates, division officers have a great deal of opportunity to talk to the department heads for whom they work and observe the stress they encounter, their successes and failures, and so on. Their colleagues discuss other department heads that they work for on the same ship. Their peers, who work for the same department head in a slightly different context or for other department heads, also discuss their experiences. In addition, reading materials about the department head position are available in the form of magazine articles, training qualification booklets, career information newsletters, and so on. The division heads can learn vicariously a great deal about the position of department head and the knowledge, skills, behaviors, and personal characteristics that appear to lead to successful performance in many of the roles associated with the job. They can then practice some department head behaviors, both directly and cognitively, decide whether to stay in the navy, determine which of the ship's three department head positions they want to strive for, and develop realistic expectations about the job, even though it will not be attained until three to five years later.

Although the immediate supervisor position is most closely related to the individual, many other positions can be experienced vicariously via members of other role sets. When officers leave the ship to learn about specific tasks, such as damage control in the training environment, they can vicariously experience what it is like to be an instructor while they are students.

Vicarious learning (Manz and Sims, 1981) supplements direct experience in career development as indicated in the following proposition (proposition 2): A significant source of influence on the learning of role incumbents is their interaction with other members of their multiple role sets. These members include peers, subordinates, and superiors who may or may not be linked to the role incumbent through the formal organization. The sources may be represented as role models, representations in reading and training materials, or social interaction. The latter may be in the form of discussion, advice, assistance, counsel, and so forth. Mentoring is a unique vicarious learning technique (see Chapter Five).

It also appears to be important for the role occupant to have sufficient time and propinquity with respected peers to develop a peer network. Managers not only trade productive resources (Kaplan and Mazique, 1983) but also learn from each other. In several interviews with commanding officers who have limited contact with immediate superiors, the interviewees described a peer network that served as a means to learn possible solutions to problems and to provide and receive social support. Members of one triumvirate had developed their relationship by car-pooling fifty miles while they were in a three-month training program. Each officer represented expertise in one of the three major departments present within a surface combatant ship.

Personal Development. Up to this point, the reader may have been inferring that the experience-based career development model focuses entirely on role development—that is, the development of knowledge, skills, and behavior. That is not true. Personal development of cognitive and emotional characteristics is a key element. Attitudes, values, personality, and some cognitive characteristics are learned and adjusted for congruence between the person and the requirements of the job and job context (Brousseau,

1984; Sokol and Louis, 1984). Work and working conditions cause changes in the individual's persona, a consideration that adds an additional perspective to selective recruitment and job redesign. (Note: Selection is an important factor, since the role occupant must have sufficient cognitive, motor, and social abilities to be able to perform the role in an acceptable time frame [Allen and Van de Vliert, 1984].) Knowles (1973) addressed this idea when he proposed that one of the differences between adult and child learning is that adults change their self-concept. They become more independent and seek out situations in which they are in charge of their own learning. Thus the third proposition of our model is: Career development consists of personal development (the adaptation of many of the individual's personal characteristics) as well as role development (the learning of knowledge, skills, and behaviors) over the life span.

Cognitive Characteristics. While proposition 3 is very omnibus in nature, more specific aspects can be addressed using recent research. Intellectual capacity (Frese, 1982) or ideational flexibility (Kohn and Schooler, 1978, 1982) appears to change in the logical direction under extreme conditions (that is, if the job is either intellectually sterile or enriched). However, the effect is minimal. Extrapolating from these limited results, our related proposition (proposition 3a) is: Cognitive characteristics of the individuals are relatively stable upon attaining adulthood, and changes as a result of work or the work environment will be limited. In this instance, since individual cognitive characteristics may not change except under unusual circumstances, the organization and the individual should collaborate in matching the individual with appropriate assignments and career patterns (a selection strategy) or altering jobs to fit the individuals placed in them (a job design strategy).

Noncognitive Characteristics. Many noncognitive personal characteristics appear to change significantly in response to the work and its context. This was proposed by Schein (1971) in the presentation of his conceptual scheme of the individual, organization, and career. Longitudinal research (Kohn and Schooler, 1982) has found such long-term effects as bureaucratization and the availability of job protections (job security) leading to feelings of *distrust*. The latter situation also produced a significant increase in *authoritarian conservatism*. Upward movement in the organization (Andrisani and Nestel, 1976) and solving tough job problems (Brousseau, 1984) have been found to lead to increases in *internal locus of control*. *Emotional well-being* (Kohn and Schooler, 1982) and *mental health* (Frese, 1982) increase as autonomy and control improve and decrease as variability, complexity, social support, autonomy, and status drop. Mental health also is hurt under conditions of work over- and underload, role ambiguity and conflict, social stress, excess overtime, shiftwork, threat of unemployment, and long-term unemployment. Brousseau (1984) reports that task significance and identity influence the *activity* and *sociability* of the incumbents. Those who are in jobs that are substantively complex (in terms of people and data and/or things) significantly increase in their *self-directedness*, assuming more responsibility and trust.

Work experience also can change *values* over time (Mortimer and Lorence, 1979; Schein, 1978). Managerial career anchors strengthen as engineers move into management. An emphasis on extrinsic rewards can reduce the salience of people-oriented and intrinsic values and increase extrinsic values. Work autonomy can create an increase in intrinsic values. For individuals with a very strong, initial people-orientation value, the environment does not appear to have much effect. In this latter instance, selection appears to be a more useful strategy than development.

The experience-based career development model does not propose that change in personal characteristics across the career is constant. Figure 1 shows it as very strong at first during initial socialization (job and job context no. 1) and very weak as the individual performs in the target position (job and job context no. 4). In the target position, the individual has a major impact on how the job is performed as a consequence of the personal characteristics that have been developed. The smooth development of personal characteristics shown here would not occur if one of the positions in the job/job context was a dramatic change from the others. In fact, it appears that the next step that a surface warfare officer takes after the commanding officer job has been completed requires a major adaptation. That position, commodore of a squadron of ships, requires him to manage a group of ships without immediate access to what is occurring—he must become a manager. At such a major transition point in the career, it may be necessary to employ a program that assesses the potential of individuals to continue successfully in their direction. This may be the point at which a move should be made into other career patterns, such as staff, technical, or staff management, in contrast to line management. These findings have led to the following additional personal development proposition (proposition 3b): Noncognitive personal characteristics will change significantly in response to the work and its context. Such change will be more rapid and significant early in the career than later.

Workers who have been promoted to foreman must adapt their values to be more consistent with management than with workers. Naval officers whose successful specialized careers in the engineering (propulsion plant) department have earned them promotions to general management as commanding officers must adjust their values accordingly. The appropriate early emphasis on the concrete, data/things, and personal achievement needs to shift toward the abstract (tactics) and toward influencing people to get the work done. A key process in the adaptation of values is modeling (Weiss, 1978), in which subordinates imitate the behaviors of their supervisors (Weiss, 1977).

To develop the whole person, job analyses should measure psychologically important variables (autonomy, intensity, and so on) that are relevant to development as well as the opportunity to learn new skills (Frese, 1982). For example, the work pace must not be so hectic that the individual must respond in a stereotypical previously learned way: There must be time to learn. Frese (1982) proposes that the key to personality development and its generalization across situations is the opportunity (time) to use a planning strategy. That is the chance to know far enough in advance when to use a certain type of skill and when to interpret an ongoing process.

Career Pattern Design. Extrapolations from learning theory present the potential that effective role and personal development can take place over a career if career patterns (sequences of jobs and job contexts) are designed appropriately. To do so, assignment patterns must be "orchestrated" so that individuals have the opportunity to experience (either directly or vicariously) key knowledges, skills, and behaviors and are rewarded for their performances. However, random exposure to such experiences would be dysfunctional to the development process.

Hierarchies of Learning. Role development should occur via a sequence of roles that are formed in an order of ascending complexity. The concept of learning hierarchies (Horne, 1983) can aid in the optimum design of such a sequence, as depicted in Figure 1. The key roles in job no. 4 are presented as probably more complex than the key roles in job no. 3, and so on. Although educators feel that learning hierarchies should be "causal" (the second task in a sequence cannot be learned until the first is mastered), this is not required in an experience-based career development model. The lives of developing adults are too unsystematic to lend themselves to such rigidity and control. It is more realistic to propose that *some* of the earlier learning experiences encountered in careers increase the efficiency and likelihood of learning and performing in subsequent experiences. This is referred to as a "likelihood" hierarchy. However, logically determined sequences of job roles designed to build a hierarchy of skills needed to perform in a target career position usually are not identified. Proposition 4 from our model concerns the design of such sequences: The closer the design of a career pattern can come to establishing a likelihood hierarchy of roles, the more career development will be enhanced.

For a surface warfare officer, it is clear that serving in the role of tactical action officer while assigned as the operations department head (seven to ten years into the career) would be the most efficient way to learn major facets of the "tactician" (ship-fighting) role of the commanding officer. However, the role also may be partially learned while the officer serves as the executive officer (fourteen-year career point) *if* his or her commanding officer provides ad hoc learning opportunities. Another substitute could be an assignment as a tactics instructor in basic surface warfare officer school. Such a variety of opportunities would be termed a "likelihood hierarchy of career development."

Mastery Learning. Formulating a developmental sequence of work roles and contexts is not sufficient. It is also essential to establish how much time is required for an individual to learn and practice a particular role. Mastery learning (Arlin, 1984; Bloom, 1971) is relevant to this concern. This concept is based on the principle that the learner should achieve mastery at each level in the learning hierarchy before proceeding to the next. As the complexity of knowledge, skills, and behaviors forming each hierarchical step increases, measuring the level of mastery attained becomes more difficult; thus, achieving a high level of mastery at each step may be unrealistic. However, at the entry level, not only may mastery be required but also considerable practice beyond it may need to be provided so that the individual receives the rewards of feeling competent and receiving feedback via achievement and personal development occurs. Simultaneously, the organization receives a return on its investment in the individual's learning. This leads us to proposition 5 of the model: At each step in the hierarchy of career roles, a level of mastery should be attained that provides the ability to quickly perform at an acceptable level in a new context or job or, if a period of time has elapsed, to quickly regain the level of performance attained in the past.

There are wide variations in the amount of time individuals need to achieve an acceptable level of mastery. As a result, the organization will need to determine what proportion of the incumbents in a position are required to staff the next level of positions in the hierarchy. The time in the position should be set so that that proportion of the incumbents achieves mastery.

In the military context, the overlearning of a skill may be critical to retaining it while the officer serves in an interim job that does not require practicing the skill and quickly relearning the skill when he or she returns to a job that requires it (Smith and Matheny, 1976). For example, the skill to drive a ship or schedule propulsion plant repairs that was developed in an initial job assignment may have to be set aside while the officer spends one to two years recruiting or working on an MBA. Then he or she may return to sea to use the skills that have partially deteriorated through lack of practice.

Organizational-Level Factors

Up to this point, we have concentrated on career development from the perspective of the individual. Obviously such development occurs not in a void but within an organizational context. Using the experience-based career development model, the organization can integrate propositions 1 through 5 by establishing sequences of related jobs and job contexts, or career patterns (middle row of Figure 1). It might be expected that the field of human resource management would have approached the problem of designing job sequences so that the abilities and personal characteristics required of individuals in the organization's future target positions would be developed. Not many have done so, but when it has been accomplished, the common approach is to use historical precedence by capturing navy officers' perceptions of the best sequence of jobs to take to achieve a key senior position or by capturing (with mathematical models) the past movement of actual personnel through the system.

The U.S. Navy's model exemplifies this approach. A surface warfare officer learns his or her trade as a division supervisor aboard ship and then becomes a department head, later an executive officer, and finally a commanding officer. Each of these positions requires that he or she be aboard ship. This sequence of promotions and career progressions with its concomitant learning goes back to the days of John Paul Jones. The navy has acknowledged the structure of its career progression system by publishing it in a booklet of career guidelines for officers, but few other organizations have done the same. Most organizations use word of mouth in the form of a folk history to pass on impressions of effective means of career progression.

Historical sequences of careers can be identified by mathematical modeling techniques. A typical example, Vroom and MacCrimmon's (1968) study of interposition mobility, assumes that (1) transitions (changes from one position to another) will be made in the same direction and rate as in the past, (2) the structure does not change, and (3) the existing system will continue to change in exactly the same way as it has historically.

None of these approaches aids in the design of career patterns based on development or provides broad-based developmental alternatives that can be used when key positions become obsolete as a result of reorganization or technical change or are plugged by nonmobile incumbents. A few corporations have applied a slightly more sophisticated approach than that of historical precedence by clustering positions according to education, behaviors, skills, or work characteristics based on job analysis (Burack and Mathys, 1977). Although for a new employee such career patterns typically concentrate on the first two to three years, at least one such pattern, based on a job evaluation system, was designed to cover logical routes from entry to senior positions (Morgan, Hall, and Martier, 1979). Even the more complex lattice or network models (Burack and Mathys, 1980; Proske and LaBelle, 1976), which design patterns according to hierarchical skill groups, are based on historical precedence and a limited set of technical skills—the same problem present in simpler techniques.

There is a need to go beyond the current technology used to design career patterns by identifying roles and work contexts that broaden our present approach and cover the breadth of skills, knowledge, abilities, and personal characteristics that individuals must learn in order to be effective as they move through a system. This approach is represented in the experience-based career development model by proposition 6: A career pattern should be defined by a sequence of positions that (1) provide the opportunity to learn a target position via prior experiences in less complex versions of the skills, knowledge, abilities, and personal characteristics required and (2) increase in the complexity of their contents and contexts from entry to the target position.

Analyzing Work Behavior. To design career patterns from a developmental perspective, it is necessary to establish what must be learned in order to perform effectively within each position in the sequence. Traditional job analysis methods (Cloonan and Squires, 1981) describe a job in terms of observable tasks that are presented as though they are unique and independent from each other. While this may be adequate for describing some lower-level, mechanistic jobs, it is wholly inappropriate for more complex and subjective jobs, such as the work done by professionals, scientists, supervisors, managers, executives, or naval officers. Their jobs consist of many interconnected formal, informal, and interpersonal activities that cannot be broken down into disassociated concrete tasks. It is more useful to reconceptualize a job as a grouping of several roles that must be enacted, where a role is defined as "a constellation of behaviors required to achieve a task or task objective." This view provides a more global, coordinated view of work activities. It is also a flexible approach that allows changes in job roles as organizational changes occur (Katzell, Barrett, Vann, and Hogan, 1968). Finally, the concept of work roles encompasses many behaviors that are *not* usually defined by typical job analysis techniques—those that have been learned from direct work experience rather than formal training or education. For example, traditional job analysis would overlook the role a commanding officer plays when he uses the power of his position to intercede and help a subordinate complete a task.

The problem with this approach is that *role* is so broadly and vaguely defined throughout the literature that it is currently difficult to apply to our model. The research literature is concerned with characteristics of roles (Arnold and House, 1980; House and Rizzo, 1972; Kahn and others, 1964; Roos and Starke, 1981; Serey, 1981) rather than the role behaviors that are required to design career patterns. The definition of role behaviors provided by Kahn and others (1964, pp. 17-18) is tantamount to saying, "We don't know what role behaviors are, but we can tell when they're ambiguous!"

However, the news is not all bad, and initial steps are available for developing the technology required to do role analysis. Some introductory steps for the development of statements describing role behaviors are available (Graen, 1976). In addition, there have been attempts to cluster roles according to underlying dimensions that can help us identify role behaviors (Child and Ellis, 1973; Katz and Kahn, 1978; Roos and Starke, 1981; Tsui, 1984). Those dimensions could be either translated into behavioral terms or expressed as outcomes of the behaviors.

Little was found in the literature (Burack and Mathys, 1980; McCormick, 1976), that adequately describes the work behaviors of professionals, scientists, and managers. This problem was present as far back as the 1930s, when Gulick attempted to define the elusive "behaviors" of managers (Gulick, 1937).

In 1973, Mintzberg conducted a study involving intense observation of managers to define their activities in behavioral terms. He felt that the activities of managers could be grouped into ten sets or constellations, which he termed *roles*. These roles fell into three categories—interpersonal, informal, and decisional—and included some informal prescribed and social (interpersonal) behaviors that are not tapped by traditional job analysis. Some examples of the roles that a commanding officer of a destroyer would need to fulfill are shown in Table 1. These were taken from research (McBer and Company, 1984; Rundquist, West, and Zipse, 1971) and from our pilot interviews.

Table 1. Examples of Commanding Officer (Destroyer) Roles Requiring Expert or Advanced Levels of Proficiency.

Tactician (fight ship)	Judge and jury
Ship handler/Navigator	Reward system administrator
Weapons system manager	Personnel manager
Communicator	Planner/Scheduler
Engineering manager	External command representative
Command image builder	Peer problem-solving network member
Priority setter	Supervisor and role definer
Establisher of standards	Subordinate
Power broker	Role model and trainer

A difficulty of Mintzberg's (1973) approach to examining work role behavior is that his methodology/approach is frozen within a specific time. It does not take into account the strategies people employ to change and adapt their behaviors over the course of their careers as the context of their work changes. This dynamic character of organizations, jobs, and roles has to be considered if we are to accurately assess the skills and knowledge that need to be acquired for satisfactory career performance and for reaching target career goals.

There are two conditions under which individuals must adapt to new stimulus environments and learn new behaviors. First, the roles one is required to perform within a particular job can be expected to change. Changes in organizational structure and practices or changes in the environment in which the organization exists place new demands on individuals' jobs. If these new demands are not met, career stagnation or obsolescence may result. Second, changes in role behaviors inherent in an existing job *sequence* or changes in the job sequence itself will occur. Ideally, the behaviors one needs to perform new job roles have been partially acquired in previous job roles. Under this condition, the transition from job to job is smooth and efficient unless the prior experiences conflict with those required in the new job (Brett, 1984). Usually the lack of attention to the sequence of job/job contexts and learning concepts causes organization members to enter new jobs (containing new roles) either "cold" or with radically different experiences and expectations than those required. Thus the experience-based career development model includes proposition 6a: Career patterns should be constantly updated because of the dynamic nature of work role behaviors and the context within which they occur.

Considering only the content of career patterns as stated in proposition 6 and 6a is not sufficient. The context is also a critical factor. Learning theory again contributes to the model by formulating the requirements for the context that makes the career pattern functional. The learning theory that contributes in this instance is instrumental conditioning.

Instrumental Conditioning. Instrumental conditioning is present when voluntary behaviors, such as learning what is required to perform well in a work role or to obtain a required qualification, are learned (or unlearned) because of the consequences of performing or not performing them. Such consequences may not occur for several years but can be anticipated by combining constellations of experiences that do not necessarily have close temporal relationships. For example, success as a department head may lead to selection as an executive officer, but one or more assignments may intervene between the two assignments. The experiences may be random or planned, effective or ineffective, averse or rewarding, or external or internal to the person (Unruh, cited in Krumboltz, 1979). Past consequences will cause individuals to approach some situations and occupations and use some behaviors while avoiding others altogether. This leads us to proposition 7: The formal and informal reward and punishment policies and practices of the organization that are administered consistently over a sustained period of time (more than three years) contribute to career development. Those that are stated but are not applied consistently or that vary markedly in their application over shorter periods of time (three years or less) stultify career development.

Experiences at work provide continuous opportunities for feedback about past, present, and future performance. The work itself is a constant source of such feedback, as are subordinates, peers, superiors, and other occupants of the various role sets. The receptivity of the individual to performance-related information determines the effectiveness of both instrumental conditioning and vicarious sources of learning. Characteristics of the job and its context also serve as attractors to and rewards within a career pattern (Roos, 1978). For example, while overall job satisfaction may be similar, managers tend to enjoy the prestige, power, and pay of their work while technical personnel are attracted by the relatively greater autonomy in theirs (Schoner and Harrel, 1965).

Naval officers are attracted to the surface warfare career pattern by the opportunity for command and promotion. The path (via different assignments) that is sought is based heavily on the precedence established by successful predessors and not just statements by navy policy. If the navy does not place top-notch officers in the assignments that policy indicates should have such officers, the more junior officers ignore the policy and avoid those assignments.

Work/Person Interaction

Our model is based on the premise that there is potential for interaction between individuals' role development and their work/ work context that changes the balance between the two as they move from job to job throughout their careers (Schein, 1971). Initially, work experience (job no. 1 in Figure 1) contributes heavily to individual role development by increasing knowledge and skills, and individuals do not contribute significantly to their work. The balance of this relationship between the contribution of the individual and that of the work experience shifts until equal contributions are being made by the time the target position (job no. 4 in Figure 1) is attained. This premise is based on the assumption that work experience is the primary source of career development.* It is also predicated on the consideration that the jobs experienced are so dissimilar in content and context that an individual must develop new behaviors rather than apply stable previous behaviors (Brett, 1984).

As noted previously, it is not essential that each role be present in ascending order of complexity in every job in the sequence. The officers interviewed reported many experiences that were mastered at one point in their careers and recalled several years later. It appears that the keys to effective recall and performance are (1) initial mastery of the behaviors, (2) vicarious learning of the behaviors through a highly admired or disliked individual, or (3) the immediate perception that the behaviors are relevant and valuable. The contribution of the relationship between the supervisor and subordinate (vertical exchange) to career development appears to be significant (Wakabayashi and Graen, 1984).

A clear example of the use of a role model in learning was provided by one of the commanding officers who was interviewed. He was learning about propulsion plant management from one of his subordinates because of the role model provided by the commanding officer (CO) he had had when he was an executive officer. The model CO was an individual from aviation who had had previous command of a squadron but no experience on board ship. While the model CO was coaching the executive officer on how to be a CO, the executive officer taught him ship handling and other surface ship CO skills. Now that the interviewee had been advanced to the position of CO, he was playing the same role: He

---

*In Bray, Campbell, and Grant's (1974) longitudinal study of early career managerial personnel incorporating assessment center techniques, three administrative skills and two of six interpersonal skills did not change. The four remaining interpersonal skill scores actually dropped. Although the authors observed that basic management skills of their subjects did not change over the first eight years of employment, they did not describe their subjects' jobs as management positions that would emphasize such skills.

was learning engineering from his immediate subordinate, the executive officer. In exchange, he was coaching the executive officer in command roles. The interviews supported Wakabayashi and Graen's (1984) findings and added the role-modeling element of vicarious learning that the officer was using to fill his job proficiency void. Another CO was using a network of peers to fill the same gap in his engineering management proficiency.

Personality characteristics help create the interaction effect. The behavior of the individual is not just a reflex to the work environment but is activated by cognitively interpreting and actually changing the environment while simultaneously being influenced by it (Frese, 1982). The interaction effect leads to proposition 8: There is an interaction between individuals and their work. Initially, the influence is primarily unidirectional, with minimal effect of the individual on the work role and context (see job no. 1 in Figure 1). With experience, the individual's influence on the work role and context increases with the level of role and personal competence the individuals develop.

Implications of the Model

The model has a broad array of implications for both research and practice. A few key examples will be reviewed here, but much will be left to the creativity of the reader.

Career Research Implications

The model points out many voids in research that should be filled in order to make the design of career patterns effective. From the individual perspective, we still know very little about the stability or instability of personal characteristics. A start has been made, but our knowledge is incomplete. We also know very little about how long it takes to master a work role and, once it is mastered, how long the role should be practiced to the advantage of the individual and the organization. We also do not know how to set a target for a career pattern so that there is sufficient stability in the pattern for the goal to be achieved yet enough flexibility to allow adaptation to a changing environment. Both the type of goal and the temporal distance to the goal appear to be key variables. Another question is how much time can intervene between the practice of a role at one level of complexity and the utilization of what was learned in the same role at a higher level of complexity without any signficant degradation in ability. There are many more implications for new research, but there is not sufficient space to cover all of them.

Implications for Application

The eleven propositions and the model that summarizes them are of limited value if they cannot be applied to a "real world" situation. As with the implications about research issues, there is not enough space to cover all of these, but we will introduce a few of the most salient ones. It is clear that if the organization wants its personnel to follow certain developmental patterns, clear, stable career reward and punishment policies and practices must be established that are consistent with the requirements of the patterns. To make developmental process and work performance effective, realistic training programs must be designed and used to support individuals as they move into new or significantly more complex work roles. Career patterns should be designed so that they are consistent with the central mission of the organization and provide the development for personnel that is necessary for a high level of performance throughout a career. An example of how the experience-based career development model can be applied to the design of a career pattern is presented in the next section.

Career Pattern Design Steps

To demonstrate the need for a systematic approach to the design of a career pattern, an example of an inadequate pattern will be provided. Then, changes in that pattern will be proposed as stipulated in the experience-based career development model. A schematic that shows a poor pattern through which many surface warfare officers in the navy have been progressing is shown in Figure 2. The driving factors behind the assignments these officers have received are short-term operational expediency (keeping a

Figure 2. Poorly Designed Twenty-Year Commanding Officer (Destroyer) Career Pattern.

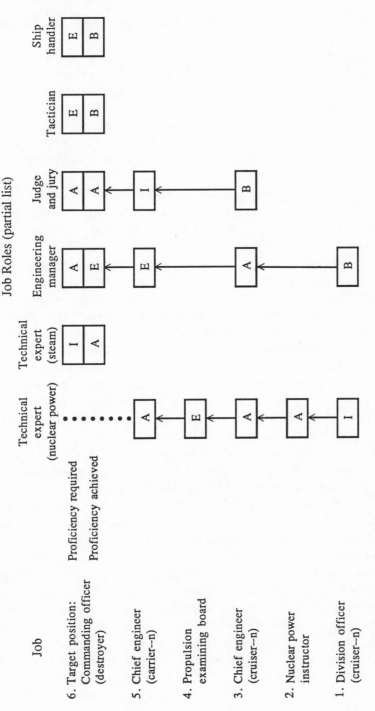

Job Roles (partial list)

Note: Capital letters denote proficiency level achieved in role.
B = Beginner   I = Intermediate   A = Advanced   E = Expert

competent person in a problem situation), manning requirements (making sure jobs are filled), and tradition. Neither target position role competency requirements nor developmental growth in knowledge, skill, and personal characteristics were considered. No system had been established to make developmental consideration a coordinated, systematic part of the sequential decision process. Out of the three most critical roles of the commanding officer's position, two—tactician (ship fighter) and ship handler—were overlooked as key aspects in any previous position's *required* roles. (This refers to roles formally prescribed by the navy as part of the job. A familiarization process for both roles and an introductory training course for one was prescribed by the navy, but the opportunity to learn vicariously or gain mastery via practice was dependent upon the individuals' previous commanding officers. Some commanding officers established ad hoc command programs to provide key developmental experiences beyond the required position roles, but most did not. Because of their informal nature, the quality of the programs that were present varied widely.)

It is important to determine the best sequence of experiences, because that is the primary source of career development and the period of work life is limited (Porter, Lawler, and Hackman, 1975). Appropriate sequencing is important because having had an experience at the beginning level makes an individual more or less ready to learn from another at a more advanced level. Our biggest problem is determining what experiences and sequence of experiences should be included in the career pattern.

Step 1: Identifying Target Positions. Eight steps are required to establish a career pattern or sequence. The first step is the identification of key organizational positions or families of positions (London, 1985) to serve as career targets or goals. Such positions should be: (1) central to the purpose of the organization, (2) distant enough in time from entry positions to serve as an effective career goal and provide a developmental opportunity, and (3) located within the organization's structure at a point that requires transition across intraorganizational boundaries. The latter would include such characteristics as continuance within the same career sequence to another significant hierarchial strata, changing to another career sequence, or early retirement, (Louis,

1980). These key positions should not be positioned within the organization so far down the career sequence that there is not sufficient time for the additional developmental experiences required to perform effectively in the organization's most senior class of positions. The job of commanding officer meets the requirement, since a destroyer plays a primary fighting role in a wartime navy. The commanding officer will have served sixteen to twenty-one years in the navy, with a potential of serving five to twenty more.

Step 2: Analyzing the Key Positions. Step two is the assessment of job/role behaviors (not just tasks) and requirements for the key organizational positions or classes of positions. For example, most commanding officers of ships indicate that "setting high standards" is a critical role (see Table 1). One of the behaviors used to set high standards is the constant inspection of living and work spaces for neatness and cleanliness during a daily walk through the entire ship. Rewarding comments for a top-notch job are made when warranted, and corrections are made when necessary. Meticulous attention to detail appears to be common among the commanding officers with the top ships. An important ingredient in this analysis is an assessment of the complexity of each task/role, not just its presence. Thus, the level of knowledge, skill, and personal characteristics required to act out the behaviors and tasks necessary to perform effectively in the key position(s) must be noted, as presented in Figures 2 and 3.

The personal characteristics should be divided into those that change very little as a result of career experience and those that can change markedly as postulated in the model. The former characteristics become factors in the selection of individuals for portions of a career sequence and the latter are those that can be planned as part of the personal development process.

Step 3: Identifying Potential Pattern Positions. The third step is identification of the positions that are candidates for providing the experience that develops the knowledge, skill, and personal characteristics required in the key position(s). Theoretically, all line and staff positions at or below the target positions should be included in this step. However, this is not feasible in very

Figure 3. Improved Twenty-Year Commanding Officer (Destroyer) Career Pattern.

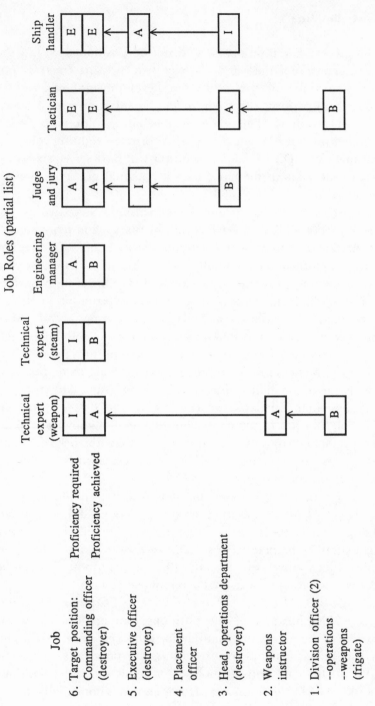

Job Roles (partial list)

Job	Technical expert (weapon)	Technical expert (steam)	Engineering manager	Judge and jury	Tactician	Ship handler
	Proficiency required					
	Proficiency achieved					
6. Target position: Commanding officer (destroyer)	I / A	I / B	A / B	A / A	E / E	E / E
5. Executive officer (destroyer)						
4. Placement officer						
3. Head, operations department (destroyer)	A			I	A	A
2. Weapons instructor	A					
1. Division officer (2) --operations --weapons (frigate)	B			B	B	I

Note: Capital letters denote proficiency level achieved in role.
B = Beginner   I = Intermediate   A = Advanced   E = Expert

large organizations. The list can be narrowed down by going through four procedures.

First, identify the roles in the target positions (see Table 1 for examples) that are most critical to effective performance (tactician), that demand the highest level of performance (ship handler), and that require a long period of development (judge and jury), a change in role perspective and behaviors at some transition point in the sequence (technical expert [steam] to engineering manager), or a major increase in the complexity of the behaviors between two steps in the career pattern.

Second, determine the level in the organization at which the eventual candidates for the target position typically enter the organization (division officer in Figures 2 and 3).

Third, eliminate any positions that require a level and type of technical expertise that is significantly beyond entry-level or target position requirements. Examples of these would be medical staff, chief chemist, and supply officer if the target position is line management. If technical knowledge and skill requirements are paramount in the target position, then this third step means eliminating any positions that do not require a level and type of expertise that is significantly near the target position requirement.

Fourth, omit from consideration any positions that the organization is not able and willing to denote as legitimate assignments for viable candidates for the target positions (Officer Candidate School instructor, for example). In other words, recognize and discard from consideration those dead-end positions that the organization does not consider central to its purpose and that it staffs with personnel who are no longer candidates for the target positions.

The positions remaining after these four procedures have been completed are now candidates for the analysis required in step four.

Step 4: Establishing a Hierarchial Position. The initial action to take in step four is to cluster the positions identified in step three according to common levels of perceived value to the organization. This organizational value may be expressed in terms of responsibility and authority, a standardized organization chart, or some other means acceptable to the members of the organization.

For example, division officer positions in destroyers and frigates might be grouped at the entry level, but division officer jobs on cruisers might be in a different cluster. The clusters are then placed in a hierarchical sequence according to the same perceived value used to form them.

Step 5: Analyzing Job Content and Context. Step five is an analysis of the content and context (Brett, 1984) of each of the clusters. The role requirements of each of these positions need to be carefully spelled out. The content analysis of the jobs uses the procedures applied to the key position(s) in step two plus one additional dimension: time to achieve mastery. While the socialization process is most powerful just before and after a particular boundary is passed in an organization (Frese, 1982), more time will be required to achieve mastery. This unique dimension— not normally part of job analysis—is an assessment of the time that the average incumbent will take to achieve mastery learning for each important task/role. The longest time period identified to achieve mastery of a single task/role within the set of important ones becomes the minimum time that someone should be in that job. The achievement of mastery should contribute to effective performance for the organization and provide the individual with a developmental experience that contributes to learning the related, more complex task/role in the next job requiring it. The achievement of mastery also should provide the positive consequences that make the job and career pattern attractive and that enhance feelings of competence and self-esteem.

Naval officers have made it clear that the time spent in entry-level positions that are developmentally demanding must be greater than the period spent in later assignments. For example, an eighteen-month assignment as executive officer (see Figure 3) seems to be adequate to achieve mastery of roles after thirteen years in the navy. However, the same time may not be sufficient to achieve mastery as a division officer in the operations department.

The context analysis should describe the opportunity that the incumbent will have to learn appropriate behaviors for present and future tasks/roles. An example is obtaining appropriate counsel from and observing the performance of effective role models. This analysis should describe the environmental opportunity for vicarious learning to occur.

Step 6: Designing a Developmental Career Pattern. Step six is the application of hierarchical learning as a developmental process to the design of a career pattern. First, the tasks/roles common to two or more jobs or job clusters are arranged in a hierarchical sequence according to their complexity—that is, their developmental demands. Next, this sequence of tasks/roles is used to arrange the jobs or job clusters in a complementary hierarchy that becomes the career path. Although preferred, it is not essential that every set of related tasks/roles be arranged in a perfect developmental sequence. A "likelihood" rather than a "causal" hierarchy of learning has been assumed in the model of experience-based career development.

It is important that key roles be experienced at least once earlier in the career at a less complex level than that required in the target position. For example, in Figure 2, the commanding officer of a destroyer has had no previous exposure to the key roles of "tactician" and "ship handler" that require performance at the level of "expert." In Figure 3, this problem has been resolved, although the commanding officer has not performed in earlier beginning-level roles as "engineering manager" and "technical expert (steam)." However, the level of proficiency required in the target position for the two latter positions is not nearly as high as for the two former positions. If early experience in such key roles is not available, return to step 4 and redefine jobs or clusters so that such experience can occur.

It also is not necessary for the sequence of tasks/roles to appear in immediately adjacent jobs or job clusters. It is not desirable that they occur many years apart, but real life experiences do not appear to be forgotten as rapidly as the material depicted in laboratory studies (Loftus, Fienberg, and Tanur, 1985). Thus, a job assignment that is outside the career path and does not require practicing any of the central tasks/roles can intervene (see "placement officer" in Figure 3). Such a career interruption should not be detrimental as long as performance on the new tasks/roles does not interfere by requiring that previously learned behaviors and personal characteristics be "unlearned" first.

Steps 7 and 8: Assessing Training Requirements and Individual Potential. The final steps are not key to the design of a career path but are essential to its implementation. One of these steps is the assessment of the jobs/job clusters to establish what training should be conducted to help individuals perform their jobs quickly and well. The other step is the assessment of the individuals to determine if they: (1) are able to develop the behaviors required in the career path, (2) are motivated to learn them, and (3) have career plans consistent with organizational requirements (Porter, Lawler, and Hackman, 1975). These last steps will not be developed further here because the theme of the chapter is career path design, not its implementation.

Conclusion

Researchers and practitioners are beginning to recognize that the contribution of work experience to career development is significantly greater than the contribution of education and training. While education and training may provide an intellectual knowledge base, they seldom provide skill development and do not include effective social skills or personality development. The management of tasks and assignments over the course of a career can provide the opportunity for work experience to systematically contribute to an individual's career development—that is, the learning of increasingly appropriate and complex work knowledge, skills, and personal characteristics. In contrast to London's (1985) assessment, it would appear that the benefits of managing assignments effectively throughout a career are numerous. The cost of developing a systematic approach to doing so may be high, but the continuing administration of such a program would cost much less.

Very little has been done to apply adult learning theory to the experience-based learning process. This application is essential since adults use experience as their primary medium for learning. Four separate theoretical approaches—instrumental conditioning, vicarious learning, learning hierarchies, and mastery learning—are available to be assimilated and applied to the experience-based career development process. The aggregation of approaches is essential to the analysis of career learning because it occurs over long periods of time (ten to forty years) and over many work assignments and situations.

In this chapter, an experience-based career development model is proposed that considers both role development (learning the knowledge and skill required to perform a role) and personal development (changing such personal characteristics as values and attitudes so that they are congruent with role requirements). Using examples from navy officers' career experiences, we have described the process of career development as an interaction between the individual and the job/job context. Initially, the interaction is dominated by the job/job context. Later in the career, role development comes into a balanced interaction with neither dominating because the job and job context can be adjusted by individuals at the same time that they are learning. At some later time, the interaction between personal development and the job/job context reverses the initial influence pattern, with the individual affecting the job/job context more than vice versa.

The last section of the chapter is the translation of the introductory constructs and experience-based career development model into an application: the design of career patterns. The following six steps of career pattern design are described using navy officers' career policies, practices, jobs, and job contexts as examples: (1) identifying career goals in the form of target positions, (2) analyzing those key positions for tasks, roles, and associated personal characteristics, (3) identifying positions that potentially could provide the development required to perform effectively in the target positions, (4) establishing a hierarchy of the positions spotlighted in step 3, (5) analyzing the content and context of the positions from step 3, and (6) designing a sequence of positions as a career pattern that focuses on development and provides effective alternative choices at each level.

However, two technologies must be developed before any further progress can be made. The techniques for designing sequences of work assignments (career patterns or ladders) has not progressed far enough to provide a systematic, developmental approach. The available career patterns concentrate on the intellectual knowledge and skills combinations that can be covered in training programs, which is only a small portion of the developmental experience. The methodology of job analysis suffers from the same problem. It must be developed further to identify and analyze the roles and role behaviors that need to be learned so that they can be incorporated into such a design.

The experience-based career development model and its application to the design of developmentally oriented career patterns require a large amount of research before they can be considered either theoretically robust or operationally effective. The research designs and analytical approaches to such longitudinal work have become available only in the last two decades. Now it is time to take advantage of both that technology and the early findings that have been described to build a much greater understanding of how people develop in their careers and how individuals and organizations can collaborate to make career development more effective and satisfying.

References

Allen, V. L., and Van de Vliert, E. "A Role Theoretical Perspective on Transitional Processes." In V. L. Allen and E. Van de Vliert (eds.), *Role Transitions.* New York: Plenum, 1984.

Andrisani, P. J., and Nestel, G. "Internal-External Control as Contributor to and Outcome of Work Experience." *Journal of Applied Psychology,* 1976, *61,* 156–165.

Arlin, M. "Time, Equality, and Mastery Learning." *Review of Educational Research,* 1984, *54* (1), 65–86.

Arnold, H. J., and House, R. J. "Methodological and Substantive Extensions to the Job Characteristics Model of Motivation." *Organizational Behavior and Human Performance,* 1980, *25* (2), 161–183.

Baltes, P. B., Reese, H. W., and Nesselroade, J. R. *Life-Span Developmental Psychology: Introduction to Research Methods.* Monterey, Calif.: Brooks/Cole, 1977.

Bloom, B. S. "Mastery Learning." In J. H. Block (ed.), *Mastery Learning: Theory and Practice.* New York: Holt, Rinehart & Winston, 1971.

Bowen, E. "Schooling for Survival." *Time,* 1985, *125* (6), 74–75.

Bray, D. W., Campbell, R. J., and Grant, D. L. *Formative Years in Business.* New York: Wiley, 1974.

Brett, J. M. "Job Transitions and Personal and Role Development." In K. M. Rowland and G. R. Ferris (eds.), *Research in Personnel and Human Resources Management.* Vol. 2. Greenwich, Conn.: JAI Press, 1984.

Brousseau, K. R. "Job-Person Dynamics and Career Development." In K. M. Rowland and G. R. Ferris (eds.), *Research in Personnel and Human Resources Management.* Vol. 2. Greenwich, Conn.: JAI Press, 1984.

Burack, E. H., and Mathys, N. J. "Career Ladders, Pathing, and Planning: Some Neglected Basics." *Human Resources Management,* 1977, *18* (2), 2-8.

Burack, E. H., and Mathys, N. J. *Career Management in Organizations.* Lake Forest, Ill.: Brace-Park Press, 1980.

Cairo, P. C., and Myers, R. A. "The Quantification of Progression Status in the Officer Personnel Management System." *The Career Center Bulletin,* 1984, *4* (2), 13.

Cairo, P. C., and others. *The Quantification of Career Progression Status in the Officer Personnel Management System.* Research Note 84-66. Alexandria, Va.: Army Research Institute for the Behavioral and Social Sciences, 1984.

Child, J., and Ellis, T. "Predictors of Variation in Managerial Roles." *Human Relations,* 1973, *26* (2), 227-250.

Cloonan, J., and Squires, H. "Job Analysis: Key to an Integrated Human Resource System." In D. H. Montross and C. J. Shinkman (eds.), *Career Development in the 1980s.* Springfield, Ill.: Thomas, 1981.

Feldman, D. C. "The Multiple Socialization of Organization Members." *Academy of Management Review,* 1981, *6* (2), 309-318.

Frese, M. "Occupational Socialization and Psychological Development: An Underemphasized Research Perspective in Industrial Psychology." *Journal of Occupational Psychology,* 1982, *55,* 209-224.

Goulet, L., and Baltes, P. *Life-Span Developmental Psychology.* Orlando, Fla.: Academic Press, 1970.

Graen, G. "Role-Making Processes Within Complex Organizations." In M. D. Dunnette (ed.), *Handbook of Industrial and
Organizational Psychology.* New York: Wiley, 1976.

Gulick, L. H. "Notes on the Theory of Organization." In L. H.
Gulick and L. F. Urwick (eds.), *Papers on the Science of
Administration.* New York: Columbia University Press, 1937.

Gutteridge, T. G. "Commentary: A Comparison of Perspectives."
In L. Dyer (ed.), *Careers in Organizations.* Ithaca, N.Y.: New
York State School of Industrial and Labor Relations, Cornell
University, 1976.

Hall, D. T., and Fukami, C. V. "Organization Design and Adult
Learning." *Research in Organizational Behavior,* 1979, *2,* 125–
167.

Hall, D. T., and Hall, F. S. "Career Development: How
Organizations Put Their Fingerprints on People." In L. Dyer
(ed.), *Careers in Organizations.* Ithaca, N.Y.: New York State
School of Industrial and Labor Relations, Cornell University,
1976.

Horne, S. E. "Learning Hierarchies: A Critique." *Educational
Psychology,* 1983, *3,* 120–135.

House, R. J., and Rizzo, J. R. "Role Conflict and Ambiguity as
Critical Variables in a Model of Organizational Behavior."
Organization Behavior and Human Performance, 1972, *7* (3),
467–505.

James, L. R., Hater, J. J., Gent, M. J., and Bruni, J. R.
"Psychological Climate: Implications from Cognitive Social
Learning Theory and Interactional Psychology." *Personnel
Psychology,* 1978, *31,* 783–813.

Kahn, R. L., and others. *Organizational Stress.* New York: Wiley,
1964.

Kaplan, R. "Trade Routes: The Manager's Network of Relationships." *Organizational Dynamics,* 1984, *12* (4), 37–52.

Kaplan, R. E., and Mazique, M. *Trade Routes: The Manager's
Network of Relationships.* Technical Report No. 22. Greensboro, N.C.: Center for Creative Leadership, 1983.

Katz, D., and Kahn, R. L. *The Social Psychology of Organizations.*
(2nd ed.) New York: Wiley, 1978.

Katzell, R. A., Barrett, R. S., Vann, D. H., and Hogan, J. M. "Organizational Correlates of Executive Roles." *Journal of Applied Psychology*, 1968, *52* (1), 22–28.

Kaufman, H. G. *Obsolescence and Professional Career Development*. New York: AMACOM, 1974.

Knowles, M. *The Adult Learner: A Neglected Species*. Houston, Tex.: Gulf, 1973.

Kohn, M. L., and Schooler, C. "The Reciprocal Effects of Substantive Complexity of Work and Intellectual Flexibility: A Longitudinal Assessment." *American Journal of Sociology*, 1978, *84*, 24–52.

Kohn, M. L., and Schooler, C. "Job Conditions and Personality: A Longitudinal Assessment of Their Reciprocal Effects." *American Journal of Sociology*, 1982, *87*, 1257–1286.

Krumboltz, J. D. "A Social Learning Theory of Career Decision Making." In A. M. Mitchell and others (eds.), *Social Learning and Career Decision Making*. Cranston, R.I.: Carrol Press, 1979.

Livingston, J. S. "The Myth of the Well-Educated Manager." *Harvard Business Review*, 1971, *49* (1), 79–89.

Loftus, E. F., Fienberg, S. E., and Tanur, J. M. "Cognitive Psychology Meets the National Survey." *American Psychologist*, 1985, *40* (2), 175–180.

London, M. *Developing Managers: A Guide to Motivating and Preparing People for Successful Managerial Careers*. San Francisco: Jossey-Bass, 1985.

Louis, M. R. "Career Transitions: Varieties and Commonalities." *Academy of Management Review*, 1980, *5* (3), 329–340.

McBer and Company. *Command Effectiveness in the United States Navy: An Interim Report on the Pilot Command-Effectiveness Study*. Boston: McBer and Company, 1984.

McCormick, E. J. "Job and Task Analysis." In M. D. Dunnette (ed.), *Handbook of Industrial and Organizational Psychology*. New York: Wiley, 1976.

Manz, C. C., and Sims, H. P. "Vicarious Learning: The Influence of Modeling on Organizational Behavior." *Academy of Management Review*, 1981, *6*, 105–113.

Mintzberg, H. *The Nature of Managerial Work*. New York: Harper & Row, 1973.

Morgan, M. A., Hall, D. T., and Martier, A. "Career Development Strategies in Industry: Where Are We and Where Should We Be?" *Personnel,* 1979, *56* (2), 13–31.

Morrison, R. F. "Utilizing Discretionary Research Funds to Support an Applied Laboratory's Goal: An Exploratory Investigation." Paper presented at 41st annual meeting of the Academy of Management, San Diego, Calif., Aug. 1981.

Morrison, R. F., and Holzbach, R. L. "The Career Manager Role." In C. B. Derr (ed.), *Work, Family, and the Career.* New York: Praeger, 1980.

Mortimer, J. T., and Lorence, J. "Work Experience and Occupational Value Socialization: A Longitudinal Study." *American Journal of Sociology,* 1979, *84,* 1361–1385.

Porter, L. W., Lawler, E. E., III, and Hackman, J. R. *Behavior in Organizations.* New York: McGraw-Hill, 1975.

Proske, A., and LaBelle, C. D. "Human Resource Matrixing." *Administrative Management,* 1976, *37* (1), 22–25.

Roos, L. L., Jr. "Institutional Changes, Career Mobility, and Job Satisfaction." *Administrative Science Quarterly,* 1978, *23,* 318–329.

Roos, L. L., Jr., and Starke, F. A. "Organizational Roles." In P. C. Nystrom and W. H. Starbuck (eds.), *Handbook of Organizational Design: Adapting Organizations to Their Environments.* Vol. 1. New York: Oxford University Press, 1981.

Rowe, M. W. "Manpower Models as Tools of Military Planning." *Defense Management Journal,* 1982, Fourth Quarter, pp. 21–25.

Rundquist, E. A., West, C. M., and Zipse, R. L. *Development of a Job Task Inventory for Commanding Officers of Amphibious Ships.* Research Report SRR 72-2. San Diego, Calif.: Navy Personnel and Training Research Laboratory, 1971.

Schaie, K. W. "Beyond Calendar Definition of Age, Time and Cohort: The General Model Revisited." Paper presented at 91st annual meeting of the American Psychological Association, Anaheim, Calif., Aug. 1983.

Schein, E. H. "The Individual, the Organization, and the Career: A Conceptual Scheme." *Journal of Applied Behavioral Science,* 1971, *4,* 401–426.

Schein, E. H. *Career Dynamics.* Reading, Mass.: Addison-Wesley, 1978.

Schoner, B., and Harrel, T. W. "The Questionable Dual Ladder." *Personnel,* 1965, *42* (1), 53–57.

Serey, T. "A Multi-Measure Comparison of Role Conflict and Ambiguity." *Dissertation Abstracts International,* 1981, *42* (5-B), 2116.

Smith, J. F., and Matheny, W. G. *Continuation Versus Recurrent Pilot Training.* Technical Report No. AFHRL-TR-76-4. Brooks Air Force Base, Tex.: Air Force Human Resource Laboratory, 1976.

Sokol, M., and Louis, M. R. "Career Transitions and Life Event Adaptation: Integrating Alternative Perspectives on Role Transition." In V. L. Allen and E. Van de Vliert (eds.), *Role Transitions.* New York: Plenum, 1984.

Tsui, A. S. "A Role Set Analysis of Managerial Reputations." *Organizational Behavior and Human Performance,* 1984, *34,* 64–96.

Vineberg, R., and Taylor, E. N. *Performance in Four Army Jobs by Men at Different Aptitude (AFQT) Levels: 3. The Relationship of AFQT and Job Experience to Job Performance* (HumRRO TR 72-22). Alexandria, Va.: Human Resources Research Organization, 1972.

Vroom, V. H., and MacCrimmon, K. R. "Toward a Stochastic Model of Managerial Careers." *Administrative Science Quarterly,* 1968, *13,* 26–46.

Wakabayashi, M., and Graen, G. B. "The Japanese Career Progress Study: A 7-Year Follow-Up." *Journal of Applied Psychology,* 1984, *69* (4), 603–614.

Weiss, H. M. "Subordinate Imitation of Supervisor Behavior." *Organizational Behavior and Human Performance,* 1977, *19,* 89–105.

Weiss, H. M. "Social Learning of Work Values in Organizations." *Journal of Applied Psychology,* 1978, *63,* 711–718.

8

꒰꒰꒰꒰꒰꒰꒰꒰

Careers from an Organizational Perspective

Richard J. Campbell
Joseph L. Moses

Much writing and research on careers is motivated by interest in individuals, their interactions with the world of work, and their development. This traditional individual perspective has focused appropriately on such issues as occupational interests, career choice, advancement, career stages, and, in more recent years, dual-career families and other phenomena stemming from a more diverse work force. In this chapter, we purposely take a different perspective—that of the organization and how it structures careers to support achievement of its mission and objectives.

Fundamental changes in careers instituted by organizations themselves are difficult to recognize. They are relatively rare and usually are introduced gradually, and they may be neither explicitly stated nor even the result of a clear organizational plan. These fundamental changes stand in stark contrast to the more frequent, visible, and highly involving job changes that occur daily for countless individuals. The heavy emphasis on the study of individual career choice is both understandable and appropriate.

The focus of this chapter, however, is not on individual changes. Our concern is how the organization structures long-term careers for its people, factors that stimulate the organization to modify these structures, and organizational responses to these forces. This examination uses long time frames for two reasons: One is to gain perspective on how the organization makes fundamental shifts in careers as the organization itself changes in response to internal and external pressures; the other is to seek insights on the effects of these shifts on individual careers as they unfold over the life span. Hence, this review emphasizes a dynamic view, not a static look at one time slice. The assumption is that these more macro shifts, while less obvious to the observer, are of critical importance both to the organization's success and to the lives of its members.

This chapter is intended to be heuristic. Its purpose is to inform both practice and research. It presents research findings and attempts to draw lessons, but its primary aim is to direct attention to a class of fundamental career issues that we believe have been underemphasized until recent years, particularly in research and theory building. Our approach to this task is essentially the presentation of a case history of one very large organization, AT&T, nee the Bell System. The slice of organizational history to be covered is rather substantial, roughly the 30-year period from 1955 to 1985. Yet this time frame seems small in contrast with the 100-year history of the organization and the average working life or career of an individual. The time period should be sufficient, however, to chart some of the significant factors influencing careers at AT&T. Our intent is to be illustrative rather than exhaustive in highlighting the types of issues that merit the closer attention of the scientist/ practitioner.

The reader must wonder what can be learned from an analysis of an organization that is as unique and different as the Bell System/AT&T. What can be generalized from such a review? Our expectation is that there is considerable correspondence with other organizations, at least large ones, in the specific area of careers. A brief look at the dominant characteristics of AT&T will suggest some of the variables to be considered in making judgments about generalizability. The dynamic nature of the organization over the period to be covered enriches the data yet complicates the analysis. The rapid change in the organization greatly increases its value as a case study while simultaneously making any snapshot description of its characteristics invalid for the full period.

The differences between AT&T in 1985 and the Bell System in 1955 are more striking than the commonalities. Comparisons at these two times for a number of key characteristics are shown in Table 1. The Bell System was a huge organization in 1955. It employed almost 745,000 people—approximately 1 percent of the civilian labor force. It was a regulated monopoly that provided service to over 80 percent of the nation. It had assets of $15 billion and annual revenues of $5 billion. Despite Bell's uniqueness as an organization, its environment was similar in important respects to other large organizations. It competed with these firms for management recruits. It was comparable in terms of salaries and benefits. A more comprehensive evaluation of generalizability can be made following a description of the organization's evolution to the slimmed-down, partially unregulated, and broadly restructured AT&T of 1985 and the concomitant changes in careers that occurred during the last three decades at AT&T.

Developments Influencing Careers

Five specific developments that influenced careers have been selected for description and analysis. Four of these originated in the external environment of the company, while the fifth was internally generated. The latter had its beginnings in a research study, the Management Progress Study (Bray, Campbell, and Grant, 1974). It was the company's decision both to undertake the study and to make significant changes in management careers based on the findings. The changes were not implemented without conflict, but the organization had a high degree of control of the process.

Two of the external developments resulted from shifts in society. The first of these was the result of a general societal thrust toward greater participation of minorities and women in business institutions. This movement was epitomized in the Bell System by the Consent Decree of 1973, which called for improved employment and advancement opportunities for women and minority group members. The consent decree was an outcome of a charge by the Equal Employment Opportunity Commission that Bell had

Table 1. Major Organizational Characteristics of the Bell System
in 1955 and AT&T in 1985.

Organizational Characteristics	Bell System 1955	AT&T 1985
Size	Huge	Very large
Markets	Regulated	Mix of regulated and unregulated; competitive
Industry	Telecommunications	Information management and movement
Organization	Functional; regional	Line of business; national
Organizational structure	Geographically positioned in state or region	Nationwide

discriminated against groups protected under Title VII of the Civil
Rights Act of 1964. The other development was less time or incident
specific and also emerged during the 1970s. This time it was not
only protected groups that were the focus of concern but also all
managers entering the business, as well as many of those with
considerable experience. The issue was the apparent changes in the
attitudes and motivation of those who matured during or simply
experienced the social upheavals of the 1960s. How were the
managers drawn from these generations going to fare as they joined
the institutions that were generally devalued by those coming of
age? Should the organization adapt? How should this be
accomplished?

The final two developments originated in the basic business
environment of the company. One was the introduction of
competition in the telecommunications market in which the
company operated. This trend accelerated rapidly during the 1970s
and fundamentally altered the nature of the industry with
concomitant effects on the organization itself. The final event was
the most dramatic and powerful of the five. Once again, it took the

form of a consent decree. It began with an antitrust suit brought by the U.S. Department of Justice against Bell. The result was a divestiture of a magnitude rarely seen, the spinoff of AT&T's operating telephone companies. The net result was a slimmed-down AT&T with 25 percent of its former assets and 40 percent of its Bell System force.

Each of these events called for a strong organizational response. Several had the force of law. Others could be ignored, but the company would miss an opportunity for revitalization. The key environmental forces impinging on the organization and its career systems were technological advances, marketplace changes, cultural changes in society, and government intervention. They were interrelated and so firmly rooted in the environment that their profound impact on the company eventually was recognized as inevitable.

Values and Their Effects on Careers

Neither the organization nor its individual managers pursuing their careers could have predicted these changes in 1955. The Bell System of the 1950s had a very strong and clear set of values and norms. Its mission was simply and effectively defined as universal service: providing end-to-end high-quality telephone service to everyone in the United States. It was the cornerstone of a unified organization that stretched across the country in the form of twenty-two telephone companies, Long Lines, Bell Laboratories, Western Electric, and other subsidiaries. The principal values that drove careers at Bell were prompted by and consistent with this pervasive service ethic. The managers of the 1950s understood and shared these values and expected organizational behavior and actions to be governed by the values and characteristics of career systems summarized in Table 2.

Five Career-Changing Developments at AT&T

These organizational values and characteristics formed a very strong set of norms and a culture that became entrenched over

Table 2. Bell System Organizational Values and Characteristics
of Career System in 1955.

Organizational values

Strong service ethic
Strong company loyalty
Commitment to a socially important goal

Organizational characteristics

Nationwide corporate identity among employees
Strong identification with geographical unit
Well-defined organizational structure
Well-defined hierarchical structure
Strong identification with work function

Characteristics of career system

Promotion from within
Stable and well-defined patterns of advancement
Career opportunity
Rigorous performance standards
Rigorous potential standards
Development of management generalists
Commitment to an AT&T career
Supervisor as the key person who manages career development
Primacy of work career

decades. Such cultures are highly resistant to change, and Bell's strongly influenced its response to five career-influencing events and the outcomes of attempts at organizational adaptation. Let's look at these events in more detail.

The Management Progress Study. The particular interest in this intervention in career systems is that it was internally generated: It was self-initiated as a way to improve the vitality of the organization. The Management Progress Study (MPS) is a major study of the development of managers, massive in scope and fully supported by the organization over a long period. The purpose of the study was twofold: The organization was committed to long-term careers and promotion from within. Its success depended heavily on effective development of its managers. Also, it wanted a better understanding of the impact of its career systems on the individual. The loyalty between company and employee was reciprocal.

Several MPS findings led to major changes affecting the career system. One was the establishment of rigorous selection procedures for promotion into management. Historically, promotion to management was based largely on technical skills and seniority. Reviews of promotion procedures showed that promotions went to longer-service employees who had demonstrated strong technical skills, knowledge, and performance. The final decision on promotion was heavily influenced by the immediate supervisors, who typically considered a small group of candidates—those who reported to them. MPS findings clearly demonstrated the characteristics, such as leadership and decision making, that were related to advancement in management and illustrated effective methods for measuring them (Bray, Campbell, and Grant, 1974). The findings were communicated across Bell, and assessment centers were established to evaluate managerial skills as input to promotion decisions. Eventually, promotion decisions were based more heavily on managerial potential, and the stream of promotees to management came from relatively low seniority ranks as well as the highly experienced group.

A second MPS finding led to substantial changes in the early career experiences of new management recruits from outside the organization (about 15 percent of new managers). The development process in the 1950s for the typical recruit, a recent college graduate, called for two years of service in a series of trainee positions in order to learn the "nuts and bolts" of the business. The rationale was that the recruit had to perform such jobs as installing telephones before assuming a supervisory position. The top management of the business had passed through this system, and the organization was strongly committed to it. The MPS findings demonstrated that giving recruits challenging jobs early in their careers provided a potent stimulant to development. The new recruits reported that rotation through a number of trainee jobs had a stultifying effect on their development. The early development program was revamped in the early 1960s and a new program, the Initial Management Development Program (IMDP), was initiated. Two new features formed the core of the change: Early job assignments were designed to be challenging and managerial in scope, and decisions were made early in a recruit's career concerning potential for middle management. Only those demonstrating this potential were asked to stay with the company. Experience with the new program and additional research findings increased confidence in the approach. A study by Hall and Nougaim (1968) showed a circular and reinforcing pattern of success. The more capable managers tended to get the more challenging jobs, which, in turn, led to more rapid development. This spiraling effect became an important underpinning of the high-risk/high-reward program for new managers.

Both these MPS interventions encountered strong resistance within the organization. It took five years for the new development program to become general practice across the Bell System. The assessment center approach was not operational in all companies until ten years after its introduction. This *gradual* implementation of highly important career programs with strong research documentation was a good indicator of the difficulty of altering the firmly entrenched and widely accepted career systems. They were considered major interventions in the late 1950s and early 1960s, and management's endorsement of gradual change indicated the importance attached to maintaining a career system that is highly endorsed by its managers. Yet in comparison with some of the changes to come, the interventions were relatively minor. Only one of the principal values was affected: Immediate bosses played a less important and powerful role in the selection and development of managers. The disturbance of the overall career system was minor. It was more a case of new methods to serve old rules.

Women in Management. In 1971, the Equal Employment Opportunity Commission (EEOC) intervened in a Federal Communications Commission hearing on a proposed Bell System rate change and charged the Bell System with discrimination against women and minorities in employment, advancement, and other personnel actions. As the largest private employer in the United States and an organization regulated by various levels of government, the Bell System was a prime target for the EEOC, and the regulatory process gave the EEOC the opportunity to intervene quickly with charges against Bell. The reaction within Bell was one of surprise, disbelief, and embarrassment. It viewed itself, and was generally regarded, as progressive in its personnel practices and among the leaders in equal opportunity. Bell could point to favorable statistics, such as the fact that half of its 120,000 managers were women. But the statistics also showed that women were disproportionately concentrated in lower levels of management, and it was soon evident that being among the leaders was hardly satisfactory. There were strong pressures in society as well as in government for major changes in employment and career opportunities for "protected" groups.

The dispute was settled by the Consent Decree of 1973. The agreement was very comprehensive in its coverage of protected groups, jobs, compensation plans, and so on. Only one part of the response to the consent decree will be covered here, since the total response was far too massive for the scope of this chapter. The provision that will be used for our purposes dealt with the development and advancement of a specific group of management women. The high-risk/high-reward development program (IMDP) for new management recruits described earlier was identified by the EEOC as a critical career advancement program that was underpopulated by women.

The Bell System agreed that this was a prime mechanism for improving the advancement of women and negotiated a plan that it felt was feasible and would produce positive results. A special program was designed to place more women in the development program. All women hired into management between 1965 and 1971 and in lower levels (first and second levels of a seven-level management hierarchy) of management in 1973 were eligible for the program. Those who were interested in participating were to attend the assessment center used by Bell for evaluating potential to reach middle management (third level). Additional assessment centers were established to ensure that all candidates could be evaluated within a twelve-month period. Those who demonstrated potential for middle management at the assessment center would enter the development program. Those who did not would continue their careers as before. No report of their assessment performance was sent to the field organization. The latter was instructed that a person's attendance was not to influence her career in any way.

The assessment requirement was a critical piece of the program. Normally, only about half of the management recruits were placed in the high-risk/high-reward program, those deemed to have the potential to make middle management within a ten-year period. Research had shown that the assessment center was the best way to identify high-potential managers. More importantly, assessment was well accepted by managers by this time. They had confidence in the results. Thus, women who were assessed as having good potential were much more likely to be seen as very legitimate participants in the development program. A second basic ingredient in the program was a special career-planning program for the purpose of further accelerating the development of the women whose entry to the high-risk/high-reward program was several years behind that of their male cohorts.

The program was solid in design and one that all parties could support with enthusiasm. Success was hardly guaranteed, nor was it precisely defined. No one knew how many of the women would volunteer for assessment and demonstrate further management potential. It would be necessary to move women out of the departments (functions) in which they were overrepresented if they were to gain access to middle-management openings. This appeared to be the greatest potential obstacle. It was clear that the program would require vigorous support, and management was determined that it would be done very well.

Of the 2,049 women hired between 1965 and 1971 and covered by the decree, 1,838 were still employed in 1973. Over 90 percent of these elected to participate and attend the assessment center. The results were gratifying. Over 40 percent of the women (689) were assessed as having good advancement potential and recommended for the development program. This rate of success at the assessment center was very similar to that for men. Analysis of the assessment data indicated that the women were similar to men in terms of their managerial characteristics and that women provided a talent pool for advancement comparable to that of their male counterparts (Ritchie and Moses, 1983).

The next step was designing the special career-planning program for the women recommended for it on the basis of their assessment performance (Boehm, 1974). The basic components of the career plan were: (1) challenging jobs, (2) goal-setting and action plans, (3) periodic performance review and feedback, and (4) continuous support and follow-up by both the boss and a program coordinator. The support and follow-up phase required the most intensive and innovative effort. A brief review of traditional career patterns will give some perspective to the problems faced by the career planners and the women participants.

About half of all new management recruits typically were placed in the high-risk/high-reward program. The goal was to reach middle management in five to ten years. The accepted career path was progression up through the function or department the recruit entered. About half of those who stayed with the company made middle management in the targeted time frame. At that point, the high achievers began to be assigned cross-functionally into other departments for development as a multifunctional general manager. The underlying rationale was that the recruit should learn one function in great depth and direct that function successfully as a middle manager. The organization was not prepared to offer risky cross-functional developmental assignments at the middle management level without seeing a strong demonstration that the candidate was worth the risk.

Consider the position of the women. Few were in the high-risk/high-reward program. They were concentrated in such departments as traffic and commercial, which contained heavy proportions of women working as operators, service representatives, and clerks. Advancement opportunities generally were restricted to their home departments. They had to compete not only with their women peers but also with the high-potential (male) managers in the IMDP or other male middle managers who moved over from other functions for developmental assignments. The pyramid narrowed quickly to the eye of the needle for many. The situation was aggravated when growth occurred more rapidly within departments, such as plant and engineering, which were predominantly male-populated departments. The number of advancement opportunities was likely to remain limited if these traditional advancement patterns were maintained.

Formal career plans took several approaches to opening up advancement paths. A critical step was the lateral movement of substantial numbers of women to other functions, including such nontraditional assignments as supervising telephone installers and construction crews. A minority of the women followed these nontraditional paths, but lateral assignments for the women were the rule rather than the exception. Over 75 percent changed functions at least once in the ensuing years, and over half changed functions two or more times. These proved to be very important developmental moves and clearly aided their advancement. The moves to nontraditional assignments frequently required considerable expense in terms of both time and money. Special functional training programs were designed, perhaps in some cases overcompensating to be sure that the transfering woman was given a fair shot at success. The women encountered other anticipated obstacles as well. For instance, not every manager readily accepted women in nontraditional jobs. One of the programs established to help with this problem was a behavior-modeling training approach that provided supervisors an opportunity to observe effective behavior, practice it, and get feedback on their performance (Collier and Moses, 1977).

The bottom line for all of this intensive effort was the promotion rate into middle management. The consent decree did not specify how the program was to be measured beyond the general statement that the women should be given the opportunity to "catch up" to their male counterparts hired at the same time. After much deliberation, the Bell System set its own measuring stick: The percentage of women promoted to middle management should be at least 80 percent of the rate for comparable men. The ratio in 1976 was .48. By the end of the consent decree (1979), the rate was .85. And in 1982 it climbed to .92. Recall that only about half of the high-potential men who remain usually reach middle management within ten years. By 1982, 48 percent of the women had reached third-level management or higher.

The program was a definite, clear-cut winner. Both the company and the women benefited. Managers who observed the women's performance recognized their capabilities. Many sought out these women for assignments because of the reputation they established for performance. The larger test, however, was the spillover that the program was intended to have to other women outside the program. Research findings (Moses and Boehm, 1975; Ritchie and Moses, 1983) showed that the characteristics important for advancement were similar for men and women. Assessment centers for men and women considered to have potential for middle management were established on an ongoing basis shortly after completion of the special consent decree assessments. Efforts at nontraditional assignment continued. Table 3 shows the rapid increase in representation of women in middle management positions from 1.4 percent to 14.6 percent over the twelve-year period of 1971-1983. Not all of this increase can be attributed to this program and its spillover; it was but one of a number of affirmative action efforts. But it clearly was an intensive intervention whose major significance may have been as a demonstration of what could be done.

What has happened to our principles underlying the career system? Only two appear to be altered: The intervention broke many of the traditional patterns of advancement, and it opened up new talent pools for the organization and increased the internal competition for jobs. Program coordinators shared some of the bosses' power in development and career planning. The Bell System learned much from the experience, yet the basic principles of the career system survived largely intact. It was a creative adaptation.

One final comment on the importance of an external intrusion is necessary. It is very unlikely that change of this magnitude and speed could have been accomplished without the

Table 3. Increase of Women in Middle Management, 1971–1983.

| Year | Middle Managers | | |
	Total	Women	Percentage of women
1971	15,992	224	1.4
1983	9,827	1,436	14.6

consent decree. The organizational effort and unfreezing required could not have been achieved in this time frame without the constant pressure provided by the 1979 deadline for the decree.

The New Work Force and the Influx of New Values. The 1973 Consent Decree was a manifestation of some fundamental changes taking place in society during the 1960s and 1970s. The rapidly changing ethnic and sex mix of the new recruits pressed many managers into trying to learn more adaptive approaches. But this was only part of the challenge of coping with the widely heralded new breed of managers, which included the "typical" white male recruits from prestigious universities. The struggles over beards, different dress styles, and so on were the surface concerns. Both the external and the internal media carried daily warnings for managers on the other side of the generation gap that they would have to change if they hoped to manage the new breed effectively. Survey results claimed that the younger generation did not trust societal institutions and was particularly disillusioned with business organizations. There was genuine concern about the ability of traditional hierarchical organizations to function well once, and if, the new generation entered business.

Career systems were once again under strain. Though it came from new recruits inside the company, it was a reflection of the external milieu and the general experiences of the new cohorts. The changes in attitudes, values, and behavior have been attributed to many things: affluence, the extended period of education, unpopular wars, liberation, and even marijuana. Whatever the causes, the new generation was different.

The Bell System responded in various ways. It experimented with day-care centers. Dual-career families became a familiar concept, with some living examples observed in the organization. Managers reluctantly began to accept the notion that they should be more tolerant of individuals who refused a geographical move even if it meant an opportunity for advancement. Training programs were established or modified to help managers deal with the new realities.

The Bell System decided that it needed a better understanding of the abilities, motivation, and developmental needs of these new recruits. A study was begun in 1977, patterned after the original longitudinal study (MPS), to examine these issues and contrast the new cohorts with those of the 1950s. Analyses of the two hundred new recruits assessed during 1977 to 1979 provided support for the notion that this generation was different (Howard and Bray, 1981). The new cohorts had more education and contained substantially more minorities and women. Beyond the increased ethnic and sex mix, they were a very diverse group and were highly individualistic. Their assessed managerial capabilities were equivalent to those of the earlier recruits, and they shared with the earlier group a high need for accomplishment. This presented a rather positive picture for the host organization. However, a key concern of the researchers was that some of the recruits expressed both a lack of motivation for upward mobility and a definite disregard for traditional organizational hierarchy.

There was much discussion of the implications of experiences with the new recruits and the research findings. How should the career system be altered? Was it necessary to tinker with the very strong hierarchical Bell System mode of operation to respond to these motivational shifts? The organizational response was diffuse and experimental. Over a period of years, a number of steps were taken in an attempt to increase participation and introduce some flexibility into the hierarchical system. Some companies reduced the number of management levels. Surveys were introduced, along with a quality-of-work-life effort. House organs trumpeted the need for participative management. Some companies modified their socialization process. These interventions had some impact: The organization moved somewhat gradually toward changes it believed would strengthen its performance. It has in recent years articulated a point of view stressing individual accomplishment and responsibility. In this way, AT&T has shifted toward an organizational structure that more fully empowers, challenges, and rewards all of its managers while retaining a basically hierarchical structure. This evolutionary process is likely to continue for some time. It is a complicated response to a complex set of changes in recent cohorts. However, how much change is necessary to respond to cohort shifts is uncertain. There has been some evidence in the last few years to support those who argue that the 1970s cohort was a unique group and that future cohorts will look more like those of the 1950s in their attitudes toward business careers, advancement, and leadership.

The new cohorts were a threat of some unknown magnitude to several of the principal values: loyalty, career commitment and continuity, and advancement from within. They also questioned the basic order of its structure and its hierarchy. Why was the organizational response so fuzzy and noncommital? Beyond the organization's reluctance to change its basic values and approaches, several factors seem salient. The forces for change were not unequivocal. They developed over a period of years, and many believed that the changes were transient. There was no time-specific incident, such as a consent decree, demanding immediate action. The result has been mainly some attenuation of the hierarchy but no real dismantling of it. These new recruits have not as yet brought about major change in the organization's career system.

Competition. Our fourth change, which overlapped the last two in time, began in the late 1960s. It developed slowly initially, became a major movement in the Bell System during the 1970s, and continued to increase in importance and impact in the early 1980s. The change it wrought is clearly of a different order of magnitude than that produced by the three events described earlier. It was no longer simply an issue of wider competition for the usual set of jobs and career opportunities. Nor was it only a matter of new jobs and new career paths. The mission and method of operation of the organization itself were under challenge, as were its organizational values and career systems.

Technology was the prime stimulant of the change. It spurred competition, change in the markets, and regulatory rulings. It began rather quietly with a petition by a small company to market a radio-phone coupler (Carterphone) that was to have access to the telephone network. In 1968, after a lengthy court battle, the instrument was approved for access to the network. This opening up of the market to non-Bell companies reached major proportions in the 1970s. By the 1980s, there were a number of companies offering various makes of telephone sets and other communication devices. The consumer also had the option of having a company other than AT&T provide its long-distance service. Vigorous competition had taken hold in the telecommunications business. It was to have far-reaching consequences for the organization and the careers of its employees. How did the organization respond?

The tangible effects of competition were dramatic. AT&T launched a new marketing function. There had been several marginally successful attempts to establish a marketing function in earlier years. The organization made it clear that this time the need was critical and a strong marketing function *would* be established. Marketing was structured as a department—but one that was more centralized than the traditional Bell departments. The department was given authority to move out of the traditional geographical structure into a national organization. A significant aspect of this movement was the power to establish and/or modify jobs and career paths along with considerable control over the hiring and placement of individuals in marketing in the telephone companies. New jobs were formed, such as account executive and communications system representative, that required new skills and training. Career paths were designed that specified little movement either into or out of marketing. The marketing specialist was the order of the day. The compensation system was changed, with a greater percentage of salary at risk, to encourage performance and provide rewards for staying within the function. *Risk* was a hot word, and risk takers were wanted. Many harbored doubts about the ability of long-service Bell employees to compete for and in these positions. This was one indication of a fundamental shift taking place within the organization.

The initial task was to establish an essentially new function in a large, stable organization. It was to be a major function with over 10,000 employees, and its success was crucial to the success of the company. There was no precedent for such a change in the annals of business organizations. Below the surface of new function, jobs, and career paths, the organization had the more difficult job of changing perceptions and values and constructively resolving organizational conflict. Marketing was to be more than a function: It was to pervade the entire organization. The push toward a "market-driven" company created more than power issues. It raised questions about the fundamental values of the organization: Would the key value of service be sacrificed for profits? The values of the organization regarding its people, which had been forged over many decades, also were to be tested.

Recognizing that it would need to make some basic changes in its operations if it were to become an effective marketing organization, Bell hired an outside change agent—a senior marketing manager—into the executive level of the marketing function. He was to spearhead the move to an effective marketing organization as well as the building of the marketing function. The act of bringing in an outsider at a high management level was a very unusual and clear signal. Additional high-level outsiders were to follow. There was strong pressure from this core group to staff the marketing function with outsiders who would have not only the new skills required but also the appropriate attitude and motivation (that is, people who were not socialized in the ways of the Bell System).

At the same time, this was a period of little growth in the work force. Technological and market trends led to the shrinking of some traditional jobs and career paths. There was surplus in some areas and growth in others, such as marketing. The organization's dilemma was honoring its commitment to its employees and its commitment to forging a marketing-driven organization to maintain leadership in telecommunications. Should the organization try to change people or replace them? The issue struck to the heart of the organization's values and the beliefs that people would hold about careers in the company. Could the organization be revitalized while retaining the commitment and loyalty of its long-service employees?

Attempts to resolve the conflict were threefold. First, there was the reshaping of the corporate mission and values that built on the old while adapting to new demands. Since universal service had been virtually achieved, AT&T redefined its mission as the more encompassing one of providing individual customer satisfaction. This triggered an examination of what constituted outstanding service in the new environment. As a result, the underlying service value also began to take on new meanings. Next, appropriate new screening devices were developed and validated. Both internal and external candidates were examined, and a vigorous effort succeeded in identifying and placing a substantial number of internal candidates in these new jobs. However, many existing employees did not qualify for the newly created marketing function, and there was a substantial infusion of external hires. Some sizable surpluses remained. The third step was implementation of a special outplacement program designed to move surplus or difficult-to-place employees out of the organization in an acceptable manner. The plan was voluntary and provided a payment of up to one year of salary, six months of continued medical insurance for those not eligible for retirement, and outplacement counseling. The plan was offered to groups of employees in areas in which surpluses existed. It was well received by those who volunteered. Those who remained were reassured that the company had done its best for its employees in a trying time.

The marketing function has gone through many transformations as markets and regulatory policies have changed. The function is established, but it is still young and proving its mettle. The external change agent is gone, but many of the outsiders remain. The integration of new and old continues. Career pathing into and out of marketing is still limited. The issue is not yet settled regarding proper development of marketing people and development of all managers for a marketing-focused organization.

Competition had introduced some fundamental changes into the telecommunications business and altered the mission and operations of the organization. Every one of the basic characteristics underlying the career system was under challenge. The organization went to great lengths to maintain career continuity, yet managers wondered if it would be able to do so in the future. Patterns of advancement appeared to be changing. Managers were expected to behave differently, and some questioned whether "monopoly-bred" managers were suited to or could adapt to the new world. Assessment programs were reviewed for relevance in identifying managers for the future. Promotion from within was less honored than in the past. Specialists, not generalists, were wanted for many jobs. Many questioned whether the transformed goals were worthy of the organization. Loyalty was hardly gone, but the climate was changing. Individuals were sensing that they would have to become more active in managing their development and careers. Simply put, the career system was becoming more dynamic, with no apparent stable state in the offering.

Divestiture. The last, most dramatic, and most far-reaching event during the period under review was the split-up of the Bell System. It is hard to imagine a more significant change in organizational careers than the fragmentation of the organization itself. The incident, of course, was AT&T's agreement in January 1982 to divest itself of its operating telephone companies (OTCs). Various reasons have been cited for the split-up. Perhaps the most fundamental cause was the rapidly changing technology that blurred the distinction between telephone and computer or between data transmission and data transformation. Other obvious factors were the burgeoning markets and the general governmental thrust toward deregulation and competition.

This was to be an unusually complex divestiture for reasons beyond that of the sheer size of the Bell System. The consent decree did not stipulate a simple divestiture of the OTCs intact; rather there was to be shifting of functions between the OTCs and AT&T. For example, a substantial piece of intrastate long-distance service was to be transfered from the OTCs to AT&T, with the corresponding assets and people also moving to AT&T. The organization had two years in which to complete the divestiture, a very short time considering the magnitude and difficulty of the job.

The first task of the organization was to reconfigure AT&T and the OTCs into viable organizations within the stipulations of the consent decree. The plan that emerged essentially called for grouping the somewhat scaled-down OTCs into seven regional holding companies and the reconfiguration of AT&T into a national organization, a high-tech company providing information systems and long-distance service. All organizations faced an enormous amount of change and uncertainty. This was particularly true for AT&T, which would become a research-and-development-, manufacturing-, and marketing-oriented company, along with its national telecommunications network. In addition, some aspects of AT&T's business would be regulated and others unregulated. All its business would be open to competition.

No phase of the divestiture was more vexing than the assignment and managing of the people. The success of the future organizations formed from the divestiture would depend heavily on getting the right people in the right places and maintaining their high motivation, commitment, and loyalty. How was this massive placement task to be conducted? How were the people to be shifted geographically to match the new organizational configurations? What would be done about the inevitable mismatches and surpluses that would develop? There were a million employees involved. It had to be done quickly and well. There were two basic steps in the assignment of people. The first was the determination of the number and types of people to be assigned to AT&T and the OTCs. These numbers flowed directly from the allocation of functions and assets. In most cases, an entire work group would be allocated to an organization. Frequently, however, each organization was assigned a portion of the work, which necessitated a sharing or allocation of the work group involved. Once these numbers became available, the process moved on to the second major step: the assignment of specific individuals to an organization.

The establishment of principles to guide the assignment of individuals was recognized from the outset as crucial. The announcement of the divestiture had been a surprise and a shock to the employees. They were learning to expect and to deal with change in their organizations and careers, but they were not prepared for anything of this magnitude. Although they had joined a particular company, they were part of the Bell System; they were intensely loyal to the system and committed to its goals and values. Universal telephone service was the core mission of the system. Many feared the divestiture would by its nature threaten the goal that had guided all their efforts. It was difficult to envision very precisely what the "new" organizations would be like. What would the career opportunities be? What would the jobs be like? Would there be jobs for everyone? Would the new organizations continue the personnel policies and share the same values of the Bell System? The questions were riveting, the answers fuzzy and slow to materialize. While employees were expected to be treated fairly, there were new realities and constraints, which led to uncertainty and anxiety.

The organization responded by developing a set of eleven staffing policies with the dual purpose of producing organizations prepared to meet the new environment and satisfying as much as possible the needs and concerns of its people. Five key policies dealing with careers were: (1) The initial staffing of new organizations would be accomplished through the use of existing Bell System employees wherever possible. (2) The basic premise for assignment was that employees follow their work. (3) Employee preferences would be considered where business needs permitted. (4) Human resources would be shared equitably between entities. (5) At divestiture each entity would contain adequate management resources in order to ensure senior management continuity.

The organizational needs were paramount. The provision for people following their jobs was an attempt to maintain skill and experience levels on the job, keep work groups intact where possible, and keep the placement effort within manageable bounds. The provisions for sharing human resources equitably and ensuring senior management continuity were essential for meeting the legal test of fairness as well as the needs of the new entities.

The organization's needs placed constraints on the individual's choices regarding both job and organization. In the main, individuals would follow their work according to the allocations of the Plan of Reorganization (U.S. District Court, District of Columbia, 1982), and the need to share talent meant that there would be a balancing of people that could override individual preferences. The policies contained some strong assurances for employees, however. The new organizations would be staffed with existing employees wherever possible, thus preserving as many jobs as possible for them. In cases in which work forces were split, their preferences for entity would be solicited and honored as much as possible. Some employee voice in career decision was maintained, although the extent of his or her influence would depend on the individual's particular situation.

Individuals faced a difficult task in expressing their preferences for assignment. They had to make their choices on the basis of the information available, knowing full well that there was considerable uncertainty as to how things would work out in the entities. It was a choice they had never expected to have to make.

The individuals were provided with written materials about the new entities and the assignment process, and they attended meetings at which they could seek further information. They then indicated their preferences in writing, followed by individual meetings with their supervisors to discuss their situations. Following these sessions, the supervisors made recommendations for placement of their people.

Actual assignments were based on employee preferences and supervisory recommendations within the overall constraint of balancing the split groups in terms of skills, training, experience, and performance. This already complex assignment process was confounded by two events in the second half of 1983. One event was a three-week strike that impeded the assignment process. The second was the recognition that serious surpluses and mismatches were developing due to the reconfiguring of the entities both organizationally and geographically. In September 1983, a massive outplacement program was launched to reduce the surpluses. The program was the same one used earlier in marketing; it was voluntary and contained attractive incentives. By the end of 1983, 11,000 employees had opted for the program and left the system prior to the split. On January 1, 1984, the divestiture became effective, and many individuals began reporting to new organizations.

Managers working in AT&T in 1984 found a slimmed-down company with a new mission. Many of the general organizational values had shifted. Certainly one of the major shifts was toward a more bottom-line orientation. Cost containment resulted in freezing of salaries, reductions in management levels, and limited promotional opportunities for the near term. Managers heard of the need to take risks, to be more responsive to the customer, and to be flexible and adaptive in managing in the new environment. The growth patterns remained uneven, with hiring in some functions and surpluses in others. The organization continued to use its outplacement program to deal with surpluses. Advancement patterns were fuzzy. The "new" management style and the managerial characteristics required were only beginning to become evident. Bosses faced the same ambiguities, and identification of role models for the future was problematic. Managers sensed that if they could not meet the changing requirements, career continuity would become tenuous. Loyalty remained high, but all were carefully watching the organization's behavior. AT&T was in the middle of a transformation and under considerable stress. Managers were learning what their new organization was to value and helping to shape it, trusting that it would remain an organization that captured their commitment.

Organizational Adaptation

Our retrospective look at the last thirty years suggests massive organizational changes that none of the recruits hired in the 1950s could ever have anticipated. The 1950s recruit expected a continuous career in a stable organization that had many interchangeable units and thus provided many opportunities for growth and advancement as part of an established nation-wide system. Today's recruit works in a much more uncertain environment. Loyalties have shifted, career patterns have changed, and many career characteristics have become open to question or significantly altered.

This is quite evident when we look at Table 4. The table indicates whether the organizational values and characteristics and the characteristics of the career system have remained stable, are of uncertain status, or have been transformed during the last thirty years. Only three of the seventeen values or characteristics listed have remained stable. AT&T managers have maintained a strong identification with their work function, and to a large extent the same hierarchical form of organizational structure has continued. Rigorous performance standards are still expected. These values are strong ones, and the fact that they have remained constant has certainly helped maintain career continuity for both an organization and its people during a period of unparalleled change.

Turning to the remaining characteristics, it is interesting to note how many organizational characteristics and characteristics of the career system have been transformed during this thirty-year span. The massive organizational shifts resulting from both competition and divestiture certainly changed the outlook of the organization and its managers. Similarly, shifting managerial

Table 4. Shifts in Organizational Values and Characteristics of Career System from 1955 to 1985.

	Stable	Uncertain	Transformed
1. Organizational values		• Loyalty • Commitment to a socially important goal	• Service
2. Organizational characteristics	• Well-defined hierarchical structure • Strong identification with work function	• Well-defined organizational structure	• Nation-wide corporate identity among employees • Strong identification with geographical unit
3. Characteristics of career system	• Rigorous performance standards	• Stable and well-defined patterns of advancement • Career continuity • Development of management generalists • Commitment to an AT&T career • Primacy of work career	• Promotion from within • Potential standards • Supervisor as key person who manages career development

values reflecting changes in society also influenced the nature and direction of careers. We have gone from a period in which managers expected stable, well-defined career patterns to an era of much less certainty and predictability of career continuity.

Examining the career and organizational continuities and discontinuities from a case study perspective highlights the complex interaction between these forces. The changes in society and the changes in work force composition both occurred gradually. While the impact of competition and divestiture was more specific, the organization had changed in many ways. Because these were visible business shifts, they probably produced greater change in the career systems. Both the organization and its managers were different.

What conclusions can be drawn from our review of organizational adaptation? Six key learnings seem to be important.

1. An organization and its people are amazingly resilient. Despite the massive upheavals in organizational and career values, dislocation of employees to units that may be very different from initial employment expectations, and shifts in organizational focus from a service orientation to a product and service perspective, the company continues to run fairly smoothly, its people are generally upbeat, and its management is optimistic about the future. An organizational change of this order of magnitude—resulting from the breakup of an organization with 1,000,000 employees into eight different (and mostly new) units ranging in size from 90,000 to 350,000 employees—is not an everyday occurrence, but for the most part the change has gone smoothly. New employees have been hired and trained, promotions have occurred, and staffing issues that at one time seemed insurmountable have been resolved.

2. Predicting the future and its impact on both individual and organizational careers is extremely tenuous. No one in 1955, 1965, or even 1975 could have predicted or even anticipated the major shifts that would occur in society, in the organization, or in its people. Yet throughout this period selection and development programs designed to ensure organizational vitality have continued. How they are used will vary, and an

adaptive organization will modify its procedures to meet and anticipate changes as appropriate. For example, AT&T's assessment center programs now stress placement and development along with selection, an adaptation to the staffing needs of the business.

3.   Cultural change forces new organizational characteristics and new characteristics of the career system. This raises several unresolved issues, not the least of which is strategies for understanding these shifts. For example, what early warning signals are important organizational barometers of change? Next, assuming that we do understand such shifts, how do new values compete with old ones? What does it mean in terms of organizational effectiveness to note that loyalty has shifted from identification with the company to identification with one's work unit? How are entrenched values such as service modified as the organization moves from a monopoly to a competitive environment, and what effect does this have on long-term individual and organizational performance? What impact do these value shifts have on careers? Take, for example, an "institution" such as marriage. In the 1950s, marriages were for the most part "career" decisions, with both parties expected to remain together "for better or worse . . . until death do us part." Few marriages in the 1980s fit this stereotype. If marriages tend to be short term, reflecting shifts in our society's values, what can be said about long-term careers? These questions are not easily resolved, yet the answers to these types of questions are essential in forming a long-range development strategy to ensure organizational vitality.

4.   More attention must be given to understanding and anticipating *future* management requirements. Shifts in markets suggest that a different skill mix and style will be required. For example, managers need to tolerate and cope with ambiguity, be more creative, and be more effective risk takers. These are not new skills, but their importance has increased. At AT&T, a major shift in problem-solving focus has occurred, from problem solving in certain environments to problem solving in unpredictable environments. Managers trained and rewarded for having a short-term "fix the crisis" orientation have to shift

to a longer-term focus, which will necessitate dealing with many complex issues, some of which may not be resolvable. To what extent should the organization rely on internal organizational staffing? How can managers trained in one "culture" adapt to another? There are many advantages to a promotion-from-within staffing policy, not the least of which is the internalization of values important to the organization. This also can have a down side, particularly when its managers resist new ideas and change. How can an organization balance the development of new skills to make it effective in the marketplace? How can it retain key skills that have led to its success in the past?

5. Career continuity issues must be articulated and understood. This is a major issue for both an organization and its people. From an organization's perspective, does it make sense to offer its managers a lifetime career? If it does, how should the organization go about equipping managers to be more flexible, to adapt to change and new markets? If the organization wants to selectively retain only some of its managers, how does it go about doing this? If the organization wants to develop strategies that retain only some core of its management body, how does it instill loyalty, direction, and continuity? The organization itself also has changed, including its approach to development. It has shifted from a rational, slow, and deliberate pace of development to one that encourages trial and error, experimentation, and risk. Development in the 1950s had strong advancement overtones. However, decreased promotional opportunities, a smaller organization, fewer interchangeable units, and a shift in the skill mix desired have resulted in development strategies of the 1980s having a strong placement focus. Desired developmental experiences changed as well from those leading to the development of management generalists to more emphasis on experiences leading to specialist or expert knowledge. All of these affect career continuity strategies.

6. Individuals need to manage their careers. Changes in expectations about career continuity come from many sources. Societal and organizational shifts are important forces. Yet the

expectations of the individual are also important determinants of career continuity. Part of the transition in career continuity comes from individuals who are seeking more career changes today. In the next section, we will review some shifts in career expectations that have occurred in the last decade. One of the most important lessons here is the need to help managers come to an early understanding of career continuity issues. Equipping people to be more responsible for their careers may be a major departure for many managers, but it may be a major determinant of both individual and organizational vitality.

Individual Perspectives and Expectations

Our focus up to now has been on the organization. However, we cannot ignore shifts in individual perspectives that significantly affect expectations about careers. While other chapters in this book cover this topic in greater detail, we have identified six themes, listed in Table 5, that have changed during the last thirty years. These themes reflect significant changes in the expectations of managers, shifts in society, and changes within the company itself. They represent a complex mosaic of career expectations.

Implicit Length of Employment. This is one of the major areas of change during our review period. Career perspectives significantly decreased during this period. Recruits hired during the 1950s were expected to remain with one major employer and viewed entry into the business as entry into a lifetime career. Today's recruits have a much shorter time perspective, often thinking of employment in terms of two to three years. This shift reflects a much more mobile society. It also mirrors the increased diversity in jobs, the rapid emergence of new technologies, and the relative ease of movement across organizations.

Motivators. Advancement was the major career reward offered during the 1950s and 1960s. Managers expected to remain with an organization throughout a career, and one of the major inducements offered was advancement and the status, power, money, and prestige that came with increased levels of re-sponsibility. During the early 1970s, a change was noted. New recruits seemed to be motivated by an intrinsic sense of job

Table 5. Changes in Development Themes from 1955 to 1985.

Development theme	1955	1985
Career perspective	Lifetime	Short-term
Motivation	Advancement	Accomplishment/ Advancement
Career managed by	Supervisor	Individual/Third party
Number of careers	One	Several/Many
Family income/Dual careers	One primary wage earner	Dual careers
Development focus	Long-term, general	Next job, specialist

accomplishment and job challenge rather than by advancement. There were many reasons for this change, not the least of which was the social change occurring during this period. The 1980s saw a return to more traditional themes of advancement, but a strong sense of accomplishment theme continues as well. Again, these motives reflect shifts in our society.

Who is Responsible? The concept of responsibility for managing development also saw significant shifts during the past decade. For many years, one's immediate supervisor was viewed as the person who was primarily responsible for assisting (or preventing) availability for different assignments. With the advent of equal employment legislation, third parties—mainly personnel or departmental coordinators—became involved with career management issues. Supervisors had to report on the number of movement opportunities for protected groups, and procedures were instituted for these third parties to help supervisors with developmental planning. With divestiture and a total reorganization of work groups, the responsibility for career planning became much more an individual matter. While bosses and third parties still play a role, the shift to shorter career perspectives, along with the dissolution of previous networks resulting from divestiture, forced the individual to try to manage his or her career.

Number of Careers. Perhaps one of the most significant changes affecting career perspectives is the realization that multiple careers are socially acceptable. The recruit of the 1950s and 1960s was expected to have *a* career. Individuals with many major career changes were viewed as eccentric at best and unstable at worst. Partially as a result of increased life span and increased retirement ages, multiple careers became realistic options for many.

Family Income/Dual Careers. One of the major outcomes of fair employment legislation was the growth of women managers in the work force. This, and the inflationary period in the 1970s, resulted in the need for many couples to seek full-time employment. As women began to advance into higher-status jobs, a significant shift in career focus began to emerge. Decisions about job change, advancement, or relocation took on a very different perspective when viewed through the eyes of a dual-career family.

Focus of Development. Shortened career perspectives, multiple careers, dual careers, and shifts in career motivation affect the focus of development. Managers in the 1960s expected to have a lifetime of development. In this sense, development was general and positive. On-the-job developmental assignments were given to high-potential managers with the expectation that such learnings would be useful as they gradually moved up in the business. Today's focus has changed considerably. In many areas, development is geared to the next job rather than thinking in terms of long-term career development. Just as importantly, managers are encouraged to capitalize on their existing knowledge and strengths by seeking situations that make the best use of their current abilities. We will return to this theme in the next section, when we examine how to help people manage their careers.

The Future of Organizational Careers

We identified two dominant themes that occurred at AT&T during the period reviewed. We believe that these themes are more generic than specific and apply to most large organizations. These should be kept in mind as we examine the future of organizational careers: (1) The forces that inhibit or facilitate changes in career patterns are increasing. (2) Organizational values are as significant as any other determinant in shaping career patterns.

Organizational career practices are incremental, often building on precedent and an established order. Yet future organizations will need to be more responsive in order to adapt career patterns to changing times. The ability of organizations to shift and adapt their career development strategies will result in manpower pools that are sufficient to meet ongoing staffing needs. Large excesses or deficiencies in such pools may be a clear signal that career development practices are "out of synch" with marketplace, environmental, or social forces.

For a variety of reasons, careers traditionally have been viewed from the perspective of the individual. We agree with this point of view, as individual differences in job skills, motivation, abilities, and so on are important determinants of career success. Yet we need to balance our knowledge of career patterns with a better understanding of how organizational values shape careers. This can help us understand why people change organizations, as well as how people accommodate to shifts within organizations.

Our case study suggests that statements about the long-term future of careers are risky at best. The case is a study in dialectics containing stability and change, order and uncertainty. Some swings are subtle and incremental, while others are abrupt shifts between extremes. Prescriptions in such a setting would be foolhardy. However, identification of critical issues and alternatives for dealing with them are essential. The observations that follow are intended to stimulate discussion, action, and research regarding the basic career characteristics organizations must fashion in adapting to a rapidly changing environment.

How Long Will Organizational Careers Be? Perhaps the fundamental issue to be resolved by the organization is the length of the career it offers individuals. Will it strive to provide life-span careers, short-term careers, or something in between these extremes? This decision should influence the remaining characteristics of the career system. The more fundamental shifts in career characteristics at AT&T resulted from changes in the environment and the nature of the business. Technological, marketplace, and governmental developments were the primary causes, and their reverberations on career systems were not fully controllable by the organization. It is quite likely that many large organizations will face similar circumstances in the future. Deregulation has had enormous impact on the airlines and banks. Mergers of large organizations are no longer unusual. The pace of technological development and the emergence of the information age portend a period of rapid, large-scale shifts in the mission and operations of many major organizations. Decisions concerning career expectations will be key ones for both the individual and the organization.

What Features of a Career System Should Be Stressed? While organizations can be expected to vary in the extent to which they offer long-term careers, the design of career systems and the preparation of managers are likely to become more crucial factors in the success of organizations in the future. Our case analysis suggests some strategies that could prove useful and mesh with the changing expectations of individuals. Multiple careers within the organization would help meet this organizational need and satisfy those individuals seeking career change for personal reasons (Levinson, 1978). Ways of conceptualizing career development experiences along the lines suggested by McCall, Lombardo, and Morrison (forthcoming) appear very appropriate for the multiple-career environment. The socialization of new managers (Schein, 1985) can be designed to predispose managers to expect multiple careers. Experienced managers can be screened, developed, and advanced, with more emphasis placed on their ability to cope with ambiguity and uncertainty (Moses and Lyness, 1983). In the end, it is the behavior of people that establish the norms, standards, and values of the organization. Establishment of an adaptive organization with multiple internal careers for individuals will depend on effective interventions that enable people to develop appropriate perspectives and behavior.

How Do We Prepare People to Take on a More Active Role in Their Career Management? If the trend toward more rapid change in organizations continues, individuals should anticipate more varied careers and the need to be very active in managing their careers. Those who opt for commitment to a specialty or occupation, whether with one or many employers, face some of the same uncertainties as organizations. Keeping pace with changes brought about by technology will call for lifelong learning. Those who obtain multiple experiences and competencies, preferably relatively early in their development, should be in a better position to deal with multiple career opportunities.

We also need to have a better understanding and anticipation of future development needs. We need to understand emerging skills and their impact on organizations. For example, coping with ambiguity may become an increasingly important skill for managers in many organizations. Equipping managers to deal with an uncertain world requires both diagnostic and intervention efforts. We also need to expand our diagnostic information about jobs and people into effective early warning systems concerning major shifts in careers and development needs. For example, we need to expand our taxonomy of developmental experiences. Much of today's development relies on training, education, or on-the-job experiences. We know very little about the appropriate sequencing, duration, and benefits of each of these. We need to integrate job analysis with developmental analyses in order to ensure the best fit between individual and organizational needs. These are all important inputs to help people better manage their careers.

What Impact Will Career Shifts Have on Motivation and Productivity? Some important research questions emerge from these long-term career themes. One is the effect of multiple careers on individual and organizational motivation and performance. What can individuals and organizations do to maintain high levels of commitment and productivity in the face of shifting values and missions? The ability to manage change well depends on rapid response to fundamental organizational needs while avoiding overresponse to transitory forces. More imformation is needed on effective ways to induce change through the hiring of outside talent. What kinds of people should be recruited? How are they grafted onto or integrated into the organization? How will organizations match their espoused values as they compete in the marketplace for future talent? What should a recruiting brochure of 1995 look like? What values will be important, and how will they be expressed?

None of these issues is easily submitted to empirical research. Most involve study of behavior over substantial periods in what is posited to be a very dynamic environment. The quest seems worth the effort in terms of the need for both better knowledge and improved practice in the development of career systems worthy of individual commitment and organizational support.

Conclusion

As both organizational members and researchers, we have been struck with the impact that the organization itself has on the careers of its members. Often difficult to recognize, organizational shifts in response to market, environmental, or social forces are frequently subtle and rarely direct. These shifts are hard to detect when they occur, but they are easy to recognize in retrospect. Each organization has its passages. Learning to identify which event will be transitory and which will or should affect career systems can be most beneficial in developing career and staffing strategies for the future.

References

Boehm, V. R. "Changing Career Patterns for Women in the Bell System." Paper presented as part of the symposium, *Employment Status of Women in Academia, Business, Government, and the Military.* 82nd annual convention of the American Psychological Association, New Orleans, Aug. 1974.

Bray, D. W., Campbell, R. J., and Grant, D. L. *Formative Years in Business.* New York: Wiley, 1974.

Collier, B., and Moses, J. L. "Applying SRT to Outside Plant." *National Society for Performance Improvement Journal,* 1977, *16,* 3–5.

Hall, D. T., and Nougaim, K. "An Examination of Maslow's Need Hierarchy in an Organizational Setting." *Organizational Behavior and Human Performance,* 1968, *3,* 12–35.

Howard, A., and Bray, D. W. "Today's Young Managers: They Can Do It, But Will They?" *The Wharton Magazine,* 1981, *5*(4), 23–28.

Levinson, D. J. *The Seasons of a Man's Life.* New York: Knopf, 1978.

McCall, M. W., Lombardo, M. M., and Morrison, A. M. *The Lessons of Experience.* New York: Harper & Row, forthcoming.

Moses, J. L., and Boehm, V. R. "Relationship of Assessment Center Performance to the Management Progress of Women." *Journal of Applied Psychology,* 1975, *60,* 527–529.

Moses, J. L., and Lyness, K. S. "A Conceptual Model for Studying Ambiguity." Paper presented as part of the symposium, *Ambiguity, Uncertainty and Change: A Theoretical View.* 91st annual convention of the American Psychological Association, Anaheim, Calif., August 26, 1983.

Ritchie, R. J., and Moses, J. L. "Assessment Center Correlates of Women's Advancement into Middle Management: A 7-year Longitudinal Analysis." *Journal of Applied Psychology,* 1983, *60,* 227–233.

Schein, E. H. *Organizational Culture and Leadership: A Dynamic View.* San Francisco: Jossey-Bass, 1985.

U.S. District Court, District of Columbia. Civil Action 82-0192, *Plan of Reorganization.* December 16, 1982.

9

𐠒𐠒𐠒𐠒𐠒𐠒𐠒𐠒

A Critical Look
at Current Career
Development Theory
and Research

Edgar H. Schein

Career theory and research is a relatively young field within the
social sciences, and it is not yet clear whether it will survive with
its own identity intact. Positive indicators are volumes such as this
and the fact that the Academy of Management has elevated the
"career interest group" into a full-fledged division. On the negative
side is the fact that the field is fractionated, lacks coherent concepts
and theories, and has a strong ethnocentric and managerial bias.

The chapters in this book certainly show that there is a high
level of effort, activity, creativity, and constructive intent in this
field. New technologies are being invented every day to enhance
career planning and development, new concepts are being suggested
to increase our understanding of career dynamics, and organizational programs are being described and advocated to show how
these systems and technologies should work.

Problems of Career Theory and Research

All this is well illustrated in the chapters of this volume and
should make us quite optimistic about the future. Yet I find little

cause for optimism. What, then, is the problem? I have divided my discussion into several major points, followed by some case materials to illustrate some aspects of the problem as I see it.

Fractionation. The field is fractionated, partly because it falls between the various academic disciplines that inform it. Sociologists and anthropologists who study careers start with a descriptive bias and illuminate what organizations do or do not do for people in their occupational lives (Hughes, 1958; Becker, Geer, Hughes, and Strauss, 1961; Glaser, 1968; Perrucci and Gerstl, 1969; Van Maanen, 1973). In contrast, occupational psychologists are preoccupied with predicting who will enter what type of career. They know a great deal about testing and counseling young people, but they know relatively less than the sociologists and anthropologists about what it actually is like to be a doctor, lawyer, engineer, clerk, production worker, manager, and so on (Osipow, 1983; Holland, 1973; Super, 1980; Tiedeman and O'Hara, 1963; Gysbers and Associates, 1984). However, knowledge of what members of those occupations look like when one gives them interest inventories is hardly an adequate criterion for what the properties of those careers really will turn out to be.

Organizational and industrial psychologists have partially remedied this situation, but they are biased toward improving rather than describing and thus have focused on developing techniques and tools to enhance the process of selection, promotion, development, and matching of job requirements with individual talents and needs (Hall, 1976; Storey, 1976; London and Stumpf, 1982). The concern is with predicting success, advancement, productivity, and satisfaction, a bias that is certainly relevant and important, but a bias nevertheless.

Those psychologists who have spent their time in personnel and industrial relations departments often develop a bias toward improving the management of "human resources," which usually means the lower levels of the organization, while managerial psychologists (who are well represented in this volume) focus primarily on the selection and development of managers. This managerial bias is rationalized by authors through the argument that managerial resources, especially at the higher levels, are, after all, the most critical resource in most organizations. In recent years,

I have come to doubt this conclusion, as more and more companies acknowledge their dependence on key technical or functional people who may be individual contributors (Schein, 1978).

In the meantime, another troop of social scientists with more of a sociological bent has attempted to uncover what is *really* happening on the factory floor and has found evidence of outrageous levels of exploitation and inequity (Terkel, 1974; Schrank, 1978; Balzer, 1976). Such findings sometimes lead to political biases against the "establishment" and occasionally even against the entire capitalist system. A few brave souls leave the shop floor and actually study the establishment itself, leading to some interesting questions and concerns about how careers are actually lived in organizations, as contrasted with how they are supposed to be lived (Dalton, 1959; Rosenbaum, 1984; Manning and Van Maanen, 1978; Bailyn, 1980, 1982; Schein, 1978).

Why is such fractionation a problem or source of concern? Because when one reads the various accounts from different fields it would appear that the researchers do not really understand and take seriously the "realities" uncovered by points of view different from their own. If the various fields do not understand the realities that are revealed by the other fields, *none* of them will represent accurately what actually happens in real organizations. Or, worse, their generalizations will appear to be valid when, in fact, they are not.

For example, many of the chapters in this book reflect a managerial bias in being concerned on the one hand with improving career development and human resource systems and procedures while on the other hand also being concerned with how technological changes will create organizational problems that may make career development more difficult. Research reflects this bias in being concerned primarily with the evaluation of various tools, programs, and methods rather than attempting to describe in either clinical or ethnographic terms what actually happens in organizations when they attempt to use the tools and when economic times get better or worse.

The irony of this bias is that, especially at critical times when there is a major technological change and careers disappear or when a company is forced to lay off hundreds of people because of an economic downturn, what happens most often is that the kinds of career development programs that are advocated in many of the chapters are abandoned as being frills and too costly.

At this stage of the development of the field, I think it is particularly important to maintain the descriptive approach, because I have observed—both as a member in and as a consultant to organizations—that there is little connection between the career systems that are prescribed and what actually goes on when they are administered. Except for a few longitudinal studies, we have very few bases for connecting any given career programs with levels of success; my own research indicates that formal criteria for success, such as attaining a middle-management rank, may not correspond at all with what career members regard as success, since levels of ambition vary so widely (Bray, Campbell, and Grant, 1974; Bray, 1982; Schein, 1978).

Subfields Ignore Each Other. The fact that career researchers come from many different fields is healthy. But when researchers in one field seemingly actively ignore the work of researchers in other fields, this is distinctly not healthy for the evolution of the career area. For example, there is reason to believe that *technically* based careers both at the staff and managerial levels will become more important in the future. Yet there is hardly any reference in the chapters of this volume to any of the work done on such careers by Dalton, Thompson, and Price (1977), Bailyn (1980, 1982), Ritti (1971), Kopelman (1977), and many others who have concerned themselves in a major way with the question of what a technical career is all about. How engineers and scientists differ from each other, how one makes the transition from technical to managerial work, whether or not general managers can or do evolve out of technically anchored functional managers, and other critical questions are almost totally ignored in this volume.

If our career theories and research do not answer such questions, we cannot help either future career participants or organizations. Yet I have observed much concern in the senior levels of many organizations about human resource strategy pertaining to technical resources: (1) How can one evolve sensible policies of recruitment, selection, job placement, and development in a world in which one cannot predict accurately what the nature of technical

work will really be like even five years down the road? (2) How can
one write job descriptions, develop consistent placement policies
and reward systems, and make development plans for people when
it is not known what the basic strategic thrust of the business will
be a few years down the road? (3) How can one create the time for
"developmental assignments" when the very survival of the
company depends on full utilization of people in their present
assignments?

      If, as some have argued (Zuboff, 1985), the computer will
fundamentally change the nature of the work, then how will careers
be defined in this uncertain future? One of the most interesting
possibilities is that most of the systems that have been built up in
traditional organizations for the management and development of
human resources will become obsolete and will have to be replaced
by systems and procedures that have not yet been invented.

      For example, it may well turn out that the only way to deal
with the reality of having to get rid of employees who are
technically obsolete or who have been made redundant by
automation is to give them several *years'* pay in order to permit
them to reeducate—not merely retrain—themselves. In 1980, I heard
an Australian entrepreneur tell his managerial colleagues that he
got rid of obsolete programmers by offering them $100,000 to go
away. His colleagues were shocked by what seemed to them a very
costly and inhumane process. Recently, I mentioned this story to a
group of managers in a number of European companies and was
told that many of them are already talking in terms of three years'
pay as the minimum that must be given to an employee being
terminated for other than performance reasons in order to allow
that person to reeducate himself or herself.

      What we need in this area is not cases from "typical"
organizations but data from organizations that are themselves on
the frontier. Our research is too biased by the survey logic of looking
for what the average or typical company is doing and not
sufficiently biased toward clinical/ethnographic investigation of
the most untypical cases, both in terms of what may seem most
healthy and what may seem most pathological (Kets De Vries and
Miller, 1984). We need to look for organizational inventions that
deal with the problems of the future, and our role as researchers and

scholars should be to create clear concepts and theories around such advanced practices rather than continuing to study what may soon be outmoded anyway.

Cultural Biases. Much of our career research is culturally biased. We talk of "management," "career development," and "success" as if these were *general* concepts and forget that we are talking about particular aspects of United States culture. If there were evidence that principles of management are indeed general, this might be acceptable; but, if anything, the evidence is beginning to point in the direction of cultural specificity (Hofstede, 1980; Laurent, 1983; Schein, 1984). We act as if the only obligation we have academically is to unravel the problems of our society.

If it is true that most business organizations, whether in the United States or in other parts of the world, are going to become more internationalized and be forced to think on a global basis, what will this trend do to career concepts and career systems? There is virtually no reference in any of the chapters to the major dilemmas the multinationals face in defining what a "career" is in the international context. If it is true that people today want less geographic movement, how will organizations manage single or dual careers internationally?

Who will address the problems of training for multicultural management, of getting employees to think globally even if they themselves do not move to other countries, of getting managers to look at United States management principles as only one way to do things? There *are* career researchers who worry about and study these problems, but the fractionation of our field makes them seemingly invisible if one is not closely connected to them (see Adler, 1983; Harris and Moran, 1979; Moran and Harris, 1982; Zeira and Banai, 1985; Desatnick and Bennett, 1978; Hofstede, 1980). The price we may pay is that the members of each subset of researchers will be relevant only to their immediate academic colleagues and will not contribute to the building of theory and knowledge on a broad enough basis to be relevant to the academic community at large or to practitioners.

Lack of Integrative Constructs and Theory. This point is directly derivative from the above points. Each academic discipline happily develops its own concepts but does not feel obligated to connect them to the concepts that flow from other disciplines. For example, one should explicitly connect theories of *ego development* (Loevinger, Wessler, and Redmore, 1970), theories of *cognitive development* (Driver and Streufert, 1969), theories of *adult development* (Levinson and others, 1978; Osherson, 1980; Vaillant, 1977), and theories of *career development* (Super, 1980; Hall, 1976; Schein, 1978; Driver, 1980), yet one rarely sees a research study in one of these fields that makes any reference to all the other fields.

In the meantime, the practitioner and/or teacher is faced with compendia of readings and applied articles that use none of the concepts developed in any of the subfields (Morgan, 1980; London and Stumpf, 1982; Jelinek, 1979; Montross and Shinkman, 1981). Integrative studies that draw concepts from many disciplines tend to be ignored (Evans and Bartolome, 1980). This situation is not necessarily a problem as a field develops, but many of the writers represented in this book write as if there is a mature and integrated field. The reader is then confronted with a myriad of potentially conflicting concepts and models and no one seems to own the responsibility for straightening out the theoretical mess.

To give one example, London and Stumpf, in Chapter One, propose the construct of "career resilience" to measure the capacity of people to shift and change careers, to deal with career uncertainties, and to cope with organizational disappointments. The concept implies that this dimension applies to all kinds of people and all kinds of careers. In contrast, my longitudinal studies (1975, 1978, forthcoming) have led me to the concept of "career anchor," which implies that different people in organizations come to define their careers very differently in terms of their evolving image of their own talents, motives, and values.

The two concepts together might illuminate in a constructive way why some people are upset about a given kind of career event (for example, a failure to get promoted or the failure of a proposal to be transfered to another function) while others seem not to be bothered by it at all. The answer is that the person who is anchored in general management defines progress and success in terms of formal promotions, while the person who is anchored in technical or functional competence cares less about promotion and more about his or her ability to remain challenged in that area. Being moved out of the area becomes tantamount to being moved into an area of incompetence; the argument of the developmentally oriented boss that "rotation is a good thing" will have little persuasive power for such a person. In other words, subjective definitions (what I call the "internal career") specify for the individual the meaning of success, what path should be followed to success, and, by implication, what kinds of events will be stressful and disappointing. Measuring resilience as as *general* property without relating it to other career variables is much less powerful.

How does better theory come about? First of all, we need to build concepts and models around what I call the "realities" of how things really work in organizations. We need more and better descriptive studies of how things work so that concepts and models mirror what really goes on rather than what we normatively wish would go on. Being normative is very comfortable until one starts to take the concept of culture seriously. One then discovers that the career field is shot through with cultural biases, that even the concept of career itself has no clear meaning independent of an occupation, a particular organization, or a country (Schein, 1984). The effort to define it sociologically as a culture-free concept has clearly not been successful, as a reading of the chapters in this volume will show. Different authors focus on very different aspects, all under the single label of career research and theory.

Second, we get better theory if we escalate academic debate. Perhaps the compartmentalization and fractionation bothers me so much because it deprives us of the academic debate that might lead to clarity. "You keep your concepts and I'll work on my concepts" seems to be our norm, and that is a wonderful way to keep things vague and static. *Some* of us must be working on the wrong end of things or have concepts that are less useful, but we never seem to confront each other about this; we just ignore each other. If we continue to do that, we will not improve our theories.

Content Versus Process Orientation. The obsession with tools, programs, and normative solutions to career problems leads to a systematic myopia about the degree to which all of these solutions hinge more on *how* they are done than on what is done. Performance appraisal systems can be designed to be "perfect," using all the best psychological insights and research results available, and still can fail dismally because senior management (1) is lukewarm about the use of any system, (2) sends signals of indifference on the use of the system, and (3) never punishes any manager who subverts or misuses the system. Another company may use all the wrong techniques but because senior managers are deeply committed to the idea that people need to be appraised and given feedback, they muddle through with their own inventions and do a fine job (as measured by the satisfaction of the subordinate that good performance information is provided to him or her by the boss).

We have all observed that no matter how perfect the tools are that we give to managers, they will use those tools for whatever purposes they see fit and in whatever way they care to. And such purposes often will go beyond individual biases that could be overcome by training, reflecting instead shared assumptions that come to be embedded as elements of the organizational culture (Schein, 1985).

The architects of tests, assessment centers, career development systems, computerized data banks, and inventories put too little emphasis on the process of installing the system, teaching people how to use the tools, dealing with resistance to change or outright subversion. Some of the most interesting stories told by human resource managers have to do with the *processes* they have invented to get a system or tool implemented, to tap into managerial motivation, to help management manage better regardless of the tools used, and to adapt a tool to the local culture. It may well be that whatever we have to offer in the career development area will always have to be fine tuned and altered in a particular organizational context, and we should start doing research on these processes of implementation so that we can teach others how to succeed in installing anything at all.

Some Illustrative Realities

I have frequently referred to "realities," but I have not yet given enough attention to what some of these realities are. The case examples offered here are intended to be descriptive, to lay out what actually happened as I observed it, and to provide some observations as data on the basis of which a more complete understanding of career dynamics eventually can be built.

Case 1. Who Controls the Career Development System? I attended a meeting of the executive committee of a rapidly growing high-tech company to review its strategy for determining the company's human resource needs. I had been attending all of the committee's meetings as a process consultant (Schein, 1969), but this meeting was described by the president as an especially relevant one because human resource policy in several areas was to be reviewed. Also on the agenda was the "stock option plan" and some "contingency planning" for what to do if the economic downturn continued.

The senior manager in the human resource area presented a six-step plan for determining the needs of the business. He proposed that the company make some reasonable growth projections, check the needs thus identified against the human resource inventory, and select on this basis its recruitment policies, development planning steps, and succession planning steps. It was a model presentation, fitting all the latest best thinking in the human resource area.

As soon as the presentation was over, one of the two senior division managers impatiently said that he did not know "what all this 'bullshit' was about anyway, since they knew who their good people were, those people were all utilized fully already, there was no time to develop anyone, and, in any case, [he had] never seen any general manager developed by any means other than just doing what was needed at the time anyway." The other division manager did not feel quite as strongly but echoed the sentiment that this would all be a waste of time, since the cream rises to the top anyway.

The president did not intervene on behalf of either the line managers or the human resource manager but let the discussion run its course. I attempted to clarify the issue but was overridden by the general impatience of the division managers. After some further general discussion, a new insight emerged: The reason they were so impatient with all these development plans and procedures was that they had too much dead wood in the system—managers who were blocking the progress of high-potential people—and that senior management had never been willing to face up to the problem of what to do about moving people out of blocking positions.

With this insight came the further recognition that there was a real problem with the performance appraisal system and the manner in which rewards had been allocated in the past decade. The company had been so successful for so many years that even average and below-average performers were being utilized in the rapid growth of the organization and were genuinely needed. Now that the growth had leveled off, these same people were perceived to be blocking but were not aware of it because they had been given positive feedback all along.

What the company now needed was *not* a set of procedures to routinize what the managers felt they knew anyway but a way of confronting the low performers. This led to a completely different concept of what kind of human resource inventory they needed. Once the committee members had defined the new categories that put the emphasis on identifying blockers, they quickly agreed to have a meeting soon to share their lists of promotables and blockers.

They also realized that they were much more worried now about the economic downturn and that developing people was not as high a priority as was getting rid of marginal performers. This step was necessary as a prelude to the more difficult later steps of freezing wages and possibly laying off even good performers. The discussion of career development really was intertwined with the central business concerns of the key line managers, and one could not possibly have predicted why the proposed development system would be rejected without knowing what was on their minds at that time. The human resource manager understood these dynamics and quickly adapted his proposals to what the group wanted next.

Ironically, when the group members later discussed the stock option plan as a way of holding and rewarding their key people, they needed to develop a process for identifying who would get how much stock. The process they adopted forced them to make the very same kind of inventory that had earlier been rejected as part of the career development system.

What all of this illustrated for me was the degree to which career issues are intertwined in unknown ways with other issues in the mind of the line manager, and that it is the line manager who controls what will happen to the system. Identification, development, appraisal and reward processes must fit into the culture and task structure of the powerful line managers of the organization or they will simply be sidelined and viewed as irrelevant.

Case 2. Do Organizations Want Systems or Help? A vice-president (VP) of human resources was hired away from an old consumer goods company by a large newspaper chain to bring some enlightened human resource policies, such as career development, systematic performance appraisal, succession planning, job description, and so on, into the organization. This person was given carte blanche but was told that the senior management (chairman and president) hoped that the new innovations wouldn't be "that bureaucratic stuff that big corporations do."

The human resource VP discovered that the company thrived on creativity, impulsiveness (people are fired on the spot and rehired the next day), professional traditions of journalism, and politics (in the sense that who gets ahead is ultimately a matter of who knows whom). It was the common judgment of senior managers (and the new VP came to believe it) that the success of the organization had derived largely from doing things in this fashion. So the dilemma was that bringing in "modern tools" might make the organization less effective or, worse, get the tools thrown out along with the VP of human resources.

The VP decided to redefine his job so that he would have to spend several *years* just becoming responsive to whatever issues employees and managers brought up in the broad human resource area and so that he functioned primarily as a process consultant to management, even though he had been hired as an expert. This has led to some constructive work in labor relations and has stimulated some inventions in the training area. Training has always been culturally acceptable in this organization, so the VP now "sneaks in" new ideas under the umbrella of professional training.

For example, it is clear that rotation across functions would be important for the development of future managers, but such rotation is completely unacceptable and seen as not affordable. However, cross-functional understanding can be stimulated by offering intensive seminars on business-related topics, inviting people from different functions to attend, and putting them into seminar and discussion groups in such a way as to maximize cross-functional contact. Such seminars have been seen as very useful and highly "enlightening" by managers.

What this case illustrates for me is that career development is defined very differently in different industries, professions, and organizations. Any attempts to define tools and programs that will work *across* all of these domains are doomed to be seen as irrelevant in some of them. Effective professionals in this area adapt the way they work to the cultural milieu in which they find themselves.

Case 3. The Computerized Human Resource Inventory. A large multi-national company decided to computerize its human resource inventory. Its director of management development reports directly to the president and the executive committee and has an organization that functions independently of the personnel department. The job of management development is to maintain knowledge of all future executives and to advise line management when key moves, promotions, or replacements must be made.

Since the inventory involves a thousand or more executives, it seemed logical to the management development staff members to convert their individual folders into a well-designed computerized system that would enable them to identify key candidates quickly and to cast their net more widely. They proposed the purchase of a computer to the president and were told that they could go ahead—but only on one condition: They had to buy a system that would allow *absolute security.* This resulted in the purchase of a minicomputer with floppy discs that could be put into a safe every night. In other words, the most important consideration in the design of the system was the *absolute* assurance that the files could not be penetrated.

The system itself was designed by one staff member who had an interest in it, but his decisions on how to design the system were almost exclusively driven by his own level of insight into how computers worked and by the needs of the company. No outside consultants or programmers were brought in. The operation was entirely bootstrapped from within, and the group members are very proud of the fact that they created their own system to meet their own needs. Limitations and inefficiencies are excused on the grounds that they can at least use the system they have because it was designed by them.

What I learned from this (something that the management development staff members would not have admitted) is that they put into their inventory some of their most private opinions of their potential executives and then expected such information to remain totally private. In fact, the management development function served as a kind of adjunct to senior management to help them with placement, succession, and promotion decisions. It was oriented strictly toward corporate staffing needs and was relatively unrelated to managers' developmental needs. It took the place of the little black book that many executives carry to keep track of who their high-potential people really are. Yet officially their system was described in terms of standard staffing and development terminology.

In contrast, a large retail chain began ten years ago to computerize its human resource files in order to create a data base that not only would permit administration of wage, salary, and benefits programs but also would provide instant information on all personnel, including senior management. The system was created under the leadership of the vice-president of human resources, who understood that the *process* by which it was created would determine its ultimate effectiveness. He assigned one of his best human resource executives to chair a task force that consisted of all involved line managers, the key technical people from information systems, and senior human resource people.

This task force worked for several years defining needs, opportunities, and the requirements of the system in terms of information input. The members decided to load information into the system one department at a time in order to permit debugging as they went. They found that the system evolved and improved as managers gained experience with it. Sensitive items, such as performance data or individual personality information, are coded, and the codes are kept secure so that the data base can be stored in the central computer system. The advantage of central storage is that it permits the correlation of financial data with personnel data to determine empirically what kinds of employees and managers consistently are associated with better or worse business performance. Instead of guessing about what kinds of managers it should be developing, the company will be able to determine empirically what kinds of managers actually succeed in the system, using reliable long-range financial and other information.

This organization feels that it has a state-of-the-art system. When you asked how this came to be, senior managers attribute their success to the talents of the task force chairperson and the processes the task force evolved to keep all affected parties close to the project and participating actively in debugging it.

Case 4. An Unusual Way to Conduct Performance Appraisal. The president of a large firm became convinced that he should appraise each of his key subordinates, but he found it difficult to deal with people in a one-on-one situation. He was always more comfortable talking about people as if they were "roles" and to do so in group contexts. He would say that Joe, in his role as manufacturing manager, had messed up on the inventory control and that he wanted John, his finance manager, to do a better job of creating systems that would prevent such foul-ups in the future. But when it came to sitting down with Joe or John to actually discuss face-to-face their strengths or weaknesses or development needs, he would become uncomfortable. As a result, there had been no appraisal of senior people for years.

The human resource manager sensed the need for appraisal, but he knew that the various systems available to him all involved the one-on-one meeting. To adapt to the constraint that the president preferred to talk in groups, he invented the following process:

1. The human resource manager would interview the president about each of his subordinates and prepare a written "crib sheet" to remind him of what he wanted to get across. This set of notes would be given back to the president in preparation for his meeting with the subordinates.
2. Each subordinate was scheduled for a two-hour appraisal "discussion" that would involve the president, the subordinate, the human resource manager, and an outside consultant who had worked with the group and was a trusted go-between. This process was described to each of the subordinates, and their agreement to it was elicited.

3. At the meeting, the human resource manager would prompt the president to discuss the subordinate with the whole group, using his crib sheet as needed. Because the human resource manager knew what the executive ultimately wanted to get across, he and the consultant could "lead" and "coach" the executive to get his full message out.

4. The subordinate—or anyone else at the meeting—was encouraged to interrupt for clarification, elaboration, counterargument, or whatever.

5. The consultant played the role of interviewer and clarifier, checking with both boss and subordinate on the level of understanding of what each was saying.

6. Following the meeting, the consultant met with each subordinate to discuss its impact, review its message, and work out a development plan for the subordinate with a timetable and checkpoints.

Although this process seemed awkward and time consuming at first, it was the unanimous opinion of the president and all the subordinates that for the first time a real appraisal had taken place, that the messages were loud and clear, and that it was both supportive and helpful to have the additional people in the room at the time of the appraisal. It was particularly helpful in one case, in which the boss had been unhappy with a subordinate for years but was unable to get the message across. The result was a decision by the subordinate to join another company on his own initiative.

This company has all the standard appraisal systems in operation and uses various kinds of paper-and-pencil formats. Yet all who became involved in the group process appraisal agreed that it had accomplished what their various systems could not accomplish. I learned from this to be deeply respectful of the different ways in which a given goal (appraisal) can be accomplished and not to be misled by what initially may appear to be silly, cumbersome, awkward, inefficient, or invalid.

Case 5. Performance Appraisal, Potential Assessment, and Numbers Games. One of the most dramatic examples of how systems can have unanticipated and undesirable consequences occurred in the European subsidiary of a large multinational chemical company. The company is committed to a world-wide inventory of its human resources, and it is completely convinced that the most important thing to know about future managers is their ultimate potential. Every year, every manager must submit rankings of all of his or her subordinates on the basis of their ultimate potential, by which is meant how high they feel the person will actually be able to rise in the system.

These rankings are subjected to complex statistical analyses in order to take into account the different numbers of people that may be ranking a given individual and compensate for the biases of the managers. Once freed of these biases, the rank lists for each level of supervision are published (but kept secrets so that subordinates cannot find out what their position is on the rank list) with the intention that they be used in staffing, succession planning, and other personnel decisions.

At the same time, there is a carefully administered performance appraisal system that involves rating each subordinate into a forced distribution according to whether or not he or she has exceeded, met, or fallen below the agreed-upon targets for that year. Salary decisions are made on the basis of these ratings; a clear signal is sent to the organization that potential and performance are not the same and are not to be treated as interdependent because there are many high performers who have topped out in terms of their rank yet who should be rewarded for their good performance as long as it continues.

I became involved in a project with an internal consultant to find out why the performance levels of older employees were beginning to fall off systematically. The company could show clear curves of how performance ratings climbed until about age thirty-five to forty and then began to systematically fall off so that the fifty-year-old and older employees were systematically getting lower merit raises than the younger employees.

After a modest amount of interviewing and examination of the statistical data, it became obvious what was happening. The heroes in the system were the high-potential employees, and as a person aged it became harder and harder to rank him or her highly on ultimate potential. In their efforts to defend their performance ratings, managers were systematically biasing those ratings (not necessarily consciously) toward the potential rankings so that, in spite of the company's insistence that potential and performance were independent, they were in fact highly correlated.

What made this dangerous was not that the two were correlated but that the potential rankings were overriding the performance ratings—which meant that the less reliable number (ultimate potential ranking) was biasing the more reliable one (the performance rating). We confirmed this in interviews when we were told repeatedly by supervisors that they really did not know what it took to be a very senior manager in the company but that if they had a young hotshot who sort of "looked like" a senior VP he or she not only would get high-potential rankings but would be rated as a good performer even if his or her targets were not met. This was defended on the grounds that if such individuals were given the average or low performance ratings they deserved, higher levels of management would challenge the ratings and ask how a high-potential employee could rate so low in performance. Rather than argue, the supervisor would skew the performance numbers upward.

Thus ultimate potential was driving the whole system and, as it turned out, that is what senior management really wanted: They believed that it was much more important to identify their high potentials than to accurately measure performance. They could not really see why there was a problem, and they were prepared to believe that the older, lower-potential employee really was performing at a lower level, as the curves showed.

The behavioral evidence of this bias showed up in staffing decisions. If a job opened up, it was invariably filled with the person who headed the confidential ranking list—even over the protests of the manager in whose department the job existed. I witnessed repeatedly how staffing decisions were made by the numbers rather than according to skill levels or developmental needs.

What was interesting to observe in this organization was the managers' unwillingness to see how their bias toward potential undermined their carefully designed and administered performance appraisal system. They steadfastly maintained the fiction that the performance appraisal system was totally objective and fair and that it really was a way of rewarding the steady performer who might have reached the limit of his potential. And, in this case, the personnel people colluded in the fiction in that they defended the system as much as line management did.

Conclusion

I have come to believe that the way in which an organization handles its human resource strategy, the way it defines careers, and the manner in which it recruits, selects, socializes, places, develops, and promotes its people strongly reflects (1) the national culture within which that organization exists and (2) the particular culture of that organization based on its history and the assumptions of its founders and leaders (Schein, 1985). Such cultural forces will show up particularly in the process by which standard human resource issues are handled.

Most organizations will claim that they use standard state-of-the-art performance appraisal, career-planning, and management development systems, but the ways in which they administer them may differ drastically. And it is in those processes of administration that one will find the main clues to understanding the impacts of the system.

What is missing most in our field are a theory and a technology that deal with such process issues. In our search for generalizations, we have too often glossed over process differences and, as a result, have missed the data that may in the end be the most revealing and most relevant.

References

Adler, N. "Cross-Cultural Management: Issues to Be Faced." *International Studies of Management and Organization*, 1983, *13*, 7-45.

Bailyn, L. *Living With Technology*. Cambridge, Mass.: MIT Press, 1980.

Bailyn, L. "Resolving Contradictions in Technical Careers; Or, What If I Like Being an Engineer." *Technology Review*, 1982, *85*, 40-70.

Balzer, R. *Clockwork*. New York: Doubleday, 1976.

Becker, H., Geer, B., Hughes, E. C., and Strauss, A. *Boys in White*. Chicago: University of Chicago Press, 1961.

Bray, D. W. "The Assessment Center and the Study of Lives." *American Psychologist*, 1982, *37*, 180–189.

Bray, D. W., Campbell, R. J., and Grant, D. L. *Formative Years in Business*. New York: Wiley, 1974.

Dalton, G. W., Thompson, P. H., and Price, R. L. "The Four Stages of Professional Careers." *Organizational Dynamics*, 1977, *6*, 17–33.

Dalton, M. *Men Who Manage*. New York: Wiley, 1959.

Desatnick, R. L., and Bennett, M. L. *Human Resource Management in the Multinational Corporation*. New York: Nichols, 1978.

Driver, M. "Career Concepts and Organizational Change." In C. B. Derr (ed.), *Work, Family, and the Career*. New York: Praeger, 1980.

Driver, M., and Streufert, S. "Integrative Complexity: An Approach to Individuals and Groups as Information Processing Systems." *Administrative Science Quarterly*, 1969, *14*, 272–285.

Evans, P., and Bartolome, F. *Must Success Cost So Much?* New York: Basic Books, 1980.

Glaser, B. G. (ed.). *Organizational Careers*. Hawthorne, N.Y.: Aldine, 1968.

Gysbers, N. C., and Associates. *Designing Careers: Counseling to Enhance Education, Work, and Leisure*. San Francisco: Jossey-Bass, 1984.

Hall, D. T. *Careers in Organizations*. Santa Monica, Calif.: Goodyear, 1976.

Harris, P. R., and Moran, R. T. *Managing Cultural Differences*. Houston, Tex.: Gulf, 1979.

Hofstede, G. *Culture's Consequences*. Beverly Hills, Calif.: Sage, 1980.

Holland, J. L. *Making Vocational Choices: A Theory of Careers*. Englewood Cliffs, N.J.: Prentice-Hall, 1973.

Hughes, E. C. *Men and Their Work*. New York: Free Press, 1958.

Jelinek, M. (ed.). *Career Management for the Individual and the Organization*. New York: Wiley, 1979.

Kets de Vries, M. F. R., and Miller, D. *The Neurotic Organization: Diagnosing and Changing Counterproductive Styles of Management.* San Francisco: Jossey-Bass, 1984.

Kopelman, R. E. "Psychological Stages of Careers in Engineering: An Expectancy Theory Taxonomy." *Journal of Vocational Behavior,* 1977, *10,* 270–286.

Laurent, A. "The Cultural Diversity of Western Conceptions of Management." *International Studies of Management and Organization,* 1983, *13,* 75–96.

Levinson, D. J., and others. *The Seasons of a Man's Life.* New York: Knopf, 1978.

Loevinger, J., Wessler, R., and Redmore, C. *Measuring Ego Development.* (2 vols.) San Francisco: Jossey-Bass, 1970.

London, M., and Stumpf, S. A. *Managing Careers.* Reading, Mass.: Addison-Wesley, 1982.

Manning, P. K., and Van Maanen, J. (eds.). *Policing: A View from the Street.* Santa Monica, Calif.: Goodyear, 1978.

Montross, D. H., and Shinkman, C. J. (eds.). *Career Development in the 80s.* Springfield, Ill.: Thomas, 1981.

Moran, R. T., and Harris, P. R. *Managing Cultural Synergy.* Houston, Tex.: Gulf, 1982.

Morgan, M. A. (ed.). *Managing Career Development.* New York: Van Nostrand Reinhold, 1980.

Osherson, S. D. *Holding On or Letting Go.* New York: Free Press, 1980.

Osipow, S. H. *Theories of Career Development.* (3rd ed.) Englewood Cliffs, N.J.: Prentice-Hall, 1983.

Perrucci, R., and Gerstl, J. E. *Profession Without Community: Engineers in American Society.* New York: Random House, 1969.

Ritti, R. R. *The Engineer in the Industrial Corporation.* New York: Columbia University Press, 1971.

Rosenbaum, J. E. *Career Mobility in a Corporate Hierarchy.* Orlando, Fla.: Academic Press, 1984.

Schein, E. H. *Process Consultation.* Reading, Mass.: Addison-Wesley, 1969.

Schein, E. H. "How 'Career Anchors' Hold Executives to Their Career Paths." *Personnel,* 1975, *3,* 11–24.

Schein, E. H. *Career Dynamics.* Reading, Mass.: Addison-Wesley, 1978.

Schein, E. H. "Culture as an Environmental Context for Careers." *Journal of Occupational Behavior,* 1984, *5,* 71–81.

Schein, E. H. *Organizational Culture and Leadership: A Dynamic View.* San Francisco: Jossey-Bass, 1985.

Schein, E. H. "Individuals and Careers." In J. Lorsch, *Handbook of Organizational Behavior.* Englewood Cliffs, N.J.: Prentice-Hall, forthcoming.

Schrank, R. *Ten Thousand Working Days.* Cambridge, Mass.: MIT Press, 1978.

Storey, W. D. *Career Dimensions.* New York: General Electric, 1976.

Super, D. E. "A Life-Span, Life-Space Approach to Career Development." *Journal of Vocational Behavior,* 1980, *16,* 282–298.

Terkel, S. *Working.* New York: Pantheon Books, 1974.

Tiedeman, D. V., and O'Hara, R. P. *Career Development Theory: Choice and Adjustment.* New York: College Entrance Examination Board, 1963.

Vaillant, G. E. *Adaptation to Life.* Boston: Little, Brown, 1977.

Van Maanen, J. "Observations on the Making of Policemen." *Human Organization,* 1973, *4,* 407-418.

Zeira, Y., and Banai, M. "Selection of Expatriate Managers in MNC's: The Host-Environment Point of View." *International Studies of Management and Organization,* 1985, *15,* 33-51.

Zuboff, S. "Technologies that Informate." In R. E. Walton and P. R. Lawrence (eds.), *Human Resource Management.* Boston: Harvard Business School Press, 1985.

10

꒜꒜꒜꒜꒜꒜꒜꒜꒜

Career Development
in Organizations:
Where Do We
Go from Here?

Douglas T. Hall

As discussed in the Preface, the field of careers has blossomed over the last ten to fifteen years. I hope that this volume has provided the reader with some sense of the wide range of territory that is represented by this field in terms of both current frontiers activity and trends for the future. At this point, let us look back at what the various authors have had to say and then conclude with some thoughts on the future.

Overview

In the opening chapter, I provided a framework for the *career spectrum*. This spectrum ranges from macro, organization-level work (such as succession planning) on the career management end to micro, individual-level activities at the career-planning end. I also talked about the tendency for organizations to work primarily at one end of this spectrum or the other, although it is entirely possible to engage in activities all along its range. And, in fact, Chapters Two, Six, Seven, and Eight show clearly what cutting-edge organizations are doing to tie together these different approaches to career development.

Part One of the book examines the overall cultural context of careers as well as the system-wide organizational setting in which career processes function. In Chapter One, Manuel London and Stephen A. Stumpf give a cultural overview of the changing personal values, managerial styles, and corporate career programs that are resulting in radically altered approaches to defining and managing organizational careers. New employee values, such as decreased commitment to organizations, which initially may appear to be negative, may in fact be beneficial to the organization, as well as to the individual. Since organizations now need to be free to adapt quickly to rapid change, they will need to have employees that are equally adaptive and flexible. With less organizational commitment, the individual may be less dependent on the organization for total career satisfaction, realizing instead that much of the responsibility for career development is his or her own. Indeed, major themes growing out of Chapter One are the importance of *career resilience, personal responsibility, new competencies,* and *multiple careers.*

The most critical aspect of this chapter, however, is the call for the development of specific research and programs to facilitate needed adaptive qualities, such as career resilience, insight, and identity. The trigger factors that assist in breaking midcareer routines (as discussed in Chapter Four) also can provide useful inputs to the guidelines presented by London and Stumpf. And the innovative career programs described in Chapters Two, Six, and Eight are all in-depth examples of what London and Stumpf are calling for.

Another example of research that addresses the issues raised by London and Stumpf is a forthcoming book by McCall, Lombardo, and Morrison. This is a study of executives, some of whom have "arrived" (are successful) and some of whom have "derailed." A major factor that distinguishes the two groups is *diversity of experience.* Arrivers are much more likely to have had a range of quite different types of assignments throughout their careers, while derailers are more likely to have remained in one type of activity (that is, worked within just one function or in one area

Career Development in Organizations

of specialization). Another major developmental experience of arrivers is *failure*. Most successful people have encountered a major disaster at least once in their careers and have been able to examine it and learn from it. Derailers also are likely to have had failures, but they are less able to learn from them. Thus, it appears that the capacity to adapt and learn from experience should be developed early in the career and is enhanced by variety in career experience.

Chapter Two, by Thomas G. Gutteridge, is an excellent summary of where the practice of career development in frontier organizations is today. It should be stressed that he is not describing typical organizations; these are exemplary organizations with pathbreaking programs. So, while he is describing the present state of innovative organizations, he is showing us the future of the typical organization. This chapter provides an excellent brief model of the context in which career programs operate. Career development takes place as part of a larger process of human resource planning, which in turn is part of a basic process of organizational design, which is affected by control and evaluation activities. And these control and evaluation activities, in turn, are affected by career development processes. All four of these processes affect each other in a cyclical manner, and their interactions are influenced by elements of the external and internal environments of the organization. The cases Gutteridge provides illustrate the operation of these environmental factors; these are the same sorts of factors reported by Edgar H. Schein in Chapter Nine. As Schein argues, we need these descriptive data in order to truly understand career behavior.

One of the important lessons of organizational career programs is that the specific content of the activities may be less important than the *process* by which they were created. Gutteridge makes this point well, as does Kathy E. Kram (see Chapter Five) in her call for an *organizational change approach* (a system-wide process of data collection, diagnosis, action planning, intervention, and evaluation). It is not possible to take a single method or career intervention and simply "plug it into" the organization. Like any other intervention, the change must fit with the existing culture, and the principles of good planned change must be used. The cases in Chapter Nine present compelling evidence for this point.

Part Two moves on to career processes that affect the individual. Much discussion in the literature recently has addressed the issue of work versus personal life, primarily regarding what type of interaction exists between the two (is it spillover? complementary? some other type?). In Chapter Three, Donald E. Super takes a new approach, focusing on the nature of leisure and why this aspect of personal life is important for its own sake. His Life Career Rainbow, familiar to career counselors but probably new to many industrial/organizational psychologists, provides a striking way of placing work, leisure, and other experiences in the context of a lifelong course of development. This life-span focus seems analogous to the cultural perspective at the organizational level in the sense of seeing the "big picture" from the person's point of view.

One of the most intriguing possibilities raised by this leisure concept, in addition to its intrinsic value, is the notion of *leisure as career preparatory*. An examination of one's leisure preferences and a clarification of what one values in leisure pursuits can be an extremely useful guide to career planning. If career change and adaptability are going to become ever more important elements in the career experience, it is important to find new ways to help people get in touch with what they find rewarding in various activities. Examination of leisure provides important clues as to what a person finds meaningful and fulfilling. In fact, one avenue to pursue in planning midcareer change is exploring ways one can convert a leisure activity into a paid career. We see this being done now in the case of people who take early retirement from one organization and then start second careers by converting an avocation into a vocation. The same principle could also be applied by people making less dramatic changes earlier in their careers. For example, women reentering the job market after a period as homemakers also often correct this process by identifying transferable skills and interests from volunteer work and hobbies, which may lead them into careers in fields such as management, sales, and education.

Another important original contribution of Chapter Three is the process Super proposes for utilizing leisure concepts in corporate career-planning programs. These could be useful ways of facilitating the career resilience, insight, and identity proposed by

London and Stumpf, in Chapter One. To my knowledge, few
organizations have attempted to incorporate leisure planning into
formal career programs, although many companies have invested
heavily in leisure programs for employees (such as IBM's country
club). Also, leisure planning is sometimes included in retirement-
planning seminars. It would be a short step to also include leisure
planning into more general career-planning programs.

As we said earlier, a major theme of this book has been the
need for adaptability and self-generated change throughout the
career. The notion of spending an entire career in one line of work
and in one part of an organization is becoming less feasible with
each passing year. The question, then, is how do people make shifts
in direction after they have become established in a particular career
field? This is the issue addressed by Douglas T. Hall in Chapter
Four. He examines the issue of the career routine, which is the
pattern of behavior that develops after the person has completed the
initial exploration and entry stages of the career. The career routine
is functional in the early stages, as this scripted behavior frees the
person from thinking about routine, everyday tasks and leaves him
or her free to attend instead to more creative or nonroutine
activities. Also, having routinized many of his or her activities, it
becomes easier for the person to shift time and energy more
into personal life in order to achieve the balance needed in midcareer. So the career routine serves a definite function early in the
career.

However, in midcareer the routine has the important
dysfunction of making the person resistant to change: It becomes
threatening to contemplate giving up familiar behavior and
initiating new, untried, unfamiliar activities. This is a good
example of how something that is functional at one career stage can
actively impede success at the next. Thus, the person may not
change until certain trigger events or influences come into play.
Chapter Four describes some of the more important trigger events
that might arise in the environment, the organization, and the
individual. It also describes a *midcareer learning cycle,* which
describes how these trigger events can stimulate exploratory and
trial behavior and ultimately lead to the development of an altered

self-identity. This discussion further extends the work of London and Stumpf (Chapter One) on promoting career insight and identity.

Chapter Four includes guidelines for programs to promote midcareer identity change. By creating *surprise* in midcareer, organizations can effectively reverse the socialization process that created the career routine in the first place (since the career routine is the result of the person's attempts to reduce surprise in a new environment). This points to an important and underexamined area in career learning: the unlearning of old skills and the leaving of old roles. Much of the research and practice related to career transitions has focused on entering and mastering a new role. Much more work is needed now on how people can more effectively leave and give up old roles.

Chapter Five, by Kathy E. Kram, provides an in-depth analysis of a "free resource" for career development: other people in the organization. Not only is mentoring free, but it is beautifully reciprocal: It develops the mentor at least as much as the protege. Kram shows clearly how development through relationships can occur at all career stages and thus makes an important contribution to career stage theory as well as to the mentoring literature.

A critical factor impeding the success of women has been the lack of senior female role models for women. Often the only form of mentoring available to women has been that provided by men. As Kram shows, this cross-gender mentoring is fraught with problems, such as perceived intimacy and public scrutiny. The elements of an effective mentoring relationship and effective organizational programs are useful ways of getting around these cross-gender and other problems. In particular, Kram's warning about formal mentoring programs seems especially sound. What seems far more appropriate is devoting energy to *identifying* who is doing good mentoring and *rewarding* them for it. Also, building on Edgar H. Schein's comments (Chapter Nine) on the pervasive impact of culture, the more top management espouses and models mentoring, the more it will be built into the culture and fabric of the organization.

In Part Three, we move from the individual to the organization. Here we see some of the impressive work organizations have done in recent years to promote career planning and career management. Chapter Six, by Frank J. Minor, describes some of the rapidly expanding work being done with computer-based career development programs and provides an excellent summary of some of the historical approaches to this work. Indeed, this had been an area of perennial promise, largely unfulfilled, for career planning for years. Now, with the ubiquity of personal computers, we are finally seeing the explosive growth of career information and planning aids available to individual employees.

As Minor's research on the IBM computer-based system indicates, in addition to the information he provides from other organizations, these technology-aided processes appear to be an effective means of promoting the self-directed career planning and adaptation that has been advocated throughout the book. It is ironic that machines provide an area of great promise for individualizing and humanizing the career management process. It appears that these methods result in greater job satisfaction, higher organizational commitment, more realism in career plans, and a stronger focus on one's own career goals and plans.

Remember the gap we discussed earlier between career planning and career management? It appears that computer-based systems also can be of service here, as Minor finds that organizations are beginning to link up their career-planning systems with their career management systems, such as succession planning. If this link does turn out to be a major trend in the future, it could be a major breakthrough in career development. This integration of career planning and career management would provide important organizational support to the individual in implementing his or her career plans; and it would give the organization much better information about individual career interests and predispositions in planning for human resources. Having all of this information integrated in one information system makes for excellent research opportunities, as well. The developments discussed in this chapter are tremendously exciting.

Chapter Seven, by Robert F. Morrison and Roger R. Hock, provides a creative integration of theory and research related to cumulative learning over the course of the career. By utilizing a diverse body of literature, Morrison and Hock have produced a unified set of propositions that describe how a complete "portfolio" of career skills is developed. Although there has been much work to date on how people make transitions and learn and adapt to one work role, there has been little work that considers a longer-term process of adaptation and skill acquisition. It would be intriguing to use their model to specifically address the question of how to build flexibility and adaptability into a person's skills portfolio. The work in each subfield would be strengthened by the use of concepts and methods of other subfields.

Morrison and Hock's work is the basis of a multiyear research study in the U.S. Navy. It is hoped that it will also become the basis for making changes in career patterns. Thus, the chapter is useful in guiding both research and practice. It would appear that the method of career analysis the authors have devised would be most useful in large organizations with fairly well-structured job classifications and a clear organizational structure.

In Chapter Eight, Richard J. Campbell and Joseph L. Moses take us through thirty years of history at AT&T (1955 to 1985). Since my first research was conducted with AT&T's Management Progress Study data, this chapter is for me a sort of "sentimental journey." Indeed, the Management Progress Study and its resulting programs, such as IMDP, represent landmark work in industrial/ organizational psychology. As this chapter so well describes, this work provides a model of the close interaction among theory, research, and innovative practice. Theory and practice on assessment, such as the World War II OSS work, guided the design of the initial MPS data collection. Results were analyzed, and new concepts (such as early job challenge) were developed. These concepts were then translated into programs to upgrade initial jobs, train managers of new hires, and give earlier career feedback. This long-term study has resulted in findings and practices (such as assessment centers) that have been applied in countless organizations over the years. It is difficult to overstate the importance of this longitudinal career study.

The other issues Campbell and Moses discuss provide
powerful evidence of the critical need to be flexible and adaptive in
today's organizational environments. In particular, the effect of
deregulation in telecommunications and the divestiture of AT&T
(probably the largest reorganization in business history) have
produced a radical transformation of AT&T. Chapter Eight raises
critical questions about whether an organization can maintain
career continuity (a core human resource policy in the old AT&T)
in the face of such disruption. In fact, it cannot.

Another provocative question Campbell and Moses raise is
how managers trained in one culture can adapt to another. As they
say, this is the downside of a promotion-from-within policy. Their
conclusion seems to be that the organization can provide no
guarantees to the individual—only assistance to the individual in
managing his or her own career. Again we see the theme of self-
direction and adaptability (the protean career).

In reviewing the state of the career field, Edgar H. Schein
identifies in Chapter Nine a number of issues that must be
addressed: fractionation, subfields ignoring each other, the need to
consider culture, the need for integrative constructs and theory, and
the need to consider process. These are important ideas provided by
one of the founders of the field, a caring critic. The fractionation
and subfields, ironically, are a result of the success of the field. As
the field has blossomed and grown, it has become differentiated, as
does any living system. However, to be effective, systems, especially
in rapidly changing environments, must be integrated as well as
differentiated.

Schein makes the valid point that the concepts related to
careers are spread among a number of disciplines. However, the
purpose of this book is to examine the cutting edge of industrial/
organizational work on career development; it is not to cover the
entire field of careers and all the possible different approaches to
careers.

Schein argues that the problem with the industrial/
organizational focus on improving career programs is that when
companies lay off large numbers of people, career development
programs disappear. I would argue, on the contrary, that some of
the best work on career programs has been done in organizations

that have suffered massive layoffs, such as Ford Motor Company. In fact, many companies have initiated career programs both to assist laid-off employees and to help people who stay establish more control over their career futures. This is one of the reasons careers are "hot" today.

It is very important, however, that if an organization is engaging in career programs as part of organizational restructuring and/or downsizing, it be done as part of an integrated, organization-wide process, attentive to the culture, as Schein's cases illustrate. Gutteridge's cyclical model (Chapter Two) also makes this point. Career development activities and organization development must be done in an integrated fashion. The importance of *organizational process* cannot be overstated, and Schein makes this point clearly and persuasively.

This point of process does make for a practical problem, however. In many organizations today, because the career field has become so well established and because there is a clear technology, especially in the career-planning area, the person responsible for career programs is often a specialist working at a rather low level in the organization. It is very difficult for someone at that level to plan interventions at the level of organizational processes and organizational culture. Therefore, career activities often are doomed to be simply career planning (individual activities), and career management is not adequately done.

Responsibility for career development programs must be at the same level as responsibility for organization design, human resource planning, and control and evaluation, as Gutteridge's analysis suggests. Chapter Eight also shows clearly how it was a strong concern and level of support from top management that provided the continuity for the research and programs the authors described.

Schein's call for more descriptive research provides a useful way for researchers to learn about how processes and variables outside the normal scope of their subfields might be affecting the phenomena they are studying. Theory testing research on careers often is aimed at fine points in existing theories and does little to develop new theory. And we are at a point at which we desperately need new theory (Arthur, Hall, and Lawrence, forthcoming). More

descriptive research, such as Becker, Geer, Hughes, and Strauss's classic *Boys in White* (1961), would be an important aid to the advancement of the field.

Where More Work Is Needed

We have spent many pages describing what is being done related to organizational careers, and we have heard various ideas for achieving a better integration of individual career needs and organizational human resource objectives. However, there are still some critical gaps in our knowledge of careers. Let us consider where we should go from here.

Careers of Women and Minorities. There has been an impressive amount of interest in and research on women's careers in recent years. Research centers, such as the Wellesley College Center for Research on Women, the Catalyst Organization, Radcliffe's Bunting Institute, and the Columbia Center for Research on Career Development, have produced studies that have greatly aided our understanding of the careers of women. Much of this work deals with two-career and work-family issues, as well as the process of female adult development.

Unfortunately, much of this research represents a documentation of the *problems* faced by women rather than chronicles of *progress.* Two-career relationships *do* involve trade-offs, and most people cannot have it all: successful career, happy marriage, wonderful children, charming home, a rich network of friends, and so forth (Hall and Hall, 1979). The personal stress associated with women's careers is high.

Many organizations have been successful in developing programs to identify and develop high-potential women. AT&T is a good example here, and Chapter Eight explains how an organization can successfully help women advance in management. This chapter also indicates just how much work is required here and how strong a top-management commitment is required.

A forthcoming book by Linda Moore provides a detailed examination of just how difficult the problem and pressures are for working women and what they (and their employees) can do about them. Chapters by authors such as Rosabeth Moss Kanter and

Natasha Josefowitz point out what skills women need to advance into management and what dangers await them at higher levels. Other issues that are currently receiving attention in work on women's careers are mentoring and networking, intimacy and sexual attraction at work, female-female and female-male supervisory and mentoring relationships, negotiation and competition, work versus family interactions, and dual-career couples. Whereas ten years ago "women in management" was a fairly small, well-defined area, it now has grown and become specialized and differentiated, as illustrated by the issues just described. Daniel Levinson's (forthcoming) book on adult female development will be an important addition to this literature. A new series, *Women and Work: An Annual Review* (edited by Laurie Larwood, Ann H. Stromberg, and Barbara A. Gutek, 1985) promises to be a useful vehicle for monitoring the exploding literature in this area.

A careful statistical examination of data on women in the labor market in the last twenty years (Blau and Ferber, 1985) shows evidence of progress for women in terms of labor market participation, especially for very highly educated women. There also has been a decline in occupational segregation by sex in many fields (but less progress in skilled blue-collar jobs). Men, especially young men, are doing a larger share of housework. And the sex gap in earnings in many fields has begun to decline recently, especially for younger cohorts, which provides hope for the future. (However, comparable worth as a force for change in this area may not be quite the cure-all that it was seen to be a few years ago [Rosenbaum, 1985], especially in light of the 1985 overruling of the Washington State case. It appears that salary progress for women is more likely to be made through collective bargaining than through legal approaches based on comparable worth.)

It is my impression that many women have experienced early career success but that making the move from middle management to top management is extremely unusual. In some cases, this is because the woman may opt out of the career (or cut back) in her mid-thirties in favor of devoting more time to raising a family. She may feel that she has fulfilled her career needs (or at least proved to herself that she can be successful) but that she has not yet fulfilled a personal need for parental fulfillment. And even if she initially planned to combine career and family, after a few months or years of juggling both she may have decided that either (1) the stress is not worth it or (2) being a mother is so rewarding that she wants to do it full time. There is a possibility that organizations may see large numbers of mid- to late-thirties dropouts among its women managers and professionals over the next decade. (However, my hunch is that even if a woman *thinks* she is making a permanent choice of family over career, she will resume the career, full time or part time, in the next five to ten years.)

Another part of the problem for women in middle management positions is the increased difficulty in winning promotions as they attempt to move into senior positions. Nannerl Keohane (1984), president of Wellesley College, refers to this barrier as "The Wall" and compares it to the almost physical obstacles that long-distance runners encounter when they are well into a race. Others refer to this as more informal sex discrimination or "the glass ceiling." Also, at the top, personal trust and confidences are what count, and these are often difficult to achieve in male/female relationships.

Keohane argues that part of the reason for the wall is that senior management is now the level where the old stereotypes about women still exist. The other explanation she offers is the woman's choice of family over career in response to the pressures of the "biological clock." Keohane also argues that these two issues (stereotypes and the biological clock) can reinforce each other: "It's not the desire to bear children as such that constitutes 'The Wall,' but the way our society and our culture construct the choices that surround childbearing activities for women and men. . . . One way to see the power of culture in such matters is to consider how the thesis of the 'biological clock' gets built into corporate planning. In male-dominated institutions, the fear that women will leave the company at thirty-five to raise a family often leads to pre-emptive measures. It can mean discrimination against women in promotion and support opportunities all down the line. Thus, a woman who may never marry and has no wish for children is just as much subject to the patterns of discrimination that arise from this conviction as those who personally face the choice. . . . As our society, our economy, and our corporate culture are now constituted, when a woman hits 'The Wall' she feels that she must choose between corporate advancement on the one hand and home and family on the other. She is given a choice that appears mutually exclusive, with no real possibility of putting together any successful combinations in between" (Keohane, 1984, p. 11). Keohane argues that we need more models of *flexible success* (interrupted careers, slower advancement, part-time work, and the like).

Some methods currently being practiced to help people be more proactive and career-resilient are described in Chapter One. Also, factors that help a person break out of a career routine and change behavior in midcareer are discussed in Chapter Four. Finally, ways that mentoring, particularly cross-gender mentoring, can help people develop their own particular career style, are reported in Chapter Five.

The progress of minorities has been mixed (Carnevale, 1985). Black women now earn wages comparable to white women in the primary labor market (professional, large-scale factory, and government jobs). By the late 1970s, blacks of both sexes with postsecondary education had achieved parity with whites.

However, in the secondary, low-income labor markets, blacks were doing less well, especially black men. In 1969, 73 percent of black men were employed compared to 78 percent of white men. In 1979, the employment rate for black men dropped to 64 percent, compared to 75 percent for white men. Thus, the black-white employment gap increased from 5 percent in 1969 to 11 percent in 1979. Also, black progress into upper management positions has been very slow. It appears, then, that there is a two-track career system for blacks: a relatively small group of "haves" and a larger group of "have nots" (Carnevale, 1985, p. 154). Fruitful leads for future research and practice are found in Dickens and Dickens's (1982) work on the development of black managers.

New Forms of Career Motivation. It is becoming clear that work values and motivation are different from what they were a generation ago. More and more employees are coming to feel, in the words of Beverly Kaye (1982) that "up is not the only way." People are becoming motivated more by their own values and notions of psychological success—the protean career (Hall, 1976). Yet many organizations still base their reward systems on the old assumptions about employee motivation. How does an organization create a career management system based on a more realistic view of the career orientation of contemporary employees? Chapter One, by London and Stumpf, crystallizes these new career realities and describes specific programs that help people develop more adaptive career attitudes and skills.

Systematically "Growing" Job Skills. In addition to the general career attitudes and skills described in London and Stumpf's chapter, there is also a great need to learn more about how specific job-related skills grow and develop over time. Most organizations put people through a series of "ticket punching" assignments, which are determined more by tradition than by specific job content. As mobility becomes more problematic, for reasons described earlier, organizations will need to be able to make more efficient and rational use of the moves that are available to develop people. Chapter Seven, by Morrison and Hock, provides a systematic analysis of how a progression of jobs can promote more effective development.

Work Versus Nonwork. One of the most critical areas of research and career practice is the interface between work life and home life. Much of the research to date has attempted to show relevance of nonwork experience for work behavior (and vice versa). We now seem to be at the point where the conflicts between work and home are known, and we need to understand more about how to reduce them and how people can have more meaningful nonwork lives. Not enough industrial-organizational psychology research has looked specifically at the issue of leisure behavior. We are fortunate to have one of the "founding fathers" of career psychology, Donald Super, apply his creative conceptualizing to the meaning and management of leisure in Chapter Three. His fresh ideas can provide grist for much future research and practice on how to incorporate leisure concepts in personal development.

Developmental Relationships. As we said earlier, an important theme in recent work in careers is the concept of proteanism, or self-direction. As John Naisbett (1982) said in *Megatrends,* our society is moving from a dependence on institutions to self-reliance and self-help. One of the important ways individuals can facilitate the development of their own careers is through the establishment of *relationships* with other people who have had the ability to help with both advancement and personal concerns. To date, most research and practice in this area has focused on mentoring (Levinson and Associates, 1978). In Chapter Five in this volume, Kathy Kram extends these ideas to other kinds of relationships and calls for specific programs that can help organizations promote developmental relationships. There is a rich agenda for future work in this area of person-to-person helping and developing.

Computer-Based Career Planning. For years, there has been much hope for computer-based career guidance activities. However, the early software and underlying theoretical models were quite complex, and little progress was made. The ETS system, SIGI, was a start, used mainly in educational organizations and not much in industry.

More recently, however, there are general career planning programs that can be customized for a particular organization (for example, DISCOVER). It appears that computerized career planning is just on the verge of hitting industry on a wide scale. Chapter Six, by Frank Minor, describes the work of IBM and several other organizations in this rapidly expanding area. The possibilities for integrating career planning with career management systems, as proposed by Minor, are tremendously exciting and quite feasible.

Career Change. Many of the chapters in this volume deal with how people make career decisions and develop career plans. However, much of the research and practice in careers has been on early career processes, focused on the newcomer and advancer. With growth slowing and large numbers of baby boomers hitting midcareer, it is clear that now we need to know more about midcareer change and development. Furthermore, it appears that we cannot simply take our models of early career decision making and apply them to midcareer. In fact, some factors that lead to success in early career can impede growth in midcareer. We also need to know more about how adult development and career development affect each other in midlife (Levinson, 1984). Chapter Four provides a new model of routine busting and subidentity growth in midcareer. This model invites future empirical examination and practical application.

Organizationwide Career Development Systems. All of the specific career activities discussed so far will be most effective in the context of an organizationwide effort to promote career development. The link between individual career planning and organizational career management is a difficult one to achieve, as we have said. Chapter Two, by Gutteridge, who has done considerable research on total career systems, describes elements in an integrated organizationwide approach to careers and provides several cases of well-managed career systems. The next step is to attempt to implement some of these practices in a broader cross-section of organizations. More work is needed on the diffusion of career technology in typical, mainstream organizations.

Conclusion

This, then, concludes our examination of the frontier work of some of the major people in the field of careers today. Again, we have not attempted to provide a general survey of all areas of contemporary work in careers but rather a selective, in-depth discussion of major important new areas of activity.

In reviewing the preceding chapters, I am led to the following conclusions about how and where career development work in organizations can best be done.

1. No organization has the ability (in terms of either resources or information about the future) to manage an employee's career or to plan well-ordered career paths.
2. Therefore, the employee must assume responsibility for his or her own career development (or at least 80 percent of it).
3. To be responsible for one's own career in today's turbulent organizational environments, the employee needs new *career competencies,* not just job skills. These career competencies might be called "metaskills," because they are skills in acquiring new skills. The most important metaskills are adaptability (routine busting), tolerance of ambiguity and uncertainty, and identity change.

4. It is in the best interests of the organization to help both the employee and his or her spouse assume this career responsibility and to develop their own career direction. (This makes it easier for the organization to pursue its own future directions.)
5. The organization should provide information and support to facilitate the person's assumption of career responsibility.
6. The organization should make possible wide degrees of freedom of movement for the individual. All directions of movement should be possible and valued by the culture: down, across, up, and out.
7. To provide an environment that is supportive of good career planning and career management, the organization needs a good strategic human resource management process. Career development activities are performed most effectively when they are one part of an integrated strategic human resource management system. This means that the organization must have clear business objectives and a clear set of human resource objectives and priorities growing out of those business objectives (Hall and Goodale, 1986).

The final point above means that organizations that are most effective with career development do what they do primarily because they see their career activities as simply a good way to do business. They do not see career development just as a "good thing to do" for their employees. And because career development is seen as serving important business objectives, there is a strong top-management commitment to these activities.

With massive corporate restructuring, demographic changes, value and cultural changes, and turbulent external environments, organizations will find their own adaptability increasingly dependent upon the capacity of their employees to change and adapt. The dilemma here is that while this organizational change will force more individual change, this individual change must be self-directed (protean). Thus, careers and effective career planning lie at the heart of effective organizational change. This improved integration of organizational human resource planning and individual career growth provides the challenge and excitement of the future world of career development.

References

Arthur, M., Hall, D. T., and Lawrence, B. (eds.). *Handbook of Career Theory*. Cambridge, Mass.: Cambridge University Press, forthcoming.

Becker, H., Geer, B., Hughes, E. C., and Strauss, A. *Boys in White*. Chicago: University of Chicago Press, 1961.

Blau, F. D., and Ferber, M. A. "Women in the Labor Market: The Last Twenty Years." In L. Larwood, A. H. Stromberg, and B. A. Gutek (eds.), *Women and Work: An Annual Review*. Vol. 1. Beverly Hills, Calif.: Sage, 1985.

Carnevale, A. P. *Jobs for the Nation: Challenges for a Society Based on Work*. Alexandria, Va.: American Society for Training and Development, 1985.

Dickens, F. B., and Dickens, J. B. *The Black Manager: Making It in the Corporate World*. New York: AMACOM, 1982.

Hall, D. T. *Careers in Organizations*. Glenview, Ill.: Scott, Foresman, 1976.

Hall, D. T., and Goodale, J. G. *Human Resource Management: Strategy, Design, and Implementation*. Glenview, Ill.: Scott, Foresman, 1986.

Hall, F. S., and Hall, D. T. *The Two-Career Couple*. Reading, Mass.: Addison-Wesley, 1979.

Kaye, B. *Up Is Not the Only Way: A Guide for Career Development Practitioners*. Englewood Cliffs, N.J.: Prentice-Hall, 1982.

Keohane, N. "Women and Power." Speech presented to Wellesley College alumni. New York: Oct. 1984.

Larwood, L., Stromberg, A. H., and Gutek, B. A. (eds.). *Women and Work: An Annual Review*. Vol. 1. Beverly Hills, Calif.: Sage, 1985.

Levinson, D. J. "The Career Is in the Life Structure, the Life Structure Is in the Career." In M. B. Arthur, L. Bailyn, D. J. Levinson, and H. A. Shepard, *Working with Careers*. New York: Center for Research in Career Development, Columbia University, 1984.

Levinson, D. J. *The Seasons of a Woman's Life*. New York: Knopf, forthcoming.

Levinson, D. J., and Associates. *The Seasons of a Man's Life.* New York: Knopf, 1978.

McCall, M. W., Lombardo, M. M., and Morrison, A. M. *The Lessons of Experience.* New York: Harper & Row, forthcoming.

Moore, L. *Not as Far as You Think: The Realities of Working Women.* Lexington, Mass.: Lexington Books, forthcoming.

Naisbett, J. *Megatrends: Ten New Directions Transforming Our Lives.* New York: Warner Books, 1982.

Rosenbaum, J. E. "Persistence and Change in Pay Inequalities: Implications for Job Evaluation and Comparable Worth." In L. Larwood, A. H. Stromberg, B. A. Gutek (eds.). *Women and Work: An Annual Review.* Vol. 1. Beverly Hills, Calif.: Sage, 1985.

Name Index

Subject Index

A

Academy of Management, 310
Adult Career Concerns Inventory, 114-115
Aetna, career paths at, 69
Ambiguity, and career resilience, 29-30
American College Testing Program, DISCOVER from, 65, 347
American Society for Training and Development, 53
Anchorage, Alaska: case study of, 85-90; mini career ladders in, 62; and planning model, 78
Arizona Bank, workbook for, 65
AT&T: assessment center at, 282-283, 286, 300; background on, 274-276; and career continuity issues, 301-302; career paths at, 284-285; career programs at, 17-18, 274-309, 339-340; and competition, 289-293; and consent decrees, 276-277, 278, 282, 285, 287, 293; developments influencing, 276-297; and divestiture, 293-297; and individual issues, 302-304, 306-307; Initial Management Development Program (IMDP) at, 280, 282, 284, 339; internal labor market at, 14; Management Progress Study (MPS) at, 133, 143-144, 149, 276, 279-281, 288, 339; marketing at,

290-291; and mentoring, 182; new work force at, 287-289; and operating telephone companies (OTCs), 293-294; organizational adaptation by, 297-302; and organizational careers, 304-308; and organizational structures, 22; plateauing self-initiated in, 10; staffing policies at, 294-296; values at, 278-279, 281, 286, 287-289, 290, 291, 296, 297-299, 305; women as managers at, 40, 276-277, 281-289, 342
Australia, obsolete employees in, 314

B

Baby boom cohort: and assessment of management potential, 7; and career management, 8-9; and midcareer stage, 10; and need for career development, 203
Bell System. See AT&T
Booklets, career-planning, 88

C

Canada, merger in, 23
Career coaching and counseling, in career management, 7
Career context, assessing, in placement process, 13-14

Subject Index

363

Individual Training Accounts Fund, proposed, 33
Individuals. *See* Employees, individual
Information: in career planning, 11, 207-224; midcareer need for, 146-147; and placement exchanges, tools for, 68-71, 89, 92; seeking, in placement process, 14. *See also* Computers
Information System for Vocational Decisions (ISVD), 207
Intern program, case of, 83
Internal labor market, in placement process, 13-14
Internal Revenue Service, mentoring in, 182

J

Jewel Companies, mentoring in, 182
Job posting, for information exchange, 68-69, 84, 88
Job rotation, for development, 74
Johnson and Sons, S. C., career development at, 62

L

Late career stage: mentoring in, 169-170; motivation for, 39-40
Lawrence Livermore National Laboratories, potential assessment by, 72
Learning: guides, for career resilience, 29; hierarchies of, 248; mastery, 249; research needed on, 125; vicarious, 243-244; from work experience, 236-273
Leisure: analysis of self-realization in work and, 95-119; career development implications of, 114-115; and changes, 100-101; characteristics of, 107-108; as compensation for work, 104, 105, 106; concept of, 101-103; conclusion on, 116; for downgraded workers, 110; as extension of

work, 104, 105; nature of, 103-108; as preparation for work, 106; research needed on, 346; for retired workers, 112; role of, 108-112; for static workers, 110-111; as substitute for work, 107; as supplement to work, 106; as support to work, 105; for unemployed workers, 111-112; as unrelated to work, 104, 105; for upgraded workers, 109-110
Life Career Rainbow, 96-99, 111, 114
Life career roles: concept of, 96-100; multiple, 112-113; in work and leisure, 95-119

M

McBer and Company, 253, 271
McGraw-Hill: career paths at, 69-70; job posting at, 69
Management development: concept of, 55-56; guidelines for, 26-40
Management style, changes in, 23-24
Managers, orientation for, 36
Marriott Corporation, job advancement program of, 62
Massachusetts Mutual Life Insurance Company, workshops at, 64
Mattel Corporation, career-planning seminar of, 62
Mentoring: analysis of, 160-201; attitudes, postures, and skills in, 177-180; background on, 160-161; barriers to, 181; benefits of, 196; career and psychosocial functions of, 161-163, 165; concepts of, 161-164; conclusion on, 195-198; cross-gender, 174-177, 187, 194; development role of, 164-170; in early career stage, 165-166; education for, 186-190, 193; formal programs for, 182-186; in late career stage, 169-170; in midcareer years, 166-169; organizational change approach to, 190-195, 197; organizational

W

Walt Disney Productions, 82, 83
Washington, comparable worth case in, 343
Wellesley College, Center for Research on Women at, 342
Women: in career management, 8; career motivation for, 40–41; information for, 11; and mentoring, 174–177, 187, 194; and need for career development, 203; research needed on, 342–345; wall for, 344–345
Work experience: analysis of career building from, 236–273; application implications of, 258; background on, 236–238; career development model based on, 238–257; and career pattern design, 247–248, 258–266; and cognitive characteristics, 245; conclusion on, 266–268; factors of, for individuals, 242–249; and instrumental conditioning, 254–255; and learning hierarchies, 248; and mastery learning, 249; and noncognitive characteristics, 245–247; organizational-level

factors in, 250–255; and personal development, 239, 244–245; propositions on, 242, 244, 245, 247, 248, 249, 251, 254, 255, 257; research implications of, 257–258; theoretical background of, 238–240; and vicarious learning, 243–244; and work behavior analysis, 251–254; and work/person interaction, 255–257
Work Importance Study, 100
Work roles, concept of, 252–253
Workbooks, for self-assessment, 65, 91
Workshops: for career-planning information systems, 210; and mentoring, 186–187, 189, 193; preretirement, 65; for self-assessment, 64, 83–84, 88, 92–93

X

Xerox Corporation: case study of, 90–93; supervisor counseling at, 67; workbook for, 65, 91

Y

York Russel, management style of, 23